Societies and Political Orders in Transition

This book series presents scientific and scholarly studies focusing on societies and political orders in transition, for example in Central and Eastern Europe but also elsewhere in the world. By comparing established societies, characterized by well-established market economies and well-functioning democracies, with post-socialist societies, often characterized by emerging markets and fragile political systems, the series identifies and analyzes factors influencing change and continuity in societies and political orders. These factors include state capacity to establish formal and informal rules, democratic institutions, forms of social structuration, political regimes, levels of corruption, specificity of political cultures, as well as types and orientation of political and economic elites.

Societies and Political Orders in Transition welcomes monographs and edited volumes from a variety of disciplines and approaches, such as political and social sciences and economics, which are accessible to both academics and interested general readers.

Topics may include, but are not limited to, democratization, regime change, changing social norms, migration, etc.

All titles in this series are peer-reviewed.

This book series is indexed in Scopus.

More information about this series at http://www.springer.com/series/15626

Victor Krasilshchikov

Brazil - Emerging Forever?

A Case Study of the Mid-Level Development Trap

Springer

Victor Krasilshchikov
Polish Institute of Advanced Studies
Warsaw, Poland

ISSN 2511-2201 ISSN 2511-221X (electronic)
Societies and Political Orders in Transition
ISBN 978-3-030-50207-2 ISBN 978-3-030-50208-9 (eBook)
https://doi.org/10.1007/978-3-030-50208-9

This Springer imprint is published by the registered company Springer Nature Switzerland AG.
The registered company address is: Gewerbestrasse 11, 6330 Cham, Switzerland

Acknowledgements

The first version of this book was written over ten months, from late December 2018 to the end of October 2019 with an indispensable interruption to summer mountaineering in August. It has arisen due to the favourable intellectual environment in the Polish Institute of Advanced Studies affiliated with the Polish Academy of Sciences. Director of this institute, Prof. Przemysław Urbańczyk, and office manager, Marta Chrostowska-Walenta, both helped in creating a conducive environment for this intensive research, including an opportunity to use funding from the libraries of Warsaw University, Higher School of Economics in Warsaw, and the Polish Institute of International Affairs. Hence, my gratitude goes primarily to these colleagues, without whose assistance this book would not have been written in such a short amount of time.

I would like to express my keen appreciation to Nikolay Nenovski and Jaime Marques-Pereira, professors of the Jules Verne University of Picardie, Amiens, who offered me the chance to get acquainted with some new French publications about Brazil.

I am very grateful to Greg Clark and David Durkee who helped me in proofreading of the text, modifying it, when necessary, from the global version of English, 'Globish', into British English.

In addition, I thank all my colleagues who found time to read the first version of my manuscript, making critical notes and remarks and giving useful advice to improve the book's central argument: Andrea Komlosy, Nadezhda Kudeyarova, Lyudmila Okuneva, Marcelo Weishaupt Proni, Pierre Salama, Hussein Solomon, and Arno Tausch.

Finally, I am thankful to European Association of Development Research and Training Institutes (EADI) and Spanish Network for Development Studies (Red Española de Estudios del Desarrollo—REEDES). My membership of these two academic associations allowed me access to many qualified colleagues and to information necessary for fruitful research.

Warsaw, Poland—Chernomorets, Bulgaria—Moscow, Russia

Contents

List of Figures

List of Tables

List of Boxes

Chapter 1
Introduction: Why Brazil?

This book is born as a result of my long comparative studies of modernisation and industrial development in three regions of the world: Latin America, East/Southeast Asia and the former USSR/Russia. Despite obvious differences between them, all three regions had some important common features. Namely, their modernisation was stimulated more by external challenges than by internal drivers. Additionally their modernisation was mainly imitative, copying the development path of more developed countries, and started before all the necessary internal premises for socioeconomic, institutional, cultural and political transformations were sufficiently matured. Modernisation of these regions was carried out under aegis of the state, whose role in development became somewhat hypertrophied. All three regions met serious crises in the 1980s–1990s because they were not ready to respond to the new challenges raised by the scientific-technological revolution and globalisation of the day. The latter, in particular, depreciated their past achievements in industrial development. From this point of view, the collapse of the Soviet Union in 1989–1991, *the lost decade* of the 1980s in Latin American countries and the Asian financial (and only apparently financial!) crisis of 1997–1998 are phenomena of the same socioeconomic character: they happened because of insufficient 'brain intensity' of economies and could not be explained in the terms of economics or technological policy only.

In this connection, Brazil occupies the peculiar place among all subjects in a framework of development studies. For me, also, a comprehension of the Brazilian development trajectory provides a better understanding of my native country, Russia, although there have been many differences between them. Apart from differences, there were many similarities in development paths. 'Brazil is tropical Russia' (*Brasil é uma Russia tropical*), said Fernando Henrique Cardoso, underlining that 'Brazil and Russia must march together' (*Brasil e Russia debem caminhar juntos*) in the contemporary world where new threats provide constant challenges to people in power to find adequate responses. Unfortunately, today, the tendencies observable in both countries are a concern for their future.

V. Krasilshchikov, *Brazil - Emerging Forever?*, Societies and Political Orders in Transition, https://doi.org/10.1007/978-3-030-50208-9_1

Meanwhile, there were times when these countries' development was perceived as a serious claim to a great future. In 1940 Stefan Zweig travelled in Brazil and concluded—compared to the horrible events then happening in Europe—that Brazil is the country of future. He wrote: '…the country is only at the beginning of its development. Brazil's importance for the coming generations cannot be assessed even by the most daring calculations… I had looked into the future of our world' (Zweig 1943: 3, 4). Certainly, the writer could not foresee that *the beginning of Brazil's development* would elapse some decades, remaining *nascent* up to the end of the twentieth century. However, with regard to his prognosis about *the future of the world* in Brazil, Zweig was absolutely right in this respect.

Indeed, on the one hand, Brazil has an advanced aircraft industry, being the world leader in manufacturing aircrafts for local and regional lines with a range of up to 4200 km. Brazil was also the second country in the world with the nationally made personal computer (1979). Brazil enters a narrow group of countries that keep the secrets of full cycle nuclear technologies and is capable of making A-bombs. Brazil is the second largest producer of bio-ethanol in the world, decoded the genome of rice (as well as the USA, the UK, France, China, India and Thailand) and is the only country in Latin America that expends more than 1 per cent of GDP for scientific research and technological development (R&D). Finally, Brazil has a well-computerised banking system that enables control financial flows in the regime of real time.

Simultaneously, on the other hand, there are large zones of backwardness and poverty, particularly in the North and North-East, where, as it appears at a first glance, time has been frozen many decades ago. In these places, the everyday life of millions of people does not differ significantly from life at the line of subsistence, with a lack of access to education and elementary healthcare.

Therefore, it is not an exaggeration to say: 'Brazil concentrates in itself the whole Universe of the worlds existing on the Earth'. This fact attracts the attention of many scholars and journalists, and there is a huge amount of books, papers and magazine or newspapers articles in all forms, printed and digital, devoted to Brazil, so it is not easy to say something new about this gigantic country. Nevertheless, I have risked looking at Brazil with a new approach, and only a reader may evaluate the degree to which this attempt has been successful. What is this approach?

At first, although there are many publications about Brazil, whether they are books, academic papers or magazine articles, it is difficult to find a publication where Brazil has been considered in the general context of the so-called emerging powers: from the point of view of 'the global shift from the West to the East and from the North to the South. There are only a few publications whose authors (mainly in France) scrutinise Brazil in the general world context and treat the country's problems as a specific extract of the global trends. Such an approach is the most adequate and relevant today. The attempt to realise this approach is undertaken in the proposed monograph. The author does not hide the scepticism in regard to all talks about the rise of 'non-West' (headed by China!) and explains this scepticism.

Second, this book deals with the problem of social actors in development. This problem is considered in connection with the phenomenon of the middle-income trap. Many recommendations exist for how to avoid or get out of this trap, elaborated by several scholars and international institutions such as the World Bank, CEPAL/ECLAC, OECD and Asian Development Bank. At first glance these organisations often presuppose correct solutions: stimulating innovation, technological improvements, elevation of the labourers' skills level, etc. However, they do not answer one simple question: Are there social actors capable of implementing those recommendations? In the opinion of the author, this is the key question concerning the future prospects of emerging countries such as the BRICS 'block', Argentina, Chile, Mexico, Malaysia and Thailand. Being focused on Brazil, the book demonstrates that a lack or weakness the social actors of *new development* is the main (though not the only) obstacle to the emergence of Brazil to the level of a highly developed country.

Third, the book deals with the data of social statistics in Brazil. The author, considering the national surveys of households' incomes and expenditures, concludes that the apparent social achievements of the Left-centrist governments in Brazil did not (and could not!) substantially change the social-professional structure of the country's society. The efforts undertaken since the Cardoso rule and onwards to improve the education system and to expand access of the poor to education has not created radical change in these outcomes, as the PISA (OECD tests) results for 2009, 2012 and 2015 show. Therefore, the Left-centrist social policy in Brazil could not succeed in the rise of social actors adequate to the new strategic task—transition to an innovative, knowledge-based economy. On the contrary, this policy had involuntarily been adjusting to the processes of deindustrialisation and precarisation of labour.

Fourth, I argue that the previously mentioned negative tendencies have been aggravated by the 'friendship' of Brazil with China (the same can be said about other Latin American countries as well as Russia or Kazakhstan, for example). The efforts of the Left-centrist governments of the Workers' Party (Partido dos Trabalhadores—PT) in Brazil to diversify the external economic ties and to weaken excessive dependency on the old partners, the USA and EU, turned into the second edition of the 'Open Veins of Latin America' (*Venas Abiertas de América Latina*)[1]: China has been a worse 'predator' even than the old 'imperialist powers' that exploited and spoiled the human and natural resources of the continent. Thus, this book, being devoted to Brazil, warns other emerging countries about possible threats from creating a dubious 'friendship' with China. This 'friendship' although potentially advantageous in the short-term, leads to serious losses in long-term prospects. If incomes from exportation of commodities are not invested into advanced industries and new technologies, there is no support for real economic and technological modernisation. In the case of Brazil, this has moreover strengthened agribusiness and facilitated the return of conservative, even reactionary, political forces to the political scene.

[1]The title of the famous book by the Uruguayan journalist Eduardo Galeano (1997, 2004).

Fifth, this book deals with the problem of conservatism of the lower classes. (This phenomenon was considered for the first time by Karl Marx in *The Eighteenth Brumaire of Louis Bonaparte* and is now kept in focus of attention of some Brazilian sociologists.) The premature deindustrialisation and enlargement of precarious employment make up the background for conservatism of this kind and, thereby, fertilises the social soil for strange political alliances of the upper and lower classes at the level of their political representatives (the specific alliance of the PT and the Right-centrist forces in Brazil over 13 years). And this is not only the Brazilian situation; it takes place, to some degree, in India and in Russia and may latently evolve in China. In the concrete conditions of Brazil, the Workers' Party has become a victim of its alliance with socially alien forces that block effective new development.

Finally the book puts the conception of so-called *emerging countries* or *emergence of the non-West* under scrutiny. As the reader will see later, I reject the widespread approach to global forecasting based upon (a) the one-dimensional, one-linear extrapolation of tendencies observed in the first decade of the recent century into the nearest future and (b) fetishism of quantifiable economic indicators without qualitative, social (or sociological) analysis of the processes evolving beyond the numerical figures.

The attempt of this new approach to seemingly the old, well-known and described facts predetermines the conceptual context and structure of the book.

Chapter 2 begins from the brief observation of various prognoses about (a) the rise of the Great East under aegis of China and (b) the Great Divergence of the East and West. As the author underlines, these prognoses correspond actually to the West-centred conception of modernisation and, in a broader sense, to the Western Liberal-Enlightenment universalism. In essence, they do not contradict the Western 'tradition of modernity', although often have anti-Western ideological inclination.

The concept of the BRICS is also scrutinised in this chapter. As the author argues, this concept serves to justify rising Chinese pretensions to world hegemony; it proves fruitful for adequately comprehending the real trends in our complicated world.

The chapter embraces historical reminiscences founded on the calculations of Angus Maddison and concerning the past superiority of China to western countries. That superiority hid the principal differences between the East and West in the quality of productive forces (because of principal differences in socioeconomic relationships); it turned into the strategic defeat of China in the nineteenth century. Does not the observable dynamism of some emerging countries, primarily China, hide the profound difference between the advanced Western countries and the so-called emerging powers in the character of their productive forces like it was in 1800–1820 when 'the Great Divergence' started? The next chapter is devoted to the attempt to answer this question.

Chapter 3 discusses the serious shortcomings and vulnerabilities of big non-Western countries' success stories over the last 30–40 years. Those shortcomings and difficulties are, to a large degree, the result of previous rapid but uneven development in a framework of industrial paradigm that accomplished its 'historical mission' and, thereby, exhausted itself or, at best, had come to its limit. Meanwhile, according to the author's opinion, the development of post-industrial, knowledge-based economies in emerging countries, including China, is under question today, in particular because of incompatibility of the Chinese traditions with *a realm of spontaneous creativity*' (there is a 'cognitive conservatism' of the Confucian tradition).

In this connection, as the author asserts, it is useful to remember 'the great advice' of Alexander Gerschenkron—to study unsuccessful, failed modernisations. The case of Brazil gives us a good example of such modernisation when, after the apparently visible spurt of the new success story (in the given case—in 2004–2012), a country enters a period of recession with subsequent long stagnation. As the chapter emphasises, the concrete situation in Brazil today may anticipate future tendencies in development of China and India. Indeed, some observers write about the *Brazilianisation* of China and the West, as well as about the threat to China to fall into the middle-income trap.

The chapter describes the middle-income trap's conceptions and interpretations. Approaching Brazil from the point of view of the middle-income trap problem, the author underlines the significance of both the social actors who are capable of finding an exit from the aforementioned trap and also those who are interested in conserving the *status quo*. In the case of Brazil these actors have been the 'co-products' of *conservative modernisation*, started in the colonial times.

Chapter 4 considers the specific features of conservative modernisation in Brazil. As the author intends to show, these features were rooted in plantation slavery, which provided a basis for the inclusion of local agrarian monoculture economy with a scarce population and tremendous territory into the world market. This circumstance predetermined the elitist character of Brazilian modernisation, and the chapter focuses on the latter's orientation to encouraging prestigious consumption for privileged groups. As noted in the chapter, this orientation of Brazilian conservative modernisation distinguishes it from the conservative modernisations of the nineteenth century in Japan, Prussia and Russia, where the elites, carrying out the reforms were worried about the state power, technical improvements and the domestic production of technically complicated goods for the sake of rivalry with other nations, rather than simply their own consumption.

The chapter pays attention to the peculiar path of urbanisation in Brazil where the growth of cities meant, to a large degree, the transference of the countryside into urban areas (*o campo na cidade*)—a shift of the traditional, patrimonial relationships into a new social environment. Respectively, the rising bourgeoisie was very far from 'the Weberian model' of the modern capitalist entrepreneurial class and could not become the main social actors of the emergence of highly developed industrial capitalism. Nevertheless, as the author notes in the chapter, spontaneous industrialisation began in unfavourable conditions, when the old agrarian-oligarchic system still dominated in society.

A big part of the chapter is devoted to the period after the revolution of 1930 and the subsequent start of import substitution industrialisation (ISI). The latter was the specific continuation of conservative modernisation, although now more successful and profound than in the preceding period of Brazilian history. There was a set of compromises between the new rising urban classes and old oligarchy, between the emerging industrial bourgeoisie and working class, between the state technobureaucracy and industrialists, etc. At the same time, the Brazilian ISI was accompanied by the growth of under-proletariat (*subproletariado*), numerous stratum of people who migrated from countryside to cities but could not become industrial workers because of a lack of skills and necessary education.

At the beginning of the 1960s, the so-called system of social compromises exhausted itself. The author treats the military coup d'état of 1964 as the conservative response to this exhaustion under the threat of further shift of society to the Left (in the context of Cold War!). The established military-bureaucratic authoritarian regime proceeded with conservative modernisation but now with a clearly expressed elitist inclination. The chapter demonstrates that such contemporary trends as precocious deindustrialisation and financialisation of the economy (the excessive growth of financial sector) observable in Brazil today have their sources in the economic 'miracle' of 1967–1974. In the conditions of relative closedness of the Brazilian economy in the 1970s, the premises for deindustrialisation were almost invisible but 'detonated' with the lapse of time when economic liberalisation started.

Finally the chapter emphasises the objective limits of conservative modernisation that led Brazil to the 'lost decade' of the 1980s with uncontrolled inflation and further social differentiation.

Chapter 5 considers the successful implementation of the Real Plan that oppressed destructive inflation and was aimed at active integration of the country into the process of globalisation. It is notable that the policies of the governments of Fernando Henrique Cardoso, on the one hand, and Luiz Inácio Lula da Silva and Dilma Rousseff, on the other hand, are scrutinised together, with focus on continuity instead of the differences between them, in contrast to widespread endeavour of many observers to oppose them to each other. Both political lines combined the neoliberal financial-economic policy with the social-democratic approach to acute social problems. It is underlined that the expenditures for social needs began increasing under the Cardoso administration. The main social programmes launched by the Lula government, in essence, continued the programmes of his predecessor in improved and more perfect forms. At the same time, it is noted that the policy of the PT government was more oriented to social issues than the policy of Cardoso. As it seemed previously to many observers, including myself, the inauguration of the Left president, *companhiero Lula*, on January 1, 2003, opened a new page in Brazilian history and meant a dissociation from the past development path. The main achievements of this policy—the evident reduction of poverty and decrease of incomes inequality as well as diminution of the interregional disparities—are considered in the chapter, too. However, reality appeared as being much harder than initial expectations for changes, the obvious achievements in social policy notwithstanding.

Chapter 6 concerns the costs of apparently successful social policy of the PT governments—the precocious deindustrialisation of Brazil and increased dependency on China, the factual return of the gigantic country (together with other

Latin American countries!) to the position of primary goods' supplier vulnerable to the commodities' market fluctuations.

The chapter explains the essential differences between mature and premature deindustrialisation. In the former case, deindustrialisation has been based upon the high level of industrial development; it is a result of demand shifting towards services and the increased needs of industry in services for itself (maintenance of equipment, R&D, training of skilled labourers, etc.). The case of premature deindustrialisation presupposes that it begins earlier than all its own premises matured from the demand and supply side, often under impact of the external factors. This is the case in Brazil, where deindustrialisation began in the 1980s and today has accelerated mostly due to the 'friendship' with China.

The reorientation of Brazil's economic ties from the markets of the USA and Western Europe to China has been, to a large degree, the consequence of deliberate policy of the PT with deeply rooted anti-Americanism, as it is asserted in the chapter. The Leftists anti-Americanism, although modest in the case of the PT, was keen to diversify economic ties. Nevertheless, it only succeeded in making Brazil excessively dependent on Chinese demand for primary goods. Meanwhile, the 'friendship' with China did not help to modernise Brazil and instead strengthened commodity exporters, who are not interested in significant change of the existing economic model. This aspect of Brazilian development is indistinguishable from the issue of agrarian reform. As it is underlined in the chapter, the pace of agrarian reform slowed down under the Lula presidency, and it is conditioned, to a big degree, by the consciously chosen policy aimed at searching for compromises with influential agribusiness for the sake of further financing social programmes. In addition, such phenomenon as slave labour (not formally, of course, but factually) continues to exist in some branches of agriculture (e.g. gathering of cane harvests for production of bio-ethanol), and this phenomenon is considered in the chapter, too.

The attempts of the Left-centrist governments to initiate somewhat industrial policy and to stimulate the technological innovations are under scrutiny in the given chapter, too. However, as the author demonstrates, these attempts did not succeed in the expected effects, and premature deindustrialisation proceeded as before.

Chapter 7 critically evaluates the PT social policy's achievements. These achievements have actually been very moderate, in spite of the visible positive results. The chapter contains tables composed of household incomes and expenditure statistics. The tables show how the number and share of the poorest people declined whereas the number and share of those people whose monthly incomes were between 0.5 and 2.0 and between 2.0 and 3.0 minimal wages, respectively, significantly increased. At the same time, the corresponding indicators concerning well-paid people elevated insignificantly. Therefore, the achievements of social policy under the Left-centrist governments consisted mainly in eradication of extreme poverty, in transformation of very poor into 'ordinary poor' while a big part of 'ordinary poor' lifted, at best, to the level of low-middle stratum from the point of view of their incomes.

The chapter assesses changes in the structure of household expenditure and leads to the conclusion that despite the improvements in living standards for most

Brazilians, it has been insufficient to give rise to a 'crucial mass' of labourers capable of becoming the social actors of 'new development' or, at least, capable of stimulating, by their wages, entrepreneurs to create large-scale technological and managerial innovations. This conclusion has been approved by various data that characterise a poor quality of mass education in Brazil (OECD PISA tests and assessments performed by Brazilian scholars as well). The education in Brazil remains elitist, having been inherited from the past, including, particularly, the period of authoritarian modernisation in 1964–1985, the efforts of the Left-centrist governments to change this situation notwithstanding.

Chapter 8 demonstrates that the previously mentioned shortcomings of the social policy are not the consequences of whosever mistakes; they have been conditioned by the social-professional structure of society. In its turn, this structure is partly inherited from the past, and partly formed under impact of the global processes evolving out of control of the authorities and political actors.

The chapter observes the debates among the Brazilian sociologists around former governments' assertions (particularly, under the Dilma Rousseff presidency) about the growth of a new middle class in Brazil. Really, it was the growth of a new working class, the formally employed labourers with banking and work record cards (*carteiras de tabalho*). Moreover, formal employment increased mostly in the computerised service sector (teleoperators and operators of call centres) with clearly expressed features of precariousness and low wages, at the level of 1.5–2.0 minimal salary.

Thus, neither the social-professional structure of Brazilian society nor the prevailing structure of private consumption favours profound changes in economy and education in line with contemporary challenges. The paradoxical, at a first glance, adherence of the former PT governments to conservative financial-economic policy was conditioned not only by the external circumstances (the global financial markets) and by the inevitable compromises with conservative political forces. It corresponded to the social base of the PT—to the poor social groups interested in low inflation and overvalued real; it allowed them to have access to consumer credits and to purchase cheap goods imported from other Latin American countries or from China.

The PT emerged initially as the party movement of the unionised labourers of the industrial South and Southeast, being supported by a big part of the middle class. Today the old social base of the party has been eroded and over time the PT has become the party of conservative poor; its electoral base removed to the Northeast. This chapter puts attention to the alliance of the Left-centrist PT with the political Right up to 2015–2016—the alliance that was a result of profoundly rooted coincidence of conservatisms of the lower and upper classes.

The chapter mentions the process of bureaucratisation of PT, while the mass social movements, which played a big role in its ascendance to the political power, declined. Thereby, the PT policy as itself contributed, to some degree, to maturing of premises for the parliamentary coup d'état of 2016.

Finally, the chapter scrutinises the ruling elite's attitudes in regard to the country's future. As the events of 2015–2019 demonstrate, the ruling circles of Brazil have preferred to return back to the pre-Vargas era, rejecting even several achievements of the authoritarian modernisation of 1964–1985. Moreover, there is a paradoxical contradiction in behaviour of the Brazilian political and business elite, which recognises an acuteness of the country's problems (poverty, huge inequality, poor quality of mass education, etc.) but does not want to apply efforts and resources for changing this situation.

In this connection, the problem of taxation is scrutinised because it concentrates in itself social (ir)responsibility of the dominating groups for the national development. Despite the formally progressive system of taxes, the actual taxation in Brazil is regressive; many kinds of high incomes are not subjected to taxation at all. The ruling circles are not interested to revise this system.

However, it is still insufficient to reform the taxation system. There is also the problem of effective expenditure of taxes. Will the Brazilian Left be able to reconsider previous approaches to social policy? As the experience of Brazil says, the growth of expenditures for education, for instance, has a limited effect. It does not equalise chances of children from different social groups to acquire knowledge and skills in a framework of school curricula. On the contrary, it aggravates inequality because many (fortunately, not all!) children from poor families cannot acquaint school subjects as well as children of the middle and upper classes families do. Most of them do not have necessary habits to study, to keep self-discipline and to concentrate attention on learnable subjects because their parents, being occupied by hard and often poorly paid jobs, cannot train these habits in them. Hence, it is, perhaps, not accidental that the global financial institutions, such as the World Bank, propose to intensify investments in early childhood instead of continuing increase expenditures that really maintain an already existing inequality.

Considering the content of the *last chapter* titled as *Concluding Remarks*, I anticipate here some final conclusions. The latter are performed as questions rather than as categorical assertions. In particular, what are the opportunities for Brazil to abandon the current path of conservative modernisation? Will it occur as a result of the global external shock, like in the 1930s? Or might Brazil be able to use the USA-China controversies for proper development? The answers to these questions will depend on many external and internal factors, in particular, on the attitudes of the country's elite and activity of opposition mass movements. At the same time, it is necessary to take into account that today many external and internal conditions are less favourable for development success stories than in the 1950s–1970s. For instance, Brazil is restrained by the international agreements with the WTO and Mercosul, narrowing its potential for manoeuvres in regard to the pro-development trade and industrial policy.

Unfortunately, today the most probable variant of development in Brazil is not an evolution towards the status of one of the great, leading powers but rather involution with the subsequent marginalisation of the country in the world system and losses of the own past technological achievements, as has occurred in Russia, Ukraine and other post-Soviet countries. Will the biggest country of Latin America be able to reverse this dangerous trend?

Finally, I hope that the case study of Brazil helps to dissipate a naïve belief in the 'bright future' of emerging countries, in the rise of 'new poles of power' in the world, in the global shift towards 'multi-polarity', the BRICS block and other such expressions of wishful thinking. We must yield to critical comprehension of reality whether we like or dislike it.

References

Galeano, E. (1997). *The open veins of Latin America. Five centuries of the pillage of a continent* (Translated by Cedric Belfrage. 25th Anniversary Edition. Foreword by Isabel Allende). New York: Monthly Review Press.

Galeano, E. (2004). *Las venas abiertas de América Latina. 76-a edición, revisada y corregida.* México, Buenos Aires: Siglo XXI editores (1-ra edición – 1971).

Zweig, S. (1943). *Brazil: Land of the future* (Translated by A. St. James, 282 p). New York: The Viking Press. – II. (1st published – 1941).

Chapter 2
The 'Multi-Polar World', BRICS and the Coming Chinese Hegemony: Prognoses and Daydreams

It's unnecessary to restate that the world is in the situation of bifurcation and uncertainty. Today almost everyone speaks about the epoch of uncertainty, the time of suddenness, the period of turbulence and the 'new normality' of abnormal phenomena. One of such uncertainties concerns various prognoses about the nearest future of the world economy; the essential feature of such prognoses has been constructed around the dilemma 'East or West?' Indeed, is the global centre of power moving eastwards, from the West to East Asia under Chinese hegemony? Will China be able to unite the 'Global South' against the West? The acuteness and relevance of these and similar questions are fuelled by a set of fears about the transformation of China into the new world hegemon, as the USA and West lose their global control.

2.1 The Classical Theory of Modernisation and the Rise of 'Non-West'

Many of these fears and phobias are cultivated and maintained by West-centred intellectuals. Being widespread in the Western countries, they have been picked up by various 'fighters' against 'American imperialism', from Russian traditionalists to the Middle East's religious fanatics and from 'Bolivarian revolutionaries' in Venezuela to French Leftists—by the people who intrinsically recognise their own noncompetitiveness in the world and try to compensate for it through anti-Western ideas. All these predictions concerning the decline of the West and the rise of the Great East do not correspond to, and even contradict, the Western 'tradition of

V. Krasilshchikov, *Brazil - Emerging Forever?*, Societies and Political Orders in Transition, https://doi.org/10.1007/978-3-030-50208-9_2

modernity'.[1] Indeed, why must we be wondering, watching the rise of China, India or other non-Western countries, called today as 'emerging powers', whereas such rise has been allowed and foreseen in a framework of the Western socioeconomic and political thought? In this regard, it is worth remembering Condorcet's idea about the possibility of poor people to achieving civilised nations' levels of development:

> The march of these people will be less slow and more sure than ours has been, because they will derive from us that light which we have been obliged to discover, and because for them to acquire the simple truths and infallible methods which we have obtained after long wandering in the mazes of error, it will be sufficient to seize upon their developments and proofs in our discourses and publications. (Marquis de Condorcet 1796: 257–258)

This idea, rooted in the Liberal-Enlightenment's universalism, reached its apotheosis in the views of Marx and Engels and was later borrowed from them by Marxists in simplistic, even vulgarised forms.[2] Recognising the essential differences between West European and Asian societies (the concept of 'the Asiatic mode of production'!), nevertheless, Marx believed that an expansion of capital could destroy all socioeconomic and authoritative, power-holding systems that existed in Oriental countries. In particular, critically assessing British policy in the seacoast areas of China and the outcomes of British colonialism in India, he underlined the role that the English cannons and external trade played in the subversion of the old Chinese and Indian social order, putting 'the Celestial Empire into contact with the terrestrial world' and creating genuine foundations for future Indian independence due to capitalism's accomplishments (Marx 1979a: 95, 1979b: 218). In his opinion, the Western expansion to China should succeed in a triumph of the Great French revolution's principles, *liberté, egalité, fraternité*, with an establishment of the republican order instead of the 'Celestial Son's autocracy' (Marx 1978: 267). At last, in the preface to the first edition of 'Capital', Marx formulated the principle used later—independently on adherence or hostility to Marxism—for justifying modernisation policies in non-Western countries: 'The country that is more developed industrially only shows, to the less developed, the image of its own future' (Marx 1974: 19).

Indeed, West-centred theories of modernisation, this lawful child of the intellectual life and practical politics of the twentieth-century capitalism and Cold War epoch, proclaimed not only a possibility but even inevitability for poor, backward countries of the South to attain a high level of development, though, of course, with the aid of developed nations of the North. The theory of the stages of economic growth—as the theoretical foundation for the policy of aid to development—was

[1] About the concept of modernity as the specific, Euro-centred great tradition, see Eisenstadt (1973: 203–211).

[2] One of such forms was the 'Marxist-Leninist' conception of 'non-capitalist way of development' from feudalism to socialism. Its absurdity and voluntarist character consisted not only in a naïve belief to jump over the whole stage of development – in contrast to the 'properly' Marxist classification of development stages – but also in presupposition that there was the feudalism, this exclusively European phenomenon, in non-European societies based rather on the Asiatic mode of production with all its modifications and varieties.

offered as the blueprint for action. The author of this theory, Walt Rostow, adviser to the administrations of Kennedy and Johnson, used it as the universal loadstar for all modernising nations at all times (Rostow 1960). In full accordance with such a universalistic approach to the problems of development of backward nations, the French sociologist and political scientist Raymond Aron wrote that:

> in economic and social plane all countries at all latitudes, of all races intend to the same goal under the name of fundamentally similar values. ... Nobody has more courage to declare hostility to industry and to city. (Aron 1966: 69–61)

In the opinion of Aron, 'industrialisation is inevitable, it tends to universality' (Ibid.: 93). The subsequent recognition of the variety of ways to/through modernity and, respectively, various models of modernisation ['multiple modernities' (Eisenstadt 1973: 22–46, 258–260, 2000: esp. 2–3, 14–16, 19–20, 23–24)][3] did not reject the main idea of modernisation project: to catch up with the highly developed countries by the level of incomes per capita, productive technologies, education, science and infrastructure.

Here, I refer to these old and obviously well-known views non-occasionally. Thereby, I want to underline the achievements of the East Asian industrial 'tigers' and, later, China's proving of the theory of modernisation, although these accomplishments exceed, in many respects, beyond its initial matrix which seems today, over 60 years later, as simplistic and excessively optimistic. Therefore, all either coldly academic statements or vehement worries and troubles about the rise of 'the Rest' (Amsden 2001; Kupchan 2012: 2–10, 75–86; Zakaria 2011: esp. 1–5) are performed as *a conceptual deviation* from the Great Intellectual Heritage of the West. Indeed, did you want to see non-Western countries being compared to the West on their economies, infrastructure, productive technologies, science, etc.? Then do not wonder that China today pretends to compete with you because the vector of China's development fully corresponds to the West-centred universalistic world-view by its many parameters. All fears concerning the rise of non-Western regions and countries have been based on the conviction in Western exclusiveness and on belief in the eternity of Western superiority to other civilisations. However, according to the theory of modernisation, such superiority should disappear due to modernisation.

At the same time, the prognoses predicting the forthcoming non-Western, primarily Chinese, domination in the future world have methodological fundaments in the West-centred *economical* (sic!) fetishism. They are rooted in a deification of the numerically quantifiable indicators of economic development, prima facie, GDP and

[3] 'The process of the spread of modernity beyond Europe is characterized by widely varying features' (Eisenstadt 1973: 259). 'One of the most important implications of the term "multiple modernities" is that modernity and Westernization are not identical; Western patterns of modernity are not the only "authentic" modernities', wrote Eisenstadt.—... 'the trends of globalization show nothing so clearly as ... the construction of multiple modernities; attempts by various groups and movements to reappropriate and redefine the discourse of modernity in their own new terms' (Eisenstadt 2000: 2–3, 24).

Table 2.1 The share of the biggest OECD and emerging countries in the global GDP at current prices in US dollars, as percentage, 1990–2018

	1990	1995	2000	2005	2010	2015	2018
France	5.61	5.19	4.05	4.62	4.01	3.25	3.23
Germany	7.81	8.40	5.80	6.03	5.18	4.51	4.60
Japan	13.86	17.65	14.55	10.01	8.64	5.87	5.79
UK	4.84	4.33	4.90	5.31	3.70	3.85	3.32
USA	26.45	24.83	30.61	27.57	22.69	24.19	23.91
Brazil	2.04	2.49	1.95	1.88	3.35	2.41	2.18
China	1.60	2.38	3.61	4.81	9.25	14.77	15.84
India	1.40	1.15	1.38	1.70	2.51	2.81	3.16
Mexico	1.16	1.17	2.11	1.85	1.60	1.56	1.42
The rest	35.24	32.43	31.04	36.21	39.08	36.79	36.55

Counted on the World Bank data—GDP at current prices in US$ and GDP in US$ on PPP

Table 2.2 The share of the biggest OECD and emerging countries in the global GDP measured in US dollars on current PPP, as percentage, 1990–2018

	1990	1995	2000	2005	2010	2015	2018
France	3.56	3.33	3.27	2.93	2.63	2.34	2.25
Germany	5.35	5.20	4.62	4.01	3.60	3.38	3.28
Japan	8.33	7.92	7.01	6.15	5.04	4.48	4.30
UK	3.36	3.20	3.18	2.98	2.53	2.34	2.24
USA	20.73	20.68	21.17	19.91	16.81	15.67	15.19
Brazil	3.46	3.54	3.25	3.11	3.15	2.79	2.54
China	3.88	6.08	7.62	10.10	14.03	17.13	18.25
India	3.42	3.85	4.29	4.92	5.97	6.94	7.41
Mexico	1.78	2.13	2.26	2.04	1.96	1.88	1.85
The rest	46.12	44.07	43.32	43.84	44.30	43.06	42.70

Counted on the World Bank data—GDP at current prices in US$ and GDP in US$ on PPP

GDP per capita. An emphasis on these indicators makes up the main base for all talks and predictions about the rise of non-Western poles of economic and political power.

Indeed, as it is well known, China overtook the USA by the size of GDP measured on PPP (purchasing power of parity of currency) in 2014, but not yet by the GDP at current prices measured in US$ at current exchange ratio. It is worth presenting Tables 2.1 and 2.2 to illustrate this fact as well as the weight of the biggest emerging countries in the world economy.

The share of China and other emerging countries in the world trade increased, too, but this share in the trade of goods raised to a bigger degree than the total trade that includes also services, as Tables 2.3 and 2.4 show.

Meanwhile, among all non-Western regions and countries, it is only the region of East Asia with China (and without Japan, the developed country pertaining to the West in economic and socio-political respects) that can potentially pretend to the global economic leadership and dominance. The success story of East Asia seems to

Table 2.3 The share of the biggest OECD and emerging countries in the world merchandise trade, as percentage, 1980–2018

	1980	1985	1990	1995	2000	2005	2010	2015	2018
USA	11.36	11.50	11.26	11.23	12.03	8.52	8.30	9.04	8.49
UK	5.54	5.32	5.30	4.57	4.39	3.69	2.70	2.77	2.48
Germany	9.71	9.67	12.04	10.05	8.49	9.18	8.17	7.99	7.96
Japan	6.57	9.31	8.22	8.51	7.37	5.62	5.00	3.76	3.77
France	5.84	5.35	6.19	5.78	5.04	4.38	3.40	3.05	2.97
China	0.91	1.44	1.78	2.86	3.83	7.20	10.24	13.68	12.69
India	0.43	0.48	0.51	0.59	0.65	0.94	1.47	1.61	1.66
Brazil	1.01	1.35	0.90	0.89	0.85	1.12	1.31	1.15	1.22
Mexico	0.91	1.41	1.16	1.53	2.56	2.02	1.94	2.29	2.30

Counted on the World Bank data

Table 2.4 The share of the biggest OECD and emerging countries in the world trade of goods and services, as percentage, 1980–2018

	1980	1985	1990	1995	2000	2005	2010	2015	2018
USA	12.19	13.26	12.82	12.54	13.85	10.12	9.78	10.64	9.71
UK	6.39	5.84	5.74	5.23	5.17	4.81	3.64	3.71	3.45
Germany	7.68	7.34	9.39	8.87	7.59	8.35	7.62	7.43	7.46
Japan	6.30	8.50	7.44	7.51	6.56	5.15	4.53	3.63	3.64
France	6.39	5.64	6.19	5.53	4.92	4.59	3.74	3.50	3.44
China	0.49	1.13	1.14	2.05	3.20	5.98	8.46	11.10	10.69
India	0.50	0.53	0.52	0.51	0.77	1.24	1.98	1.96	2.08
Brazil	0.92	1.19	0.88	0.90	0.84	1.05	1.25	1.09	1.08
Mexico	0.90	1.24	1.14	1.35	2.27	2.06	1.66	1.90	1.88

Counted on the World Bank data

speak of 'the Asian Century', etc., because this region since the early 1960s has performed as the world champion of economic growth. No other region or country in the world, whether Greece or Spain in Europe, Brazil or Mexico in Latin America, has seen such pace of development over such a long period of time (and pace combined with the profound changes in technologies and structure of economies!). Being enchanted by the magic of quantifiable data, even those scholars who once critically assessed capitalism shared the fetishist, 'purely economical' approaches to East Asia. Giovanni Arrighi, the outstanding representative of Fernand Braudel-Immanuel Wallerstein school of the world-system analysis with specialisation in financial issues, wrote with his colleagues in the 1990s about 'Chinese and East Asian emancipation from Western dominance' (Arrighi et al. 1999: 268, 2003: 315). His last book, published not long before his death in 2009, 'Adam Smith in Beijing' (Arrighi 2008), became the genuine manifesto for scholars and political consultants who dreamed of 'the decline of American hegemony'.

Box 2.1 Adam Smith and Giovanni Arrighi About China

Arrighi treated the development of China since 1979, firstly, as embodiment of Adam Smith market economy's idyl, and secondly, as corroboration of Smith's prediction about 'good perspectives' of China. In the opinion of Arrighi, the China success story approves the Smithian idea of a 'non-capitalist market economy' in which the growth of market is not the end but the instrument to provide well-being as much as possible for the greatest number of people (Arrighi 2008: 8, 41–50, 321, 353–361). As he underscored, 'although Smith never leaves any doubt that he favored trade liberalization, he was strongly opposed to anything resembling the shock therapies of the 1980s and 1990s' (Ibid.: 43).

Indeed, Smith in his 'Wealth of Nations' did not consider China as a poor, backward country. Smith underlined that 'China has been long one of the richest, that is, one of the most fertile, best cultivated, most industrious, and most populous countries in world'. He marked a good network of roads and navigable canals which served for communications between different provinces of the large 'Celestial Empire' (Smith 2007: 60, 565). Recognising a relative stagnation of China at the previously attained level (Smith could not, of course, imagine how else the Chinese stagnation could have been lasted over 170 years), Smith reduced the problems of China to a lack of good laws capable of stimulating the growth of division of labour and, therefore, wealth (Ibid.: 152, 78). In his opinion, it would be sufficient to supplement the potentially extant home market of China by 'more extensive foreign trade, however, which to this great home market added the foreign market of all the rest of the world—especially if any considerable part of this trade was carried on in Chinese ships—could scarce fail to increase very much the manufactures of China, and to improve very much the productive powers of its manufacturing industry. By a more extensive navigation, the Chinese would naturally learn the art of using and constructing themselves all the different machines made use of in other countries, as well as the other improvements of art and industry which are practised in all the different parts of the world'. (Ibid.: 528–529). Thus, the extension of foreign trade, on which Smith insisted, would lead China to prosperity. According to Arrighi's approach, Smith would be very glad to see how China began prospering while stimulated the foreign trade. Neither the past experience of China in the twentieth century (which was disappointing for a huge country) nor the structural changes in the Western economies, which facilitated the Chinese export expansion in the late twentieth century, nor 'the visible hand' of the Chinese developmental state that operated often in counterpoise and simultaneously as supplement to 'invisible hand' of *the global market* were taken into account in Arrighi's explanation of the recent Chinese success.

(continued)

Box 2.1 (continued)

At last, it is necessary to note that Arrighi involuntarily reduced the system of capitalist economy only to its West-centred, liberal form just like the neoliberal apologists did. Meanwhile, the twentieth-century experience gave us the examples of state capitalism when the state, personified by managerial/economic bureaucracy, accomplished the role of private entrepreneurs' class because of the social weakness.

Andre Gunder Frank who was even 'more Leftist' than Arrighi in a framework of the central-peripheral conception of the world-system expressed similar ideas in his works written in the last years of his life (Frank 2005: 217). He treated the growth of East Asian countries since the 1960s as the return to the economic superiority of Asia to the Europe that existed in the past, before the modern era.

At a first glance, such evaluations of East Asian development and prospects can be explained as an echo of the former anti-capitalism and anti-Westernism of the authors who began appearing on the intellectual scene in the 1960s, when Leftist and anti-colonialist ideas dominated the social discourse. Then any critical assessment of the West and compassion towards the Third World were 'permits' for passage into 'good society'. However, with the lapse of time the ideas about 'the global shift' of economic power to the East and South became widespread in the circles which could hardly be suspected of anti-capitalism or anti-Westernism. For example, just after the crisis of 2008–2009 ('the Great Recession'), the authors of one OECD report underlined:

> In 2009 China became the leading trade partner of Brazil, India and South Africa. The Indian multinational Tata is now the second most active investor in sub-Saharan Africa. Over 40 % of the world's researchers are now in Asia. As of 2008, developing countries were holding USD 4.2 trillion in foreign currency reserves, more than one and a half times the amount held by rich countries. These are just a few examples of a 20-year structural transformation of the global economy in which the world's economic centre of gravity has moved towards the East and South, from OECD members to emerging economies, a phenomenon this report calls 'shifting wealth'. (OECD 2010: 15)

According to the World Bank forecasting of 2012, the countries categorised as developing today will account for 62–64 per cent of the total world saving by 2030 (World Bank 2013: 2–3, 62–68). The global stock of capital will continue shifting towards developing countries with simultaneous concentration of wealth in their high-income, rich households. (It allows us to presuppose that income and social differentiation in the developing countries will be aggravating as previously—V. Kr.). The developing countries will provide an increasing volume of investment (Ibid.: 19–24), although, as we know, the growth of investment does not always succeed in the subsequent growth of output.

Almost 10 years after the quoted OECD report, the tendency towards the augmenting weight of the developing (emerging) countries in the global economy remained the focus of attention among the representatives of 'Davos elite'. For example, according to the estimations of Credit Suisse Research Institute, the biggest contribution to the world wealth increment from 2000 to 2018 is due to China. China's share of global wealth increased from 3.1 to 16.4 per cent over this period (Credit Suisse Research Institute 2018: 1–) The share of all countries with emerging markets augmented from 10 per cent of global wealth in 2000 to 24 per cent in 2018 and is projected to reach 27 per cent in 2023, including the share of China—19 per cent (Ibid.: 33–34). Simultaneously, China together with other emerging countries demonstrated the biggest and fastest increase of the number of millionaires and ultra-high net worth (UHNW) individuals with net worth exceeding 50 million US dollars each, from 6 per cent of all UHNW in the world in 2000 to 18 per cent in 2018 (Ibid.: 17–18).

Having the biggest and fastest growing economy over the last four decades among all emerging countries, China is the undeniable leader and absolute winner in an ascendance of 'the Rest' to new heights of development. It is sufficient to say that China exceeds India, another Asian giant, 4.6–4.7 times by the size of GDP and GDP per capita measured in US dollars at the current exchange ratio. By GDP measured on PPP, China exceeds India 2.4 and 2.3 times, respectively.[4] The Chinese superiority to the other BRICS participants by the size of economy, accumulated financial resources, indicators of scientific-technological development, etc., allows many observers to neglect China's BRICS partners or to consider the latter mainly as a companion grouping around China. Thus, the rising alternative to the US-led Western dominance has been seen not in the BRICS group as a whole but in China alone, often even without mentioning the other members of this group.

For example, in 2012 the US Intelligence Council in its report forecasting the world situation in 2030 predicted that China 'will probably have the largest economy, surpassing that of the United States a few years before 2030' (NIC 2012: IV), not worrying about the other regions and emerging countries in the world. This and other similar prognoses have almost become axioms, requiring no justification.

The Chinese dominance has begun to be conceived as inevitable, an undeniable fact like a change of day for night and vice versa. Some authors even assert that China will not only exceed the USA by the size of GDP and trade but will dictate one or another political course to America, primarily due to strengthening dependency of the latter on purchases of the US Treasury Bonds by the Chinese monetary authorities. In addition to this financial dependency, America, according to almost apocalyptic prognoses about the forthcoming Chinese omnipotence, will be weakened by such problems as widening socioeconomic inequality, a squeeze and decline of the middle class, reducing social and economic mobility, and so on (Subramanian 2011a: 99–105, 2011b: 68–70, 77–78). Even those scholars who do not see China through rose-tinted glasses and recognise all its well-known difficulties (such as

---

[4]According to the International Monetary Fund World Economic Outlook (data have been renovated two times per year, in April and October). Viewed on 05.04.2019 – http://statisticstimes.com/economy/projected-world-gdp-capita-ranking.php; http://statisticstimes.com/economy/countries-by-projected-gdp-capita.php

uneven growth of different industries and regions, deepening socioeconomic inequality, worsening quality of environment, poor access of many rural inhabitants to healthcare and, in the prospect, even a threat of disintegration) continue to predict Chinese dominance in the world economy as the most probable variant (Jacques 2009: 151–193).[5]

The achievements of China as well as those of many other Asian nations, including India and Turkey, in modernisation, economic growth and reduction of poverty excited Parag Khanna to argue that *the future is Asian*. As he wrote in his last book:

> Asia is the most powerful force reshaping world order today. It is establishing an Asia-centric commercial and diplomatic system across the Indian Ocean to Africa, reorienting the economies and strategies of the United States and Europe, and elevating the appeal of Asian political and social norms in societies worldwide. (Khanna 2019: 15)

At the same time, Khanna does not depreciate the role of the USA and Europe but rather talks of the elevation of Asia and concludes that:

> we are living—for the first time ever—in a truly multi-polar and multicivilizational order in which North America, Europe, and Asia each represents a major share of power. (Khanna 2019: 14; see also pp. 357–360)

Thus, according to Khanna, Asia, implicitly or explicitly headed by China, has been the main driver of the rise of the contemporary multi-polar (or seemingly multi-polar?—V.Kr.) world order.

Finally, I think, it is difficult to find analysts who did not refer to the Goldman Sachs publications about the 'leading core' of emerging countries, the BRIC (Brazil, Russia, India, China) supplemented by 'S' in 2010 when South African Republic joined this specific grouping of big countries, transforming, thereby, the BRIC into the BRICS. In 2001, when the first publication on this topic appeared, the growth of these countries had factually been treated as the main engine of the world economy as a whole with the prospect of rapid enlargement of equities market (O'Neill 2001). Very soon the analytical recommendation to put attention to the newly emerging markets took on a life of its own, catalysing not virtual but 'tangible' reality. In other words, Mr. O'Neill (since May 2015–Baron O'Neill) evoked serious problems for the West by prophesying them. Politicians, policy-makers, advisers and various political deceivers as well decided to derive as many advantages from O'Neill's prophecy as possible, primarily with a goal to raise the stakes in dealing with the USA and West as a whole. At the same time, a 'competition' of prognoses about 'the brilliant future of the BRIC(S)' began in periodical and academic publications. Many of those prognoses not only contained the expected dynamics of the BRICS countries' growth that should apparently be 'consolidating the process of economic multipolarization' (Stuenkel 2015: 147) but also favourably evaluated their 'stabilising' role as the global governance system became increasingly polycentric,

[5]'. . .China, with continuing economic growth (albeit at a reduced rate), is destined to become one of the two major global powers and ultimately *the* major global power' (Jacques 2009: 363).

leading to 'difficulties and dysfunctions in leading Western governance systems'. In addition, according to such evaluations, the observable 'recovery from a Western-centred systems crisis' has opened 'the way for the BRICS to come forward as global leaders' (Xiaoyun and Carey 2014: 3, 6–7). Moreover, the emerging countries and, particularly, the BRICS group have been perceived as the new 'saviours' of the world economy, 'benefactors' for other developing countries in Asia, Africa and Latin America. (Below we will consider what costs of this 'benefaction' for those countries are.) The BRICS members, in spite of all differences and even controversies between them, are seemingly portrayed as responsible:

> to shift global governance norms and arrangements established under a United States (US)-led post-Second World War, to reflect the present and future configuration of world economic and political power. (Carey and Xiaoyun 2016: 5)

Nonetheless, in most prognoses the rise of the BRICS group has been perceived rather as a long-term trend with unclear results than as something fully accomplished:

> Individually, the BRICS may be tomorrow's leaders who are destined to shape global political affairs", but today "the BRICS are, even as a whole, still too weak to create an alliance that would seriously threaten the United States. (Stuenkel 2015: X, 158)

Certainly, since 2014 it has become difficult to consider Brazil, Russia and South Africa as drivers of development but the two leading BRICS members, China and India, continue to be treated as the new poles of non-Western emerging economic power and influential global players (Ibid.: 5–7).[6] It is notable that assessments performed in the 2017 Report on the BRICS (published by Observer Research Foundation, the Indian think tank) were more balanced and 'flexible', less optimistic than in its preceding texts on this issue. Yes, of course, the BRICS are again considered as the emerging grouping, but the report implicitly recognises that 'the pace of movement' to the proclaimed goals, the just and multi-polar world order, larger participation of the BRICS countries in the global financial institutions, etc., has been continuing but undergoes a relative slowdown. In the opinion of the report's authors, the most realistic scenario of the BRICS future presupposes 'greater emphasis on economic and social issues' in the group's countries (ORF 2017: 72), seemingly, instead of stirring up further joint political activity in the global scale.

This more moderate optimism is conditioned by obvious (and recognised at last!) difficulties in the process of emergence of the group. Each member of the BRICS, including the leading and most successful of them, China and India, has vulnerabilities and deficiencies, so the recent forecasts concerning the BRICS prospects have become more complex and less categorical than the previous ones.

---

[6]Even in 2013, on the eve of 'the turning point' in the BRICS short history, when the first signs of serious structural and institutional diseases in Brazilian, Russian and South African economies began becoming evident, the Indian think tank, representing India in the BRICS academic community, continued to argue: 'The formerly dominant Western powers are steadily losing the ability and perhaps the will to play the hegemon's role, while the formerly marginalised "third world" finds itself newly empowered'. (Saran et al. 2013: 8).

2.2 The 'Great Convergence' and Economic Fetishism

According to the last assessments of the world trends, we observe today the Great Convergence of the West and East, mainly because of deindustrialisation of the former and decline of the US hegemony, although without the clearly visible prospect of change. As Leonid Grinin, Andrey Korotaev and Arno Tausch argue, the decade of the 1980s (when the East Asian 'tigers' rose as the response to the then Third World problems—V.Kr.) was the start of long-term changes in relations between the old core of the world system and its periphery (and semi-periphery), between the North and South (Grinin et al. 2016: 51–54). However, these authors connect the beginning of this Great Convergence with deindustrialisation of the West and relocation of a part of the world manufacturing industries and capacities to the East. In other words, they are biased in explaining this global shift not by the fascinating spurt of a part of the former periphery but, rather, referring to the start of destructive processes in the core (West).

Certainly, considering the evidently narrowing gap between the 'old' West and 'young' East, we have to take into account that the Chinese economy will not grow by the previous pace, about 10 per cent per year, up to the mid-century. A slowdown of Chinese growth was foreseen already in 2008–2010, and it has actually taken place. However, even the expected 4.5–5.0 per cent growth currently looks unachievable for the US and European Union economies, so all debates about the time when China will catch up with USA by the size of GDP may concern only the concrete year with insignificant fluctuations, plus or minus 5 years.

In addition, it is worth attending not only to the increased shares of China or all groups of emerging countries in the world GDP and trade but also to the *dynamics* of these shares. In other words, it is relevant to estimate how fast or, on the contrary, slowly the called shares changed. Then it becomes evident that the economic expansion of China has undergone a relative slowdown beginning approximately from the mid of the first decade of the recent century. Tables 2.5, 2.6, and 2.7 illustrate this slowdown clearly.

As we can see, the share of China in the world GDP increased in the last years by notably slower pace than in the 1990s or in the beginning of the century. In this respect, the pace of Indian share has been steadier over a long time than the Chinese spurts. In the total trade of goods and services, China not only slowed the pace of trade's growth but even began lagging behind the main competitors. What concerns two other big emerging countries, Brazil and Mexico, is that they have begun losing their positions in the world GDP and trade rankings, and this process has appears to be long term. Some acceleration of the growth of their shares in the world merchandise exports over the last years has been neutralised by losses in their exports of services and does not allow them to make a clear conclusion about whatever notable alteration in their positions at the global market of goods and services as a whole.

At the same time, the concrete situation in China or in any other big emerging country as well as the deep structural transformation of their economies (for instance, the shift from the export-led growth to the growth upon the domestic market and

Table 2.5 The average annual increase (+) or decrease (−) of the share of the biggest OECD and emerging countries in the total world GDP measured in US$ on current PPP, as percentage, 1990–2018

	1995/1990	2000/1995	2005/2000	2010/2005	2015/2010	2018/2015
USA	−0.05	+0.47	−1.22	−3.33	−1.40	−1.29
UK	−0.99	−0.10	−1.30	−3.22	−1.53	−1.43
Germany	−0.59	−2.33	−2.79	−2.11	−1.29	−1.42
Japan	−0.99	−2.42	−2.57	−3.93	−2.33	−3.90
France	−1.33	−0.37	−2.13	−2.18	−2.31	−1.56
China	+9.38	+4.63	+5.73	+6.79	+4.08	+2.84
India	+2.38	+2.18	+2.81	+3.92	+3.06	+3.55
Brazil	+0.42	−1.66	−0.87	+0.23	−2.40	−3.91
Mexico	+3.69	+1.21	−2.03	−0.82	−0.83	−0.73
The rest	−0.90	−0.34	+0.24	+0.21	−0.56	−0.35

Counted by author on the World Bank data (see note to Tables 2.1 and 2.2)

Table 2.6 The average annual increase (+) or decrease (−) of the share of the biggest OECD and emerging countries in the world merchandise trade, as percentage, 1990–2018

	1995/1990	2000/1995	2005/2000	2010/2005	2015/2010	2018/2015
USA	−0.05	+1.38	−6.67	−0.51	+1.73	−2.08
UK	−2.91	−0.80	−3.39	−6.07	+0.51	−3.64
Germany	−3.55	−3.33	+1.53	−2.29	−0.46	−0.09
Japan	+0.68	−2.83	−5.27	−2.33	−5.53	+0.06
France	−1.36	−2.72	−2.73	−4.94	−2.17	−0.88
China	+9.98	+6.05	+13.45	+7.30	+5.96	−2.49
India	+2.74	+2.07	+7.63	+9.31	+1.84	+1.05
Brazil	−0.12	−1.05	+5.75	+3.19	−2.58	+2.06
Mexico	+5.58	+10.87	−4.57	−0.88	+3.41	+0.12

Counted by author on the World Bank data (see note to Tables 2.3 and 2.4)

Table 2.7 The average annual increase (+) or decrease (−) of the share of the biggest OECD and emerging countries in the world trade of goods and services, as percentage, 1990–2018

	1995/1990	2000/1995	2005/2000	2010/2005	2015/2010	2018/2015
USA	−0.28	+1.85	−6.10	−0.67	+1.70	−3.02
UK	−1.87	−0.21	−1.44	−5.43	+0.41	−2.39
Germany	−1.13	−3.06	+1.91	−1.79	−0.50	+0.11
France	−1.85	−2.67	−1.39	−4.01	−1.28	−0.62
Japan	+0.44	−2.92	−4.72	−2.55	−4.30	+0.11
China	+12.43	+9.28	+13.33	+7.20	+5.57	−1.26
India	+2.93	+4.82	+10.08	+9.78	−0.18	+2.07
Brazil	+0.47	−1.31	+4.49	+3.58	−2.70	−0.44
Mexico	+3.56	+10.93	−1.94	−4.24	+2.76	−0.31

Counted by author on the World Bank data (see note to Tables 2.3 and 2.4) consumption enlargement) may require not only a diminishing rate of growth. It can also succeed in the expansion of 'non-productive expenditures'. For example, the air pollution with subsequent worsening of population's health, the acute problem in China, India and other emerging countries, will create demand for medical services many of which can hardly be included into the GDP quantified in market prices. It will inevitably diminish the rate of GDP growth for the sake of the general well-being increase. Therefore, a superiority of one or another country to its neighbours by GDP/GDP per capita does not mean the same superiority to them by well-being as a whole. A fact of bigger GDP of China than that of USA does not mean a full superiority of China to America.

Firstly, such a superiority by the size of economy in absolute terms (GDP as a whole), whether it will be reached in 2030, 2035 or later, is not the same as a superiority by the level of GDP per capita. Even according to the last optimistic (for China!) forecasts, this level in China will be three to four times less than in USA by the mid-century (Lau 2019: 187–188, 201–206), and it is a big question whether it will be necessary to catch up with America by this indicator or not. Secondly, numerous prognoses concerning Chinese economic precedence omit an insufficiency of GDP/GDP per capita and, on the contrary, absolutise its significance in quality of the indicator that characterise a state of one or another country's economy. Meanwhile, an approach to development that puts the GDP or income growth as the main objective began becoming obsolete in the 1970s when it became clear that this growth did not succeed in automatic resolution of problems tormenting the then developing countries (Stewart 2019: 136–139). It was not accidental that the concepts of development and modernisation were essentially enlarged and began being treated as 'the continuous expansion of human possibilities' (Eisenstadt 1973: 22), as flourishing and fulfilment of people's capabilities. As Mahbub ul Haq underlined, 'Development must put people at the centre of its concerns', and the human development paradigm includes four essential components: equity, sustainability, productivity and empowerment (Mahbub 1995: 20, 16–20). The essence of this approach was brilliantly expressed by Amartya Sen—*development as freedom* (Sen 2001).

Therefore, considering the emerging countries' development, it is necessary to avoid the 'economic reductionism' that reduces all achievements to the growth of incomes. Moreover, even from the point of view of material well-being (material wealth), the indicator of GDP is insufficient for full assessment of economic development, not speaking about numerous social and environmental aspects of the latter. This insufficiency has broadly been recognised, and the well-known *Stiglitz-Sen-Fitoussi Commission*[7] considered this issue in details. According to the Commission's conclusions, in some cases 'the pervasive use of GDP for

---

[7]This commission was organised on the initiative of the French President Nicolas Sarkozy who was not satisfied by the recent, widely accepted system of economic indicators.

measuring economic performance may lead us to wrong inferences...' (Stiglitz et al. 2009a: 21–32, 86–137, 2009b: 15).[8]

Certainly, an insufficiency does not mean a full unfitness or deficiency. Nobody in good mental health suggests to reject GDP and other widely spread indicators at all. However, it is necessary to take into account that such indicators can hide not only the unquantifiable aspects of well-being, whether they are state of environment, quality of medical services or accessibility of education, but also the principal differences between countries comparable with each other, the differences that can become evident much later, succeeding in notable income gaps between them. In this regard, it is worth remembering the situation that existed in the middle of the past millennium. As Angus Maddison demonstrated in his economic-historical studies, the income levels in the Western Europe, on the one hand, and China and India, on the other hand, were approximately equal to each other beginning from the fourteenth century when Europe had almost caught up with China but exceeded the latter up to 1700 only by insignificant magnitude (Maddison 2005: 2, 8–9). For example, Chinese GDP per capita calculated in 1990 international Geary-Khamis dollars was equal to 600 dollars in 1500 and remained at this level up to 1800–1820, whereas the UK's GDP per capita was equal to 714 dollars in 1500, 974 in 1600, 1250 in 1700 and 1707 in 1820; at the same time, China produced 25 per cent of the world GDP in 1500, 29.2 per cent in 1600 and 32.9 per cent in 1820 (Maddison 2001: 247, 263–264; see also Nayyar 2019: 8–21, 222–223). Martin Jacques in his book glorifying the achievements of China, marked, too, a full comparability of per capita incomes in China, India and Britain to each other approximately up to 1800 (Jacques 2009: 30–32). The gap between China and other oriental countries, on the one hand, and the West, on the other, in their GDP per capita reached a dramatic width already in the nineteenth century when the share of 'the Rest' in the total world output began promptly to diminish; for example, the share of China in the world GDP fell to 4.5 per cent in 1950 (Maddison 2001: 263).

Paul Bairoch, who has been known due to his historical-economic studies, too, estimated the gap between the poorest, least developed countries and the richest ones up to the beginning of the nineteenth century as very moderate, 1.3–1.6 to 1.0.[9] According to Bairoch's estimations, the gap between the rich Western countries and 'the Rest' began dramatically widening only since 1820–1830; to the last pre-First

[8]'Consider the problems posed by the suburbanization process underway in many countries. As a result of increases in commuting, GDP increases because of greater spending on transportation. If the country fails to provide adequate public transportation, there will be greater use of private means of transport, and an increase in traffic jams and thus higher oil consumption, all contributing to increased GDP. But the well-being of society is clearly lower. People literally lose time (commuting time is not leisure, nor, like work, does it yield a direct return) and pollution increases' (Stiglitz et al. 2009b: 15–16).

[9]Bairoch based his estimations upon the data on GNP (gross national product) but not GDP, as Maddison did. However, because of low level of development and small importance of the external trade for traditional, agrarian societies (except few cities like Florence, Venice, Genoa, Antwerp or Bremen) the difference between GDP and GNP could hardly be significant at that time.

World War year, 1913, it reached 7.0–1.0 (Bairoch 1981: 3, 5, 7–9). Moreover, what concerns some productive technologies, particularly in handicraft industries, 'Europeans still had catching up to do in many areas of textile weaving and dyeing, western working on imitating Indian and Chinese processes; the same was true of manufacturing porcelain' (Pomeranz 2000: 45).[10]

Box 2.2 Remarks About 'the Least Developed' and 'Poor' Countries
It is necessary to take into account that in the pre-industrial epoch, i.e. before 1780–1800, 'the least developed' did not always mean 'the poorest'. Instead poverty and wealth depended mostly on availability of the natural resources and their use in production—on 'the natural productive forces', as Marx would say, whereas the main 'engines' of such forces were muscles of humans or animals (horses, buffaloes, donkeys, etc.) and natural phenomena (e.g. wind or falling water). Well-being or, on the contrary, poverty did not depend, or depended only to a small degree, on the tools of production made especially for elevation of productivity. Undeniable and almost ceaseless perfection of manual tools of production in artisanship of the ancient Oriental societies of China, India, Siam, Khmers, etc., as well as fascinating prosperity of their civilisations as a whole were potentially due to good agriculture and fertile lands which allowed them to gather an affluent harvest and get a large surplus of products that provided a development of artisanship and various kinds of intellectual activity, for example, medicine. At the same time, one or another country with abundant resources could be rich, having poorly developed or even archaic system of production whether its technology was perfect and complicated or not.

Certainly, the abovementioned fascinating share of China in the total world economy up to 1820, as well as obvious skill of Chinese artisans in some handicraft industries, may console some contemporary 'admirers of the Orient' and various Leftist 'anti-Westerners' despite the multi-centurial stagnation of Chinese and Indian incomes per capita and their income lag that began widening at that time. But this big share in the world output hides, at first, a superiority of Britain (and later other West European countries as well) to China and India by agricultural productivity that almost doubled over the eighteenth century (Huang 2002: 502–513, 516–524). Secondly, China's and India's share in the world output camouflaged the principal difference between the economic systems existed then in both comparable parts of the world, East and West. Do we not see a repetition of the past situation in recent conditions? Meanwhile, the difference, hidden beyond visible appearance and later

[10]Being in disagreement with Pomeranz's explanations of the West Europe's, primarily Britain's, breakthroughs and take off in the first half of the nineteenth century, when the Great Divergence of the levels of socioeconomic and technological development between West and East had become obvious, I do not comment his explanations here.

estimated from the point of view of quantifiable indicators, predetermined the ever-widening gap between them over the next 150 years. Then the Western countries evolved within a framework of early capitalism and underwent the industrial revolution. And there were *the social actors of industrialisation*, pre-industrial entrepreneurs and their antagonists—hired workers and merchants who were ready to risk – conquering spaces of the New World, Africa and Asia with their abundant resources. The internal conflict of these rising social classes with each other contributed significant dynamics to early capitalism. In contrast to the processes in the West, Oriental societies underwent a slow, in many respects tormented, involution and disintegration of their socioeconomic systems (rooted, in the end, in the Asiatic mode of production!) and aggravated by emerging environmental problems. As a result of these destructive processes, they could neither resist colonial expansion of the West nor compete with machinery-made textile and other goods, being subjugated, in one or another form, to the western powers, and their apparent well-being had been depreciating under impact of the foreign influence.

Respectively, comparing the fascinating economic dynamics of East Asia with the 'turtle pace' of Western economies in the last 30–40 years, we must not enchant ourselves by a mystery of statistical data, remembering the historical precedent—the situation that existed in the beginning of the nineteenth century. A visible convergence of East Asia with the West can hide the principal difference: East Asia has been successful in a framework of industrial technological paradigm, whereas the West with the US hegemony, although not as absolute as in the mid-twentieth century, started to transit to a post-industrial, knowledge-based economy, in which a significance of 'intangible resources', such as ideas, a force of imagination, creative capacities, know-how, education of labourers, etc., increases in extending degree. Over two or three decades, from the early 1980s to the Great Recession of 2008–2009, the processes of post-industrialisation and industrial development, the processes of elaboration of new technologies and scientific ideas, on the one hand, and their embodiment or implementation in tangible, materially sensible goods, on the other hand, were, to a big degree, disconnected from each other in space. The post-industrial tendencies evolved mainly in the West, including Japan (where this process took very specific, peculiar forms), the industrial production, mostly in East Asia, particularly in China, but both were only different aspects of the same development. Indeed, as Grinin and Korotaev argue in their book, the recently observable Great Convergence between West and East is not an opposite process to the previously mentioned Great Divergence that started in 1800–1820. On the contrary, both processes are only different phases or stages of a single process. This process is the world modernisation transforming, since the 1980s, into globalisation (Grinin and Korotaev 2015: 1, 7, 85 et ff., esp. 96–113, 124–137; see also Nayyar 2019: 29–45, 178–200). Today, from 2009 to 2010, i.e. after the Great Recession, these different aspects of development began converging with each other in space. Such a convergence has been expressed, firstly in the partial reindustrialisation upon the new technological base of some western economies, including Britain and USA (the pioneers of deindustrialisation since the 1950s), and secondly in the return of some industries from China to their 'Western homelands'. At the same time, we can see attempts undertaken in China to restructure the proper economy in correspondence with the global post-industrial trends, to develop the own high-tech production and a system of R&D. Obviously, these efforts are aimed, in the end, at profound changes of both economic systems, in the West and East as well. They can succeed in serious reconfiguration of the world as a whole. But it is hardly possible to assert that this reconfiguration will surely mean the triumph of East Asia with Chinese leadership.

Later, in the next chapter, I shall also return to this issue. Here, it is worth noting that it would be useless to hope for capitulation of China and East Asia as a whole in front of the West like it occurred in the nineteenth century. Today, the East will hardly lag over many decades again while a diffusion of scientific ideas, educational experience and technological achievements proceeds much faster than at the dawn of early industrial capitalism. The political leaders, either business elites in China and other emerging countries, except, may be, only few of them, conceive the qualitative transformations in the advanced economies and are not going to adopt a reality passively, having nothing to do, in contrast to the situation that existed 200 years ago when the Asian rulers did not understand at all what was happening in the world.

However, will their intentions and efforts be sufficient and effective to continue catching up with the West or perhaps even overtaking it? While this race lasts, new problems and vulnerabilities of China's and other emerging countries' development rise. Some of them have been inherited from the past, but some are the negative effects of their rapid growth.

References

Amsden, A. H. (2001). *The rise of "the rest": Challenges to the west from late-industrializing economies*. Oxford, NY: Oxford University Press.

Aron, R. (1966). *Trois essais sur l'âge industriel*. Paris: Plon.

Arrighi, G. (2008). *Adam Smith in Beijing. Lineages of the Twenty-First Century*. Brooklyn, NY: Verso (1st print – 2007).

Arrighi, G., Ahmad, I., & Miin-Wen, S. (1999). Western hegemonies in world-historical perspective. In G. Arrighi, B. Silver, et al. (Eds.), *Chaos and governance in the modern world system* (pp. 217–270). Minneapolis: University of Minnesota Press.

Arrighi, G., Po-Keung, H., Ho-Fung, H., & Selden, M. (2003). Historical capitalism, east and west. In G. Arrighi, T. Hamashita, & M. Selden (Eds.), *The resurgence of east asia: 500, 150 and 50 year perspectives* (pp. 259–333). Routledge: New York.

Bairoch, P. (1981). The main trends in national economic disparities since the industrial revolution. In P. Bairoch & M. Lévy-Leboyer (Eds.), *Disparities in economic development since the industrial revolution* (pp. 3–17). New York: St. Martin's Press.

Carey, R., & Xiaoyun, L. (2016). *The BRICS in international development: The new landscape. IDS evidence report no 189. Rising powers in international development*. Brighton: IDS (Institute of Development Studies).

Credit Suisse Research Institute. (2018). *Global wealth report 2018*. Zurich: Credit Suisse AG.

Eisenstadt, S. N. (1973). *Tradition, change, and modernity*. New York: Wiley.

Eisenstadt, S. N. (2000). Multiple modernities. *Daedalus, 129*(1), 1–29.

Frank, A. G. (2005). East and west. In P. Herrmann & A. Tausch (Eds.), *Dar al Islam. The mediterranean, the world system and the wider Europe: The "cultural enlargement" of the EU and Europe's identity* (pp. 183–229). Hauppage, NY: Nova Science Publishers.

Grinin, L., & Korotaev, A. (2015). *Great divergence and great convergence. A global perspective. With a foreword by Jack A. Goldstone*. Cham: Springer. https://doi.org/10.1007/978-3-319-17780-9_3.

Grinin, L., Korotaev, A., & Tausch, A. (2016). *Economic crises, cycles, and the global periphery. With a foreword by William R. Thompson*. Preston: Springer. https://doi.org/10.1007/978-3-319-41,262-7.

Huang, P. C. C. (2002). Development or involution in eighteenth-century Britain and China? A review of Kenneth Pomeranz's The Great Divergence: China, Europe, and the Making of the Modern World Economy. *The Journal of Asian Studies, 61*(2), 501–538.

Jacques, M. (2009). *When China rules the world. The end of the western world and the birth of a new global order*. New York: Penguin Press.

Khanna, P. (2019). *The future is Asian*. Simon & Schuster.

Kupchan, C. A. (2012). *No one's world: The west, the rising rest, and the coming global turn*. New York: Oxford University Press.

Lau, L. J. (2019). Chinese economy in the new era. *Pacific Economic Review, 24*(2), 187–207. https://doi.org/10.1111/1468-0106.12300.

Maddison, A. (2001). *The world economy: A millennial perspective*. Paris: OECD.

Maddison, A. (2005). *Growth and interaction in the world economy. The roots of modernity*. Washington, DC: The American Enterprise Institute Press.

Mahbub ul Haq. (1995). *Reflections on human development*. Oxford: Oxford University Press.

Marx, K. (1974). *Capital. A critical analysis of capitalist production* (Vol. I) (Translated from the third German edition by S. Moore and E. Aveling and ed. by F. Engels). Moscow: Progress Publishers.

Marx, K. (1978). Review (January 1850). In K. Marx & F. Engels (Eds.), *Collected works* (Vol. 10). Moscow: Progress Publishers.

Marx, K. (1979a). Revolution in China and Europe. In K. Marx & F. Engels (Eds.), *Collected works* (Vol. 12). Moscow: Progress Publishers.

Marx, K. (1979b). The future results of British rule in India. In K. Marx & F. Engels (Eds.), *Collected works* (Vol. 12). Moscow: Progress Publishers.

Marquis de Condorcet, M. -J. -A. -N. C. (1796). *Outlines of an historical view of the progress of the human mind* (Translated from the French). Philadelphia: Lang & Ushtick. Republished in the electronic form by Liberty Fund, Indianapolis, 2011. Retrieved March, 27, 2019, from http://oll.libertyfund.org/title/1669

Nayyar, D. (2019). *Resurgent Asia: Diversity in development*. Oxford: Oxford University Press.

NIC (National Intelligence Council). (2012). *Global trends 2030: Alternative worlds*. Washington, DC: NIC.

O'Neill, J. (2001). *Building better global economic BRIC*. Goldman Sachs Global Economics Paper No. 66.

OECD. (2010). *Perspectives on global development: Shifting wealth*. Paris: OECD.

ORF (Observer Research Foundation). (2017). *Realizing the BRICS long-term goals: Road-maps and pathways*. New Delhi: ORF.

Pomeranz, K. (2000). *The great divergence: China, Europe, and the making of the modern world economy*. Princeton, NJ: Princeton University Press.

Rostow, W. W. (1960). *The stages of economic growth: A non-communist manifesto*. Cambridge: Cambridge University Press.

Saran, S., Singh, A. K., & Sharan, V. (2013). A long-term vision for BRICS. Submission to the BRICS academic forum. In *ORF (Observer Research Foundation)*. New Delhi.

Sen, A. (2001). *Development as freedom* (2nd ed.). Oxford, NY: Oxford University Press (1st edition – 1999).

Smith, A. (2007). *An inquiry into the nature and causes of the wealth of nations*. In S. M. Soares (Ed.), Amsterdam et al.: MetaLibri Digital Library. Retrieved March 18, 2019, from http://metalibri.uncubadora.faresp.br (1st published – 1776).

Stewart, F. (2019). The human development approach: An overview. *Oxford Development Studies, 47*(2), 135–153. https://doi.org/10.1080/13600818.2019.1585793.

Stiglitz, J. E., Sen, A., & Fitoussi, J.-P. (2009a). *Report by the commission on the measurement of economic performance and social progress*. Paris. Retrieved October 29, 2019, from http://www.stiglitz-sen-fitoussi.fr/en/documents.htm; http://www.stiglitz-sen-fitoussi.fr/en/documents/rapport-anglais.pdf

Stiglitz, J. E., Sen, A., & Fitoussi, J.-P. (2009b). *The measurement of economic performance and social progress revisited. Document de travail de l'OFCE N 2009-33*. Paris: OFCE. Retrieved October 29, 2019, from https://www.ofce.sciences-po.fr/pdf/dtravail/WP2009-33.pdf

Stuenkel, O. (2015). *The BRICS and the future of global order*. Boulder, CO: Lexington Books.

Subramanian, A. (2011a). In Peterson Institute for International Economics (Ed.), *Eclipse: Living in the shadow of China's economic dominance*. Washington, DC.

Subramanian, A. (2011b). The inevitable superpower: Why China's dominance is a sure thing. *Foreign Affairs, 90*(5), 66–70, 71–78.

World Bank. (2013). *Capital for the future: Saving and investment in an interdependent world. Global development horizons*. Washington, DC: World Bank. https://doi.org/10.1596/978-0-8213-9635-3.

Xiaoyun, L., & Carey, R. (2014). *The BRICS and the international development system: Challenge and covergence? – IDS Evidence Report No 58. Rising powers in international development*. Brighton: IDS (Institute of Development Studies).

Zakaria, F. (2011). *The post-American world. Release 2.0*. New York: W.W. Norton & Co.

Chapter 3
Thunderclouds Over the Emerging Countries and the Middle-Income Trap

The success stories of fast modernisations are often accompanied by the erecting of new obstacles to development, unforeseen at the start of their economic race. These can add new problems to old ones because of the shortage of time to resolve both simultaneously. Today we see how thunderclouds have been gathering over the emerging countries, and the suddenly emerging impediments may seriously hinder the success of growing nations to desirable heights of well-being and prosperity.

3.1 The Difficulties of Emergence

The main problems inherent to more or less all emerging countries and which can negatively impact their development are the following:

- A relative imbalance between the industrial and agricultural development. This continues to persist in China, India and many Southeast Asian as well as Latin American countries. Certainly, the progress in their agricultural output has been fascinating: it is worth remembering that some recently emerging countries started their modernisation from *the green revolution* of the late-1950s–the mid-1970s (for instance, India, Thailand and Mexico). Today there is advanced agribusiness that provides them with sufficient food and also exports, but, at the same time, we see a lot of peasant farms with low productivity. Such an uneven, dualistic development of both sectors of agriculture creates discordance between the low share of agriculture in GDP and its disproportionately big share in the total employment in almost all emerging countries. As a result, various disparities between the urban and rural areas widen (Bardhan 2010: 42–53, 99–100; Hochraich 2007: 23–38, 107–114; Huang 2002: 513–516).

V. Krasilshchikov, *Brazil - Emerging Forever?*, Societies and Political Orders in Transition, https://doi.org/10.1007/978-3-030-50208-9_3

- The success story of East and Southeast Asia has been accompanied by growing incomes and social inequalities. This is in contrast to the situation in the 1960–1980s when the rise of Asian 'tigers' coincided with a low and, in some cases, diminishing inequality. Then it was egalitarian, inclusive growth, but since the mid-1990s, the reduction of poverty went hand in hand with increased inequality. (Latin America has been the only region in the world where inequality decreased in the first decades of the new century although it remained very high.) The World Bank in one of its last analytical reports about East Asia even laid the responsibility for this widening inequality in the region on China, accusing 'the socialism with Chinese specificity' in driving inequality's increase in East Asia as a whole (Gaulard 2014: 67–78; World Bank 2018: 29, 32–39, esp. 34–36).
- The rise of wages of organised workers (in China, occupied mostly at the state-owned enterprises) does not prevent the diminishing share of labour (wages) in GDP of emerging countries. To a large degree, this diminution is conditioned by the existing informal sector of economy with low productivity and poorly paid jobs. Employment in big emerging countries as India, Brazil and Mexico grew mostly due to the informal sector and services (in Brazil, in formal service sector with low productivity). A huge part of this employment has been precarious, and China is the world leader on this kind of employment. Guy Standing, who devoted the special study to the rise of precariat, estimated the number of precarious employees in China as about 200 million people (Standing 2011: 96, 106–109). 'The Chinese precariat is easily the largest such group in the world', he concluded in his famous book (Standing 2011: 108; see also Hochraich 2007: 75–80, 148, 152–153).
- The widespread informal or precarious employment is combined with: (a) the long-lasting growth of underutilised productive capacities in some emerging countries, primarily in China; it succeeds in falling effectiveness of industry (this is particularly inherent to the state-owned plants in China) (Hochraich 2007: 129–131; Xu and Gui 2019: 57–59). (b) a shortage of skilled labourers. Even in India, the country which is the worldly recognised leader in IT and pharmaceutics among all emerging countries, IT suffers from a deficit of specialists. A similar difficulty has been observed in Malaysia, the country with a much higher than average standard of life than India. This problem has existed over a long time (ADB 2008: 61–75). Today it remains as acute as it has been 10–12 years ago and not only in the gigantic countries, China and India, but in middle-income members of 'tigers family' such as Malaysia and Thailand, too (OECD 2018: 173–176).
- All emerging countries face the problems of rapid urbanisation and aging population (the latter as the effect of demographic transition) (World Bank 2016). (Since both these processes are the result of rapid modernisation and also condition each other to a big degree, I consider them as different aspects of a single trend.) Certainly, an acuteness of these problems is different in different countries. For example, China has seen the consequences of population's aging already today, Brazil will experience them in the next 5–7 years, whereas India will face these problems in full measure around 2028–2033. But in all cases, these

processes will be relevant anywhere, while the emerging countries are catching up with the advanced ones. Therefore, the previous approaches to social policy have to be revised.

- Not focusing especially on the environmental problems in all emerging countries, it is impossible to neglect them at all. In China, for example, these problems become serious strains for further growth. Their significance and acuteness with all consequences for the population's health requires additional resources to resolve them, and they have been accumulating faster than economies can admit unless not being overcharged by them.
- I do not consider here such serious problem as corruption which blossoms in most emerging countries except only few of them. However, it is impossible not to mention this problem at all because it becomes incompatible with further development. Often it is the systemic character feature of the state and cannot be abolished without dismantling the whole system of state authority, threatening to a country's existence, as it takes place, for instance, in the case of Russia.

All these shortcomings and vulnerabilities of emerging countries do not put the attempts to counterpoise them to the 'old' West's dominance under question. On the contrary, they all are indistinguishable from the achievements of emerging countries as well as from the neoliberal paradigm of development that dominated, to a bigger or lesser degree, in the West since the late-1970s till the Great Recession and also afterwards but, so to speak, in 'softened forms'. (The used 'quantitative easing' as the main anti-cyclical remedy has been the Keynesian 'deviation' from the neoliberal principles.) In this connection, it is worth noting, for instance, that none of the BRICS countries proposed any alternative to the existing capitalist system. They instead endeavour to build their economies and political institutions into this system, being not 'junior partners' but equated to the 'old', previous hegemon(s), and do not intend, in contrast to the former USSR, to destroy it. In particular, the BRICS countries prefer not to dismantle but to reform the Bretton Woods financial institutions. They pretend to occupy positions within the latter, corresponding to their grown economies. Possible conflicts and controversies between the West and the BRICS, such as now between the USA and China or between the UK and Brazil some years ago,[1] do not spill over beyond the scope of the existing world system and do not principally differ from the past conflicts between 'old' and 'young' capitalist powers. As Ian Taylor wrote about a visible 'anti-systemic' character of the BRICS:

> [T]he BRICS concept might be seen as a political attempt to further the hegemonic status of liberal capitalism by accommodating emerging centers of accumulation and growth *within* the extant system. ... ... The emergence of the BRICs is, indeed, an attempt by finance capital to incorporate new and "emerging" powers into the extant world order—with the active assistance and endorsement of the elites of the BRICS nations themselves. (Taylor 2016: 60, 61; see also pp. 62–67, 75–76; Christensen and Xing 2016: 265–266)

---

[1]In 2008 the British ex-Prime Minister Tony Blair marked the worldwide significance of Amazonia, not only for Brazil but for all humankind, with far-reaching conclusions about monitoring this large area and establishing the international control of it.

What does essentially distinguish economies of the BRICS and other emerging countries (except a few of them like South Korea or Singapore that already emerged to the level of highly developed nations) from the West and make them vulnerable to the global market fluctuations in the long-term prospect? It is neither their economic model of development nor the internal misbalances but the low level of their economies' 'brain-intensity'. In particular, there is a problem of low value added in their manufacturing industries. The example of the Apple iPhone is the best illustration in this respect: the value added in the process of assembling this thing at Chinese plant of Apple accounts only for 3.5–3.6 per cent of its total wholesale price, whereas the rest 96.5 per cent are composed of the parts and details imported from other countries. Almost the same can be said about Mexican *maquiladoras* where the value added is about 3.0 per cent (Gilboy and Heginbotham 2012: 216–218; Salama 2014a: 23, 2014b: 33–34).[2] And, also, let 'admirers' of China's achievements, as well as various panic-makers in front of the Chinese global 'dominance', not forget that this second power in the world still loses at total labour productivity not only to the leading western economies and the first-tier 'tigers' (e.g. Korea) but to some emerging countries, such, in particular, as Chile of 2011 when the latter acquired the status of a high-income country (Mason and Shetty 2019: 1–2, 55–60).

Certainly, there are approved ways to elevate productivity levels such as scientific-technological development and stimulation of innovations. At first glance, it seems too obvious and banal that some forecasters of the Chinese forthcoming dominance do not consider this problem as the key issue of competition for the global leadership and mention it as something superficial or insignificant. In their opinion (methodologically rooted in economics of the nineteenth–twentieth centuries), only such factors of dominance in the world are important as: (a) resources and wealth, (b) position in the world trade, and (c) external financial relations, country's credits and debts (Subramanian 2011: 29–36, 39–42). Since 'admirers' of China's dominance think that it is easy to adopt and implement new technologies, hence China and 'the Rest' are capable of catching up with the West as soon as possible, and they not only catch up but will overtake and exceed it (Subramanian 2011: 70–81, 194–195).[3]

However, adoption and imitation of new technologies elaborated in other countries does not deliver from a *technological dependency*, which becomes even more significant today than 'the classical dependence' existing since the rise of the modern world-system and well described by many theoreticians of the former Third World development. And such an adoption is, in essence, not as easy as it seems initially. Meanwhile, it is still unclear whether China will be able to abolish the current

[2]'This is not China that exports but the ensemble of Asia which exports via China', Diana Hochraich noted sarcastically in connection to this (Hochraich 2007: 190).

[3]'...the diffusion of technology and information (including how to manage or rather not manage economic policy at macro and micro levels) may be proceeding so rapidly that catch-up—through not necessarily at a frenetic and uniform pace—is now becoming the norm rather than the exception that it has been until recently' (Subramanian 2011: 75).

productivity lag without using advanced western technologies (only due to self-reliance, domestic demand and the proper technological innovations) or not. As the real practice demonstrates, de-linkage from export-led economic growth and, in a broader sense, from *the associated-dependent development* is harder than to start up an engine of growth at the initial stages or to proceed on the known path.

Besides the abovementioned difficulties and deficiencies of further development of *all* emerging countries, there is the principal question about China's, India's or Brazil's capability of making the proper scientific-technological breakthroughs of global significance, for instance, creation of personal computers or discovery of DNA. Adoption of borrowed scientific-technological achievements is, of course, important for each country's development (not all countries, as we know, can adopt and implement the achievements of others), but it is insufficient for global leadership today. For global leadership, it is also necessary to have proper systems of scientific research which cannot arise from nothing, from sea foam, like Aphrodite, or being driven by bureaucratic innovative culture when innovations should rise by orders of 'clever officials'. Now no emerging country, including China, has such a system, the fascinating progress attained in this respect in the last two to three decades notwithstanding. Moreover, the system of education must orient students, beginning from the primary level of education, towards creative activity combined with critical thinking (*critically oriented consciousness*), and this is hardly compatible with 'cognitive conservatism' that had been cultivated in China over many centuries with emphasis on learning instead of studying (Krasilshchikov 2014: 167–168, 205–214; Ng 2001: 65). As Francesca Beausang noted in her book about the BRIC group (without South Africa) it has been a lack of critical thinking among the Chinese students that may impede an emergence of China to a genuinely innovative economy (Beausang 2012: 174–175). Even 'pro-Chinese' scholars who are biased to depreciate the recent and future difficulties of the China's development recognise today that:

> in China (and other East Asian countries), there is a long cultural tradition of respect and reverence for age and established authority, so that questioning attitude and challenges to accepted orthodoxy are rare, which makes truly break-through discoveries and inventions less likely. This is something that China must try to overcome. (Lau 2019: 197)

All stated problems of the emerging countries may potentially not only impede further development and transition to the status of advanced, fully developed countries but can also slow growth leading to prolonged stagnation. And it would be mistaken to assume that the recently growing countries, primarily China and India, will never fall into serious crisis.

3.2 The Great Advice of Gerschenkron and Brazil

Considering the emerging countries, including those with the development success stories, it is worth reflecting on ideas of Alexander Gerschenkron (1904–1978), well known as a scholar who studied the experience of catching up modernisations. His book *Economic Backwardness in Historical Perspective* (Gerschenkron 1979) became one of the classical books for students specialising in economic history and development studies. But few know that Gerschenkron studied not only success stories but also failures. One of his last works published 1 year before his death dealt with the attempt of modernisation that failed on various economic and institutional reasons. Namely, it was the case of economic reforms undertaken by Ernest von Körber, the Austrian prime minister (*Ministerpräsident*) in 1900–1904 and 1916.

Considering this case, Gerschenkron marked, firstly, a juvenile character of our social science. Namely, indeed, we like to study the rise of new social systems or orders and their functioning at the stage of maturity but ignore or, at best, underestimate a significance of their decline and disintegration. This preference is an obvious attempt to follow the one-linear vision of progress; the vision that is originally inherent to the specific *tradition of modernity*. According to such an approach, any development, whether it concerns a nature or human society, means an uninterruptible perfection, a transition, perhaps, uneven, from bad to good, from primitive to complicated forms, from ignorance to enlightenment, etc. In other words, any new thing, phenomenon or state is always better than an old one.[4] Meanwhile, as history demonstrates, a social development is not a one-dimensional, linear process, and achievements may alternate with failures or, at best, stagnations.

Secondly, Gerschenkron recommended to study failures and thought that such study is more useful and important than description of success:

> [But] failures rarely excite benevolence, and men's interest in them is easily suppressed. The listener's ear is eagerly lent to success stories and the reader's eye auspiciously turns in the same direction. The student of failure is likely to fail ... "I do believe that there is much to learn from some historical failures, and an economic spurt that failed may cast a ray of unfailing light upon things and events that should not be left in obscurity. (Gerschenkron 1977: 3,4.)

Perhaps it was not accidental that Gerschenkron devoted his last work to the case of unsuccessful, failed modernisation, because the concrete conditions of the late-1970s dissipated a naïve optimism of the original conceptions of modernisation born in the 1950s–1960s and gave examples of the incomplete and even fully failed

[4]Strictly speaking, this juvenile character of our social sciences is profoundly rooted in the culture and world-view of modernity, and this world-view had long ago become part of the specifically western tradition. Charles Perrault, who not only composed tales about Bluebeard, *Le Chat Botté* (Puss in Boots), Cinderella and Sleeping Beauty, also wrote the esthetical-philosophical treatise, expressing this world-view in a concentrated and simultaneously belletristic form. He asserted that new is always better than old, modern is better than ancient and therefore the future has to be better than the past (Perrault 1692).

reforms. (In this respect, the late-1970s anticipated the 1980s, known as 'the lost decade' for Latin American countries, and the 1990s when the Soviet project of modernisation finally collapsed, whereas many African countries underwent a decline of their economies and a respective fall of incomes.)

In the opinion of Gerschenkron, the most evident sign of failed modernisation is a 'disparity between aims and attainments' (Ibid.: 4). The story of the Austro-Hungarian empire with the Habsburg monarchy in the last decades of its existence was a clear case study of this disparity. Certainly, it would be wrong to say that modernisation did not occur in the empire at all, but it succeeded in a deep division of the whole country into the core and periphery. Some parts of Austria-Hungary experienced rapid development, their industries and urban areas grew fast. For instance, the Lower Austrian lands (Cisleithania), apart from Bohemia and Moravia, underwent the development of manufacturing industries, and industrialists were the leading actors of this modernisation. The Hungarian territories (Hungary and 'vicinities'—Transcisleithania) were a zone of specific *conservative modernisation*[5] where the land magnates invested in agriculture and industries based upon inputs of agricultural origin (foodstuffs and clothing industries). At the same time, many other parts of the empire stagnated, not experiencing modernisation at all (Komlosy 2014: 7–10, 29–37; Milward and Saul 1977: 289–296, 323–329). Such extreme unevenness of development aggravated interethnic and interregional disparities, thereby sowing seeds of separatism and disintegration. This problem was resolved only through the deliberate process of further modernisation aimed at more balanced development of different parts of the empire.

However, all efforts of the Habsburg's governments were subordinate to the maintenance of internal stability and to oppression of regional separatism. This oppression was combined with a set of compromises between Vienna and the local territories with different degrees of national-cultural autonomy. Such ambiguous and seemingly flexible policy of the reigning Habsburg dynasty was expressed in the existence of the Dual Monarchy since 1867, Austrian and Hungarian. This dualism relieved socio-political tensions after the Hungarian uprising of 1848–1849 and facilitated the control of limitrophe lands, neutralising the separatist tendencies, particularly of the pan-Slavic origin. Respectively, there were two governments and two parliaments. For instance, the Hungarian authorities were autonomous in many important affairs of internal life. Their power spread to the large territories with non-Hungarian (but not German-speaking) populations. However, Austria (Cisleithania) and Hungary (Transcisleithania) were united as parts of the same empire by unequal complementarity when the Vienna throne dominated over the Budapest authorities (the Emperor Franz Joseph I and the Empress Elizabeth (Sisi) had the titles of the King and Queen of Hungary, respectively). The ministries of defence, foreign affairs and finances were centralised in Vienna. In fact, it created institutional discordance with the main task of modernisation, namely, with the

[5]The concept of conservative modernisation will be considered in the next chapter.

eradication of deep disparities between the few developed regions (e.g. the Low Austria, Bohemia, Moravia, Southern Silesia) and backward periphery.

Considering the attempt of Körber to approach large-scale modernisation through stimulating the Cisleithanian economy, Gerschenkron underlined Körber's strategic vision: the ability to subordinate different aspects of politics to one main goal of the country's economic development.[6] In particular, Körber had the far-reaching plan of new railway construction and thought about measures of state protection for industries. Nevertheless, as Gerschenkron noted, all attempts to realise his plans met with strong impediments of physical (material), institutional and social-political character (Gerschenkron 1977: 50–51). There were long distances between the industrial centres and seacoasts, and the poorly developed transport infrastructure could not compensate for this shortcoming. The existing political institutions had weak linkages of different authorities' bodies to each other, and complicated, sometimes archaic bureaucratic procedures for decision-making did not allow the centralisation of the required resources for development. Various controversies between different parts of the state machine arose, often because of misunderstanding about the common strategic tasks, for example, between the central Ministry of Finances and the Austrian Ministry of Commerce. The former intended to cut expenditures; the latter, on the contrary, treated them as indispensable investments. In addition, many parliamentarians and top bureaucrats did not conceive of the problems of backwardness and development at all. As a result of a lack of the elite's interest in broad modernisation, Körber could not mount a resistance to the conservative circles to the plans of reforms, and therefore resigned. His return to the position of *Ministerpräsident* in 1916, in the conditions when the Austro-Hungarian monarchy was losing the war, could not rescue the empire. Its relative backwardness and incapability of the ruling groups to modernise their country predetermined the defeat and subsequent disintegration.

What are the implications of the 'unsuccess story' described by Gerschenkron for the emerging nations today, 120 years after the Körber's attempt to modernise the 'non-modernised' country?

Apart from the necessity to study the experience of failed reforms as a whole, this experience is significant on the following reasons:

– Any modernisation or set of reforms presupposes a widespread comprehension of necessity to change the current situation, at least, for the sake of preventing possible future threats and crises. Is there such a comprehension in emerging countries today? Certainly, it exists in the ruling circles of China, although

[6]Körber comprehended the relative backwardness of Austria in comparison to Germany and other leading West European countries. Indeed, in spite of the notable industrial output growth in Austria proper in the late nineteenth to the early twentieth centuries, even in 1911–1913, on the eve of the war, agriculture accounted for 49 per cent of the national product, whereas the share of industry only 37.9 per cent. Then foodstuffs, textile and clothing industries prevailed in total industrial output, a notable boom in metallurgical and engineering, machinery-building branches notwithstanding (Milward and Saul 1977: 296–314).

various groupings of the Chinese rulers understand a necessity and direction of further transformations to a different degree. The situation in India is more complicated and diversified in this respect. There are influential groups of the upper social strata which prefer to return back to the 'blessed times' of the Indian National Congress rule with the strong state regulation of economy. What concerns other big emerging countries (Argentina, Brazil, Mexico or Russia) is that there are serious doubts about an adequate assessment of their recent situation by their dominating elite groups. A narrow circle of the critically thinking intellectuals, 'advanced' entrepreneurs and 'enlightened' bureaucrats are out of account in the given cases.

– A profound, radical reform in economy or social sphere must be accompanied by a corresponding transformation of political and judicial institutions. Otherwise a discrepancy between the intention to carry out the economic reforms and their institutional accompaniment will inevitably succeed in twilight of the reformatory spurt with subsequent stagnation or, at best, with *the growth without development* situation. Will the state institutions in China (with the omnipotent power of the Communist party and political authoritarianism, which corresponded to the task of catching up modernisation 30 years ago) be changed in direction to bigger democratisation and pluralism? Is the Westminster-styled Indian political system with relics of the caste hierarchy able to resolve the country's acute socioeconomic and environmental problems? Has not the Brazilian democracy with a huge number of political parties been the obstacle to all attempts of the preceding presidents to implement rational, progressive reforms because the proposed reforms touch the particular interests of numerous 'groups of influence'?
– The story of Körber's attempts to modernise the core part of the Austro-Hungarian empire (he had no power in Hungary!) without the respective efforts applied to development of the large peripheries highlighted the problem of unevenness of modernisation in different parts (regions) of a large country. If, for example, the efforts of Körber were successful within the borders of Austria (Cisleithania), they should inevitably have succeeded in widening disparities between the core (Austria) and the empire's peripheries performed by Hungary, not speaking about Croatia, Galicia or Bukovina. An existence of the large internal peripheries, the zones of backwardness and poverty, would depreciate the real or potential achievements of modernisation in the core. It should become the difficultly surmountable obstacle to further expansion of market and would be a reservoir of cheap, unskilled labour force. In the light of Körber's experience, we can today ask ourselves: will the interregional disparities in China between the Southeast and West block the government's attempts to transit to the new stage of development? Will the existence of a large internal periphery in India succeed in the split between the advanced states and 'the rest', between Karnataka and Bihar (Bangalore and Patna as their capitals) with the subsequent rise of powerful social movements against modernisation under the slogans of justice? Will the other emerging countries face widening internal disparities while concentrating efforts and resources for creation of the advanced enclaves with high-tech production?

- At last, Gerschenkron's study of Körber's experience reminds us of the problem of social forces (actors) interested in modernisation or, on the contrary, in conservation of status quo. This problem is perhaps the most important among all implications of the Gerschenkron's study for contemporaneity. The main conclusion from the case study of Körber's activity consists in a necessity to search for the social groups and political actors who can carry out modernisation or, on the contrary, resist even to moderate reforms because of their egoistic vested interests.

All emerging countries have approximately the same general problem that can be reduced to one common denominator—to avoid the state of permanently emerging nations and to attain a high level of development not only in technical-economic but in all respects. Otherwise they risk losing the global competition and slipping to the world periphery with negative effects for their population. (As it is well known, according to *the Alice-in-Wonderland* principles, it is necessary to run faster if you want to stay in the same place.) In particular, the emerging countries have to reduce a qualitative gap in productivity and technologies between themselves and the West. However, they will hardly be able to do it without: (a) the crucial dissatisfaction by their proper recent attainments in spite of definite positive achievements in the past; (b) the respective combination of socioeconomic reforms, technological upgrading and institutional accompaniment; and (c) sufficient power of the social actors of further modernisation.

Can China, India, Brazil and other emerging countries meet these preliminary conditions in their attempt to make new steps through the process of development? Meanwhile, there is a threat of failure not foreseen by Gerschenkron: a failure can be the effect of a previous success story, as it has happened to the newly industrialised countries (NICs) of East Asia in 1997–1998 (a situation of 'the malaise from success'). A success story can little by little shift proper transformation into a failure story. This is often written about by the French economist Pierre Salama, who devotes many pages to comparative analysis of Latin American and East Asian countries' development (Salama 2000, 2006, 2012a, b, c, 2014a, b), and writes about the prospects of these emerging countries with unconcealed anxiety. He notes that their future has been shading (*leur avenir s'assombrie*) because the preceding model of their development, successful in the past (from the 1990s to 2008–2009 and onwards a little, to 2014–2015 in some of them—V.Kr.), came to its objective limits, whereas the rise of a new one is not yet seen (Salama 2014a: 22–26, 29–31, b: 11–12, 145; see also World Bank 2018: 29, 39–41). *The case of Brazil illustrates this situation very clearly*, perhaps even clearer than development stories of other emerging countries over the last twenty-twenty five years.

Up to 2012, as it seemed to many observers (including, to my regret, myself—V. Kr.), Brazil appeared to be a country that could perform the real alternative to 'pure' neoliberal recipes, to the Chinese model with excessively big role of the state authorities and to the Bolivarian 'socialism of the twenty-first century' which has actually been even worse than many versions of the twentieth-century socialism. Brazil provided the economic growth upon the base of market economy, being open to foreign direct investment, and combined it with strong social policy, slowly but steadily reducing the pre-existing income and social inequalities. In fact, Brazil gave a good example of *inclusive growth* (which has become a new mantra of solid international organisations, including the US-led Bretton Woods institutions). Brazil demonstrated the effective functioning of political democracy with regular free elections. Finally, Brazil successfully collaborated with western partners as well as with countries historically pertained to the South and sometimes softened frictions between the USA and Leftist governments of Bolivia or Venezuela. By the end of the first decade of this century, it was easy to find rapturous publications that predicted the Great Future for Brazil and ascension of the country to the rank of an economic superpower (Brainard and Martinez-Diaz 2009: 11–13). *The Economist*, the magazine which never regarded the Left and Left-centrist policies with favour, marked that political democracy, economic growth and low inflation sustained together for the first time in Brazil's history, and now (in 2006–2010—V.Kr.) 'the country is enjoying probably in best moment since a group of Portuguese sailors (looking for India) washed up on its shores in 1500' (Economist 2009: 3). Indeed, then Brazil was performing as one of the most successful emerging countries with democracy—implicitly in contrast to China with the authoritarian regime and permanent restraints of human rights.

However suddenly something wrong has happened, and Brazil has fallen into an acute economic, social, institutional and political crisis, suffering from the deepest recession since the early 1930s when the liberal model of economy, which existed since colonial times, collapsed under impact of the Great Depression in the core of the world-system. This quick fall from success to a quagmire of stagnation over a few years is not the first example in the country's history. The industrial spurt after the early 1930s crisis lasted with some fluctuations about 25 years, until the beginning of the 1960s, and turned into the new structural crisis culminated, in the political respect, by the coup d'état in 1964. The industrial boom of 1967–1974 under the authoritarian regime alternated with a complement of commercial, fiscal and economic difficulties that led to 'the lost decade' of the 1980s. The period of successful growth in 2003–2012 was succeeded by recession and stagnation, the longest in the modern history of Brazil. Thus, the Brazilian development trajectory over 80–90 years can be treated as a case study of the situation recommended by Gerschenkron for scrutiny but with one essential remark. Gerschenkron considered the economic spurt that was ceased at the initial stage, i.e. declined at the start. The Brazilian spurts started and proceeded over some years. Their attainments did not disappear without a trace in the depths of historical time, although they underwent a lot of negative, destructive impacts.

In light of the Brazilian experience, does China or India risk undergoing the similar period of growth and prosperity quickly turning into decline? Perhaps today any assertive answer to this question seems absurd and impossible, taken from a sphere of non-scientific fantasy. However, these and other problems are common for the group of emerging countries as a whole and can play the role of socioeconomic detonator, turning an emergence into descent. And if it is difficult to imagine that Brazil, Mexico or any other country of Latin America might follow the development path of China, it is possible, on the contrary, to recognise a risk for China, India or other Asian countries with apparent success stories to find themselves in the same situation as these Latin American countries. The current experience of Brazil can be very instructive and useful for East Asia and, by the way, for some parts of the former First World, developed countries too.

One of the important features of Brazilian development consists in a peculiar universality of this development. The latter concentrates in itself the main features of all three worlds existing in the second half of the twentieth century, and Brazil today shows many phenomena and trends, though sometimes in hypertrophied forms, from the recent reality and the nearest future of other countries as well. The idea about 'Brazilianisation' of the West and China can be found in publications since the beginning of new century not without reasons (Beck 2000: 1–9, 93–106; Gimarães 2007: 165–168). The most essential of such reasons is the observable processes of labour market precarisation in the West when a boundary between 'unemployed' and 'labourer' and between 'employed' and 'inactive' has been eroded because employment becomes, in extending degree, temporary, precarious activity resembling, in many aspects, to the labour market in Brazil. (Below we shall return to this issue, considering it in details; see Chap. 3). In connection with the precarisation of labour, some analysts write about *Latin-Americanisation of China* though not always directly using this term (Babones 2011: 86; see also Gilboy and Heginbotham 2012: 209–214). In the opinion of Pierre Salama, the current socio-economic processes in China have been resembling those in Brazil in the years of 'miracle', 1967–1974. Namely, in both cases the rise of the new middle class was rapid and accompanied by a deepening income inequality not only between the rich and poor but also between the middle and lower social groups. The production of technically complicated durable consumer goods, often by transnational corporations, grew rapidly to the advantage of this stratum, which, in exchange, supported, though with some 'remarks', the developmental authoritarian political regime (Salama 2012d: 115, 192–193).

Certainly, the current unfavourable situation in Brazil or some other Latin American countries is, in essence, the extreme variant of failed development. The Asian emerging countries have the chance to avoid it, not falling into the similar deep recession with subsequent long-term stagnation. But 'Latin-Americanisation' or 'Brazilianisation' of China and other seemingly lucky Asian emerging nations is probable, and it can lead them to the middle-income trap where some Latin American countries, in particular, the biggest of them, Brazil, have already been for a long time, since 1980–1982, with rare breaks for brief terms of growth.

3.3 The Middle-Income Trap: Is There an Exit?

The middle-income trap means a situation of prolonged slowdown of a country's growth after a successful industrial spurt at the initial stages of development. Then a country ceases being poor, least-developed and attains the middle level of incomes and production technologies. Also, this trap means stagnation in a qualitative respect: a lack of technological development when the previously obtained structures of economy and society continue existing without significant changes (*growth without development*), so it is better to speak about *the middle-development trap*. This concept is broader than the middle-income trap and reflects the possibility of temporary economic growth in the conditions of backward structure of economy with a domination of obsolete technologies. As we will see below, in the next chapters, this is just the case of Brazil over the last 20 years: good rates of the economic growth in 2003–2011 and impressive reduction of poverty notwithstanding. What concerns the middle-income trap conception, it has a peculiar 'merit' to be scrutinised for the sake of better comprehension of the emerging countries' rising problems.

A pioneering work where the term *middle-income trap* has appeared for the first time has been the book by Indermit Gill and Homi Kharas devoted to East Asian development after the crisis of 1997–1998. The authors considered the newly industrialised countries of East and Southeast Asia as *the middle-income countries* at the global scale (Gill et al. 2007: 3–5). Certainly, they understood that a group of countries under their scrutiny was diverse; it embraced Hong Kong and Singapore with per capita incomes higher than many highly developed nations had either such countries as Laos or Cambodia with incomes much lower than the middle world level. However, Gill and Kharas, considering East Asian economies as a whole, conceived that the average income per capita in the region just corresponded to that level. In this connection, they warned about a probability for these economies to stagnate at the attained stage of development like Latin American countries did over decades after their industrialisation spurt in the mid-twentieth century. Gill and Kharas marked, too, the ways to avoid such a trap: to search for the balance between diversification and effective specialisation of economies, to take into account that an importance of investment in fixed capital will decrease whereas a role of innovations will rise, and to reorient the education system from training workers to be disciplined executives to preparing them to create new products (Gill et al. 2007: 17–18).

After the Great Recession of 2008–2009, a great volume of publications was written devoted to the middle-income trap problem. Respectively, definitions of the middle-income trap reflected new nuances to a great extent, but the main sign of this phenomenon remained and remains today unchanged: it means a situation when 'countries that avoided the poverty trap and grew to middle-income levels subsequently stagnate and fail to grow to advanced-country levels' (Kharas and Kohli 2011: 281). A similar definition has been performed in the IMF working paper by Shekhar Aiyar and his colleagues (Aiyar et al. 2013: 3).

It is notable that a fall into the middle-income trap is not predetermined and inevitable: some East Asian countries passed the middle-income level and attained the high-income level avoiding long stagnation (Kharas and Kohli 2011: 281–282). The same concerns also such countries as Finland, Ireland, Spain, Portugal, Czech Republic and Estonia in Europe and Barbados and Trinidad and Tobago in the Caribbean (Latin America) (Foxley 2012: 11; see also: Im and Rosenblatt 2013: 4–5). Nonetheless, it is worth remembering that three quarters of middle-income countries in 1960 remained as middle-income or even regressed to low-income 50 years later, in 2009. Only one fourth of them became high-income countries, mainly in Western and Central Europe, but also, of course, Japan and the first-tier East Asian 'tigers' (Izvorski 2011). Therefore, the likelihood of falling into the middle-income trap is higher than the chances of avoiding it. At the same time, all comparisons of recently existing middle-income countries with those in the past are relative because the concrete structure of incomes and consumption today differs from the structure that existed even 20–25 years ago. Many things that were then prestigious or luxury goods today became accessible to poor people (e.g. cell phones and other electronic gadgets). These rapid changes in the structure of incomes and patterns of consumption do not facilitate counting the number of middle-income countries over decades, and Justin Yifu Lin and David Rosenblatt put attention to this problem of *relativity* for all attempts to calculate how many middle-income countries exist at any given time (Lin and Rosenblatt 2012: 175–176).

In this regard, it is essential to clarify the criteria (or, at least, one main criterion) of middle income: what are the quantitative terms of such income? Indeed, since the middle-income level has been changing over time, answers to this question can hardly be easy. Fernando Im and David Rosenblatt defined a middle-income country according to some quantifiable parameters: in the beginning of the second decade of the recent century (i.e. in 2011–2013), a 'typical' middle-income country would have per capita income of about $4000, an adult literacy rate of between 70 and 93 per cent, infant mortality of about 1[illegible] to 50 per 1000 live births and life expectancy—between 65 and 72 years (Im and Rosenblatt 2013: 2–3). Evidently, such a broad range of indicators allows for some poor and least-developed countries into the group of middle-income ones. Indeed, according to the World Bank classifications established in 2010, a middle-income country has per capita income between $1005 and $12,275. Until 2018 this range did not change notably; it has been between $1026 and $12,375. In addition, within the large group of middle-income countries, there are two subgroups, the lower- and upper-middle-income countries. The former have per capita income between $1026 and $3995, the latter—between $3996 and $12,375.

Alejandro Foxley, referring to IMF, regarded the middle-income countries as those with per capita income between $[illegible]000 and $22,000 on PPP (parity of purchasing power) in 2010 (Foxley 2012: 16–19). Lin and Rosenblatt proposed another criterion of a country's pertinence to the middle-income countries' group: the ratio of a country's per capita GDP to the level of the USA per capita GDP. In their opinion, a ratio between 0.3 and 0.7 can be assessed as middle-income level, and, as the authors have shown, the number of countries with per capita GDP in ratio to the US level within the called interval increased from 1990 and 2008 and continued increasing onwards (Lin and Rosenblatt 2012: 175–176). Seemingly, the criterion proposed by Lin and Rosenblatt looks more flexible and universal than that linked to the concrete amount of GDP per capita because the latter increases over a long period; therefore, the criterion of middle income cannot be unchangeable for all times. However, this criterion implicitly presupposes that the USA will continue being the world hegemon and economic-technological leader for an indefinite time, whereas the US GDP per capita is not the biggest in the world. It would be better to relate country per capita income to the average income in a group of the most advanced 10 to 12 countries of the OECD, taking into account a set of qualitative indicators of development: a life expectancy at birth, productivity of labour and the total factor productivity per one employed person, state of environment, healthcare, etc.

A relativity of the chosen criteria of middle-income countries has been approving by changes of number of such countries according to these criteria. Such changes can be performed in a form of table embracing a period of more than 25 years, 1990–2018 (Table 3.1).

A relativity and variability of the middle income's magnitude induced Lynge Nielsen to propose the proper countries' classification. He compared the classifications performed by the IMF, World Bank, UNDP (United Nations Development Programme) and, partly, OECD to each other, observing simultaneously a brief history of each classification (Nielsen 2011: 7–19, 20–23). At the same time, Nielsen introduced not dichotomous (poor/rich or developing/developed countries, poorly/highly medically protected and poorly/well-educated population, etc.) but trichotomous taxonomy of development. According to Nielsen's approach:

> an optimal partition requires that each threshold, *Xi*, is chosen such that the development outcome of country *Xi* is equal to the average development outcome of the countries in the interval from the previous threshold, *Xi-1*, to the subsequent threshold, *Xi+1*. For example, in a development taxonomy with four categories: LDC, lower MDC, upper MDC, and HDC,[7] the lowest threshold would be set such that a country at that threshold had a development outcome equal to the average development outcome of all countries in the LDC, and lower MDC groups. (Nielsen 2011: 30–31)

He proposed using three different proxies for characterising the actual level of development of each country: income, life expectancy at birth and lifetime income. The latter is a multiplication of the income and life expectancy at birth variables, 'what may be the most important economic indicator and the most important social indicator of development outcomes' (Nielsen 2011: 32). Obviously, this approach, synthesising the economic and social indicators of development, allows the determination of the middle level of development, not reducing it to the middle-income level.

Pierre-Richard Agénor observed classifications of countries with the goal to select the middle-income countries, too. He performed the detailed review of literature devoted to this issue and the middle-income trap problem as well (Agénor 2015: 3–9). Agénor underlined that the latter problem has not only the quantitative aspect (a slowdown of growth or stagnation at the middle-income level) but also the qualitative dimension, namely, poor quality of productive technologies, infrastructure, human capital, governance, public institutions, etc. (Agénor 2015: 10–11).

Since the middle-income trap problem has not only the quantitative but also qualitative aspects, it can be considered from different points of view with an

---

[7]The least-developed, middle-developed and highly developed countries, respectively.

Table 3.1 The number of countries classified by the income categories, 1990–2018

Category of income	Indicators of each category	1990	1995	2000	2005	2010	2015	2018
Low income	The number of countries	51	63	63	54	35	31	31
	The level of income (US$)	≤610	≤765	≤755	≤875	≤1005	≤1025	≤1025
Lower-middle income	The number of countries	56	64	53	57	56	52	47
	The level of income (US$)	611–2465	766–3035	756–2995	876–3465	1006–3975	1026–4035	1026–3995
Upper-middle income	The number of countries	29	28	37	39	53	56	60
	The level of income (US$)	2466–7620	3036–9385	2996–9265	3466–10,725	3976–12,275	4036–12,475	3996–12,375
High income	The number of countries	39	48	52	56	71	79	80
	The level of income (US$)	>7620	>9385	>9265	>10,725	>12,275	>12,475	>12,376

Source: the author's calculation on the World Bank data. Viewed on 04.02.2020—http://databank.worldbank.org/data/download/site-content/CLASS.xls; http://databank.worldbank.org/data/download/site-content/OGHIST.xls; https://datahelpdesk.worldbank.org/knowledgebase/articles/906519-world-bank-country-and-lending-groups emphasis on one or another aspect. Eva Paus puts attention, at least, to three approaches to the middle-income trap problem (Paus 2014: 13–24). These are the structuralist approach, which focuses mainly on a lack of the structural changes and technological upgrading in economy, the approach from the point of view of growth slowdown and the approach that stresses on globalisation and place of a country in the world economy. All these approaches do not exclude but, rather, supplement each other. In particular, according to opinion of Paus, the middle-income trap problem refers to:

> a situation where a middle-income country can no longer compete internationally in standardized, labor-intensive commodities because wages are relatively too high, but it can also not compete in higher value added activities on a broad enough scale because productivity is too low. (Paus 2014: 9; see also Kharas and Kohli 2011: 282; Agénor 2015: 5–6)

Lee Keun, who devoted a whole book to the positive experience of Korea and Taiwan in escaping the so-called trap, gave a similar definition. In his words, the middle-income trap is:

> a situation in which middle-income countries face a slowdown of growth as they get caught between low-wage manufacturers and high-wage innovators because their wage rates are too high to compete with low-wage exporters and their level of technological capability is too low to allow them to compete with the advanced countries. (Lee 2013: 5)

Alejandro Foxley extended the structuralist approach to the middle-income trap to such aspect as the difficulty to sustain the rate of growth higher than 5 per cent over a decade *in combination* with a reduction of inequality and consolidation of democratic institutions (Foxley 2012: 11). Similarly, Paus expanded the same approach to the problem under scrutiny to the large context of globalisation. Then middle income means 'the insufficient development of productive capabilities for innovation in the specific context of the current globalisation process' and can succeed in socioeconomic and technological regression with declining standards of life for a big part of population (Paus 2014: 18). Indeed, such a prospect is a real threat to many middle-income countries that find themselves between 'two fires', the increasingly sophisticated economies of the West and the rapidly technologically and intellectually upgrading China (Paus 2014: 20).

Meanwhile, a slowdown of economic growth after attaining the middle-income level does not mean a full stagnation. Economies can continue growing and technologically upgrading but at a slower pace than is necessary for competing at the world market and simultaneously resolving internal social problems.

Kharas and Kohli attempted to distil character features of all middle-income countries. According to these authors, in such countries 'growth tends to become more capital intensive and skill intensive in manufacturing... ...and to be more heavily oriented toward services' (Kharas and Kohli 2011: 285). Middle-income countries face the challenge of transition to more demand- and services-oriented economies, including their export sector. However, some countries remain with the obsolete structure of their production and exports, losing their competitiveness, in particular, because of excessive income inequality that impedes the growth of demand for services and the required accumulation of human capital (Kharas and Kohli 2011: 285–286).

A slowdown of economic growth after a country has reached the middle level of income per capita has been correlated with a broad set of factors: human capital quality, external trade conditions, financial (in)stability, functioning of the political and legal institutions, etc. (Eichengreen et al. 2013: 7–14). For example, Shekhar Aiyar and his colleagues mentioned 42 factors that can accelerate or, on the contrary, deter economic growth at the middle level. They grouped these factors into seven categories: (1) institutions, (2) demographic factors, (3) infrastructure, (4) macroeconomic environment and policies, (5) economic structure, (6) trade structure and (7) others (Aiyar et al. 2013: 13–29). At the same time, different factors play different roles in falling of a country into the middle-income trap; in other words, a significance of various factors is different by country (Ibid.: 32–36). It means that a slowdown of growth of the middle-income economies begins at different levels in different countries, but it has always been accompanied by the productivity growth slowdowns (Agénor and Canuto 2012: 3–6, 26; Eichengreen et al. 2011: 8; Eichengreen et al. 2012: 54; Paus 2014: 27–28). The average level of income, at which the signs of a middle-income trap become evident, is 16,740 US$ (in 2005 constant international prices on PPP), but a probability of falling into the so-called trap notably increases when a country reaches a level of GDP per capita equal to 15,389 $ in 2005 prices (Eichengreen et al. 2011: 9). (Obviously, this amount recalculated in prices of 2010 or 2015 is higher a little.) Another indicator that shows the increased probability of falling into the middle-income trap is the share of manufacturing in total employment around 23 per cent (Ibid.: 6–7, 14; Eichengreen et al. 2012: 50, 66). In addition, Eichengreen and colleagues have found that the probability of falling into the middle-income trap is low when the share of consumption in GDP is between 62 and 64 per cent (Eichengreen et al. 2012: 74), though they do not clearly explain why this is the case. It is possible to presuppose that this level of consumption is correlated with the rate of investment in GDP, on which the pace of growth depends. Meanwhile, as it is known, different structures of investment and consumption may have different effects on growth. Hence, the rate of consumption that prevents stagnation at the middle level of incomes and development may vary from one country to another.

Generalising data on 45 countries and territories from 1957 to 2005, Eichengreen with colleagues formulated the three essential conditions for growth slowdown after the initial modernisation spurt: (1) the rate of GDP growth has been equal to or exceeded 3.5 per cent during seven or more years; (2) the rate of GDP growth after 'good' period decreases by 2.0 or more per cent points (e.g. from 5.5 to 3.3 per cent) in subsequent 7 or more years; and (3) the minimal per capita GDP exceeds 10,000 US$ in 2005 constant international prices (Eichengreen et al. 2011: 5, 2012: 45–46, 2013: 5, 18–24).

Sh. Aiyar proposed another criterion of slowdown: the latter takes place if the rate of growth is lower than the expected growth with a given amount of capital and labour over 5 years (Aiyar et al. 2013: 9–10). Counting frequencies of slowdown episodes for low-, middle-, and high-income countries, Aiyar and colleagues came to conclusion that the middle-income countries underwent slowdowns of their economic growth more frequently over the 1960–2005 period than the countries belonging to two other groups (Aiyar et al. 2013: 12). It therefore seems that the middle-income countries are more vulnerable to the conjuncture fluctuations and crises than the least-developed and highly developed countries. Unfortunately, the performed statement of these interesting facts remained without adequate explanation.

Together with attempts to elaborate the general conception of middle-income trap, the concrete studies of this phenomenon in several countries and regions have risen, too. The main focus of such studies is directed to the case of China and other Asian countries with recommendations for how to avoid the so-called trap (ADB 2017: 47–109; Gill and Kharas 2015; Huang et al. 2018; Jankowska et al. 2012: 4–14; OECD 2013: 32–40, 275–348; World Bank 2013: 11–12, 80–83, 378; Zhuang et al. 2012: 9–14, 47–64). Latin American countries that experience a period of time in this trap over many years attract lesser attention of the middle-income trap students than Asia; nevertheless, they are not completely ignored (Domínguez and Caria 2016; Foxley 2012; Paus 2014; Paus 2018). According to Lee Keun, the best and only way to avoid this trap for Asian and Latin American countries is to use the experience of Korean and Taiwanese firms that were specialising in quickly renewable ('short-cycle') technologies for sustained catch-up with the world leaders (Lee 2013, esp. pp. 127–177, 223–228). Unfortunately, the author in his detailed study does not consider whether it is enough for success to only have the desire to follow the so-called 'tigers' path or whether it is also necessary to have many other conditions for avoiding the middle-development trap. In particular, performing the first-tier 'tigers' as the story of successfully avoiding this trap, Lee Keun does not mention a set of unique conditions, including ones such as the specific role of these countries in the Cold War in Asia, which favoured their expansion into the Western markets.

A fall into the middle-income trap with subsequent stagnation or *the growth without development situation* can be treated as a specific, particular case of failure stories. A further study of such stories, according to the recommendation of Gerschenkron, discovers the next set of problems behind a simple slowdown of economic dynamics. These problems concern an issue of *social actors* interested in the rise of new, more innovative, prospective models of development and capable of implementing a desirable alternative to the obsolete system. Indeed, as the experience of reforms and catching up modernisations in the past century shows, it is insufficient to have necessary material resources and technical capacities for successful development. The people who can use those resources in appropriate manner are also indispensable, and a lack of such people may doom all exciting modernisation plans to failure in spite of initial good material and technical premises for success.

However, numerous recommendations about avoiding the middle-income trap and elevating a country to the next stage of development ignore the problem of social actors. They do not consider elementary questions: Is society ready to accept and implement the necessary recommendations? Are labourers interested in improving their skills? Is there the long-term interest of entrepreneurs to apply new technologies, perhaps, at cost of some part of their incomes for current consumption? Can the system of education supply a sufficient amount of skilled specialists? Without answering these questions, all attempts to solve the recent problems risk becoming a kind of wishful thinking without visible efficient results.

Thus, the radical, long-term solution of the seemingly 'pure' economic problems presupposes multi-dimensional profound transformation of various aspects of social life and cannot be reduced to either technical or administrative decisions. Such transformation means, in essence, all-embracing social revolution lasting many years. Are the emerging or/and middle-income countries, China, India, Brazil or, for example, Thailand, ready to carry out such long-term revolution? This is a big question, yet without answer.

All these and similar questions concern Brazil, perhaps to a greater degree than many other emerging countries. In my opinion, the main problem of Brazil is not a shortage of material or technological resources but a lack or, at best, a weakness of social actors who can lead and carry out the process of transformation from 'tropical Russia' to tropical post-industrial, knowledge-based society with inclusion of large masses of people into the development process. At the same time, an existence or, on the contrary, lack of such social actors depends on the concrete social structure, preceding development, the existing system of education and many other circumstances and factors of tangible or intangible character. Do the recent conditions of Brazil favour the rise of actors of the twenty-first-century development? Unfortunately, there are serious reasons why this may not be the case, as we shall see below. In particular there are social actors interested in conservation of the current situation. Such influential actors are the long-term result of *conservative modernisation* which has been central to Brazil since colonial times and plantation slavery.

References

ADB (Asian Development Bank). (2008). *Asian Development Outlook 2008. Workers in Asia.* Mandaluyong City, Metro Manila: ADB.

ADB. (2017). *Asian Development Outlook 2017. Transcending the middle-income challenge.* Mandaluyong City, Metro Manila: ADB.

Agénor, P.-R. (2015). *Caught in the middle? The economics of middle-income traps.* (Fondation pour les études et recherches Sur le développement international. Working paper 142). Paris: FERDI.

Agénor, P.-R., & Canuto, O. (2012). *Middle-income growth traps. World Bank policy research working paper 6210.* World Bank: Washington, DC.

Aiyar, S., Duval, R., Puy, D., Yiqun, W., & Zhang, L. (2013). *Growth slowdowns and the middle-income trap. The IMF Working Paper 13/79.* Washington, DC: IMF (International Monetary Fund).

Babones, S. (2011). The middling kingdom: The hype and the reality of China's rise *Foreign Affairs, 90*(5), 79–88.

Bardhan, P. (2010). *Awakening giants, feet of clay. Assessing the economic rise of China and India.* Princeton, Oxford: Princeton University Press.

Beausang, F. (2012). *Globalization and the BRICs: Why the BRICs will not rule the world for long*. Houndmills, Basingstoke: Palgrave Macmillan.
Beck, U. (2000). *The brave new world of work (Translated by P. Camiller)*. Cambridge, UK: Polity Press.
Brainard, & Martinez-Diaz (Eds.). (2009). *Brazil as an economic superpower?: Understanding Brazil's changing role in the global economy*. Brookings Institution Press.
Christensen, S. F., & Xing, L. (2016). Emerging powers, emerging markets, emerging societies: Global responses. In S. F. Christensen & L. Xing (Eds.), *Emerging powers, emerging markets, emerging societies: Global responses* (pp. 259–267). Houndmills, Basingstoke: Palgrave Macmillan.
Domínguez, R., & Caria, S. (2016). Ecuador en la trampa de la renta media. *Revista Problemas del Desarrollo, 187*(47), 89–112.
Economist. (2009). "Getting it together at last". A special report on business and finance in Brazil. *The Economist, 393*(8657), 16.
Eichengreen, B., Park, D., & Shin, K. (2011) *When fast-growing economies slow down: international evidence and implications for China (National Bureau of economic research. NBER working paper series, WP N 16919)*. Cambridge, MA: NBER.
Eichengreen, B., Park, D., & Shin, K. (2012). When fast-growing economies slow down: international evidence and implications for China. *Asian Economic Papers, 11*(1), 42–87.
Eichengreen, B., Park, D., & Shin, K. (2013). *Growth slowdown Redux: New evidence on the middle-income trap (National Bureau of Economic Research. NBER working paper series, WP N 18673)*. Cambridge, MA: NBER.
Foxley, A. (2012). *La trampa del ingreso medio. El desafío de esta década para América Latina*. Santiago de Chile: CIEPLAN.
Gaulard, M. (2014). *Karl Marx à Pékin: Les racines de la crise en Chine capitaliste*. Paris: Demopolis.
Gerschenkron, A. (1977). *An economic spurt that failed. Four lectures in Austrian history*. Princeton, NJ: Princenton University Press.
Gerschenkron, A. (1979). *Economic backwardness in historical perspective. A book of essays*. Cambridge, MA: The Belknap Press (1st edition – 1962).
Gilboy, G., & Heginbotham, E. (2012). *Chinese and Indian strategic behavior. Growing power and alarm*. Cambridge, NY: Cambridge University Press.
Gill, I., & Kharas, H. (2015). *The middle-income trap turns ten. World Bank policy research working paper 7403*. Washington, DC: World Bank.
Gill, I., Kharas, H., et al. (2007). *An east Asian renaissance: Ideas for economic growth*. Washington, DC: World Bank.
Gimarães, N. A. (2007). La "brésilianisation" de l'Occident? *Revue Tiers Monde, 189*, 155–174.
Hochraich, D. (2007). *Pourquoi l'Inde et la Chine ne domineront pas le monde de demain*. Paris: Ellipses.
Huang, P. C. C. (2002). Development or involution in eighteenth-century Britain and China? A review of Kenneth Pomeranz's The Great Divergence: China, Europe, and the Making of the Modern World Economy. *The Journal of Asian Studies, 61*(2), 501–538.
Huang, B., Morgan, P. J., & Yoshino, N. (Eds.). (2018). *Avoiding the middle-income trap in Asia: The role of trade, manufacturing, and finance*. Tokyo: ADB Institute.
Im, F. G., & Rosenblatt, D. (2013). *Middle-income trap: a conceptual and empirical survey (the World Bank policy research working paper 6594)*. Washington, DC: World Bank.
Izvorski. (2011). *The middle-income trap again?*. Retrieved May 24, 2019, from https://blogs.worldbank.org/eastasiapacific/the-middle-income-trap-again
Jankowska, A., Nagengast, A., & Perea, J. R. (2012). *The product space and the middle-income trap: Comparing Asian and Latin American experiences*. OECD development Centre. Working paper N 311. Paris: OECD.

Kharas, H., & Kohli, H. (2011). What is the middle income trap, why do countries fall into it, and how can it be avoided? *Global Journal of Emerging Market Economies, 3*(3), 281–289. https://doi.org/10.1177/097491011100300302.
Komlosy, A. (2014). Imperial cohesion, national building, and regional integration in the Habsburg monarchy. In S. Berger & A. Miller (Eds.), *Nationalizing empires* (pp. 369–427). Budapest: CEU Press.
Krasilshchikov, V. (2014). *The malaise from success: the east Asian 'miracle' revised.* Saarbrücken: Lambert Academic Publishing.
Lau, L. J. (2019). Chinese economy in the new era. *Pacific Economic Review, 24*(2), 187–207. https://doi.org/10.1111/1468-0106.12300.
Lee, K. (2013). *Schumpeterian analysis of economic catch-up: knowledge, path-creation, and the middle-income trap.* Cambridge, UK: Cambridge University Press.
Lin, J. Y., & Rosenblatt, D. (2012). Shifting patterns of economic growth and rethinking development. *Journal of Economic Policy Reform, 15*(3), 171–194. https://doi.org/10.1080/17487870.2012.700565.
Mason, A., & Shetty, S. (2019). *A resurgent East Asia: navigating a changing world. World Bank East Asia and Pacific regional report.* Washington, DC: World Bank. https://doi.org/10.1596/978-1-4648-1333-7
Milward, A. S., & Saul, S. B. (1977). *The development of the economies of continental Europe 1850-1914.* London: George Allen & Unwin.
Ng, A. K. (2001). *Why Asians are less creative than westerners.* Singapore: Prentice Hall.
Nielsen, L. (2011). *Classifications of countries based on their level of development: How it is done and how it could be done.* The IMF working paper 11/31. Washington, DC: IMF.
OECD. (2013). *Economic outlook for Southeast Asia, China and India 2014. Beyond the middle-income trap.* Paris: OECD.
OECD. (2018). *Economic outlook for Southeast Asia, China and India 2019: Towards smart urban transportation.* Paris: OECD.
Paus, E. (2014). *Latin America and the middle-income trap (series "financing for development" N 250 – LC/L.3854).* Santiago de Chile: ECLAC
Paus, E. (2018). The middle-income trap: lessons from Latin America. In B. Huang, P. J. Morgan, & N. Yoshino (Eds.), *Avoiding the middle-income trap in Asia* (pp. 60–105). Tokyo: Asian Development Bank Institute.
Perrault, C. (1692). *Parallèle des anciens et des modernes, en ce qui regarde les arts et les sciences. Dialogues. Avec le poëme du siècle de Louis le Grand, et une epistre en vers sur le génie. Quatre tomes.* Paris: Chez la veuve de J.B. Coignard. Reprinted edition: Munich, 1964.
Salama, P. (2000). Do produtivo ao financeiro e do financeiro ao produtivo na Ásia e na América Latina. *Revista da Sociedade Brasileira de Economia Política, 6*, 5–47.
Salama, P. (2006). *Le défi des inégalités. Amérique latine/Asie: Une comparison économique.* Paris: La Découverte.
Salama, P. (2012a). Amérique latine, Asie: Une globalisation commerciale accompagnée d'une redistribution des cartes. *Problèmes d'Amérique latine, 85*, 37–53.
Salama, P. (2012b). China – Brasil : Industrialización y "desindustrialización temprana". *Cuadernos de Economía, 31*(56), 223–252.
Salama, P. (2012c). Globalización comercial: desindustrialización prematura en América Latina e industrialización en Asia. *Comercio Exterior, 62*(6), 34–44.
Salama, P. (2012d). *Les économies émergentes latino-américaines: Entre cigales et fourmis.* Paris: Armand Colin.
Salama, P. (2014a). Chine-Brésil : Une comparaison instructive. *Problèmes d'Amérique latine, 95*, 11–31.
Salama, P. (2014b). *Des pays toujours émergents?* Paris: La Documentation Française.
Standing, G. (2011). *The Precariat. The new dangerous class.* London: Bloomsbury Academic.
Subramanian, A. (2011). *Eclipse: Living in the shadow of China's economic dominance.* Washington, DC: Peterson Institute for International Economics.

Taylor, I. (2016). BRICS and capitalist hegemony: passive revolution in theory and practice. In S. F. Christensen & L. Xing (Eds.), *Emerging powers, emerging markets, emerging societies: global responses* (pp. 55–84). Houndmills, Basingstoke: Palgrave Macmillan.

World Bank. (2013). *China 2030: Building a modern, harmonious, and creative society*. Washington, DC: World Bank. https://doi.org/10.1596/978-0-8213-9545-5.

World Bank. (2016). *Live long and prosper: Aging in East Asia and Pacific. World Bank East Asia and Pacific regional report*. Washington, DC: World Bank. https://doi.org/10.1596/978-1-4648-0469-4.

World Bank. (2018). *Riding the wave: An east Asian miracle for the 21st century. World Bank East Asia and Pacific regional report*. Washington, DC: World Bank. https://doi.org/10.1596/978-1-4648-1145-6.

Xu, G., & Gui, B. (2019). From financial repression to financial crisis? The case of China. *Asian-Pacific Economic Literature, 33*(1), 48–63. https://doi.org/10.1111/apel.12249.

Zhuang, et al. (2012). *Growing beyond the low-cost advantage: How the People's Republic of China can avoid the middle-income trap*. Asian Development Bank.

Chapter 4
The Rise to Modernity via Conservative Modernisation

The prospects of each country depend, more or less, on its previous development and its characteristic features. This banal truth raised by mainstream economists into the status of scientific conception (Abramovitz and David 1973) has been clearly approved by historical trajectory of Brazil, may be, even clearer than in the cases of many other countries.

4.1 From the Colonial Times to the Collapse of 1930

Modern Brazil is not only a result of the preceding encounter and mixing of European (Portuguese), African and pre-Columbian, indigenous America's cultures, as it has been sometimes argued with references to Gilberto Freyre (1978: 3–4). Modern Brazil is also a product of the specific inclusion of the agrarian, mostly monoculture economy based upon slave labour into the world market, and Freyre underlined that only due to slavery had this encounter of different cultures and races occurred (Ibid.: 24–26 et ff.; see also Mota and Delanty 2015: 51–53; Souza 2017: 42–46, 49–53). Because of extensive territorial spaces and large-scale farming, the main unit ('cell') of the colonised society became the family of coloniser, not the individual who should see another individual in his neighbour. This family included not only a married couple of land-owner, his wife, children and their other relatives but also servants, chaplains, children of servants and slaves who served at home or worked at plantations (*casa-grande* and *senzala*, respectively). They all personified *fazenda*, a specific economic enterprise oriented mostly to the external market but connected internally by a network of the relationships of personal dependency (i.e. patrimonial relationships). This dependency was more important than any formal authority proclaimed and established on behalf of the Portuguese Crown.

V. Krasilshchikov, *Brazil - Emerging Forever?*, Societies and Political Orders in Transition, https://doi.org/10.1007/978-3-030-50208-9_4

At the same time, the system of slavery opposed the colonial elite to 'the rest' because it existed 'in a hostile environment faced with the perpetual prospects of slave revolts' (Mota and Delanty 2015: 51). This hard opposition, often within the same 'family', between the colonial elite owners and 'the rest', including slaves, succeeded in a strange, at a first glance, combination of the elite's endeavours to imitate their 'co-brothers' on class in Britain and France (already in the nineteenth century when the influence of Portugal decreased) in consumption and progressionist ideas, on the one hand, and the elite's adherence to 'elitist' world-view, on the other, when a society had strongly been dividing into 'their own' and all others.

In this connection, José Luis Fiori put attention to the elitist character of Brazilian modernisation. Namely, the Brazilian elite(s) never intended to get the support of the large popular masses for their modernisation plans/policy, except, perhaps, for the short period of the second rule of Vargas (1950–1954) (Fiori 2001: 506)—in contrast to the practice of late, catching up modernisations in other countries, in particular, in Germany or Japan, where the modernisational elites strengthened their power, enlarging 'a sphere of modernity' to a part of the working masses and involving them gradually into the process of development.

This difference between the ruling elites in both cases was the effect of different positions the called countries occupied in the world system. In the mid-nineteenth century, when the most advanced part of the old elites in Germany and Japan conceived the necessity of modernisations for their countries, the latter were not dependent on the periphery of their more powerful rivals. Meanwhile, the Brazilian oligarchy originally depended on the metropole, Portugal, and later, with the lapse of time, after independence, on Holland, Britain and France which then made up the core of the world system. The initial pertinence of the Brazilian inheritors of the first colonisers to the world periphery predetermined their attitude in regard to modernisation. *To be modern* meant for them to consume more and better, at least, not worse than the privileged classes in Western Europe consumed. Incidentally, such an endeavour of the colonial and post-colonial elite to imitate the achievements and standards of life of rich classes in the then advanced countries concerned not only a sphere of consumption of material goods but also embraced new ideas and intellectual vogue, too. This endeavour was accompanied by the conservation of the archaic, pre-bourgeois social order(s) and structures as long as possible instead of their dismantling and abolition.[1] Thus, we can consider the Brazilian modernisation as a kind of *conservative modernisation.*

---

[1]As Fernando Henrique Cardoso said in interview to the author of these lines (on September 17, 2009), comparing Brazil and Russia ('Brazil is tropical Russia') '[B]oth countries were heavily influenced by Western ideas stemming from the Enlightenment, aspired to be part of the Western Civilization and adopt their political institutions, were connected economically and financially to the West, but had fundamentally different social structures and cultural background from those prevailing at the core of the Western Civilization. How to square that circle was a conundrum to Russian and Brazilian elites during the nineteenth century' (Cardoso 2010: 36).

The first scholar who introduced the concept of conservative modernisation into scientific use was the American historian and political sociologist Barrington Moore. He applied this term to an analysis of modernisations that had been carried out in Germany (Prussia) and Japan in the nineteenth century and later in China under the Chiang Kai-shek rule in the 1930s–1940s. According to Moore, these modernisations presupposed the compromise between the old agrarian and new rising, industrial elites; they were initiated due to *the revolution from above*, by the most advanced and strategically thinking, far-seeing groups of the ruling class (Moore 1967: 62, 109, 141, 252, 435–441, 448). The main goals of such modernisations consisted, firstly, not in the abolition (destruction) of the obsolete social order but in its adjustment to the new conditions with conservation of the old elites' privileges as long as possible and, secondly, in successful rivalry with other, more advanced countries.

Conservative modernisation in Brazil had its own peculiarities. It had been carried out, spontaneously either deliberately, as it was already in the twentieth century, in the country where there were not relics of the pre-capitalist, feudal society in contrast to the countries where modernisation was conservative, too. The Brazilian socioeconomic and institutional system developed, being initially integrated into the world market; it existed and evolved as the reverse side or adjunct to the capitalist development in Western Europe and North America (de Oliveira 2011: 132; Singer 2018: 21). As Francisco Ferraz wrote, the essence of conservative modernisation in Brazil consisted in the dissociation between the visible form and real content of society's movement to modernity. In his opinion, any conservative modernisation meant that a form, borrowed, as a rule, from abroad, appeared as a new image of the old patterns of relationships or order, whereas the content did not essentially change but appropriated a superficial appearance of progressive transformations (Ferraz 1990: 9). In other words, the old relationships and values continued existing in new forms because modernisation in Brazil (conceived as the long-term process of social transformation since the colonial times) had been carried out mainly under impact of the external conditions. It began earlier than its proper, internal premises and matured to such a degree when they could succeed in self-sustaining social changes. Henceforth, the main principle of this modernisation was the following: 'renewal as admissible as necessary, conservation of the old order and traditions as steadfast as possible'.

Brazilian modernisation was actually even more conservative than the autocratic modernisations in Germany, Japan or Russia in the late nineteenth century because it changed the character of society to much lesser degree than 'the revolutions from above' in the called countries did. It was primarily aimed at the increase of private consumption of the rich, privileged social groups—in contrast to conservative modernisations in Germany, Japan or Russia where the initiators of reforms worried about the domestic *production of goods* for the sake of catching up with the economically advanced powers. Their conservative modernisation had not been reduced to imitation of borrowed consumption patterns; it changed the system of production and, thereby, impacted somewhat on all spheres of economy and society, including its agrarian sector, a fortress of traditionalism. The goal of modernisation in Brazil had been reached through the export of primary goods, agricultural products (mainly sugar, cotton and coffee) and raw materials, in exchange for various manufactured goods, mainly luxuries, for the prestigious consumption of the upper class. Conservative modernisation in Brazil did not essentially touch the rural areas with *latifundias* (*fazendas*) and power of landlords who were judges, administrators and 'fathers-benefactors' at the same time. Moreover, maintenance of prestigious consumption required increasing the export of agricultural and other primary goods. It succeeded in strengthening exploitation of peasants, often landless, and slaves. A widespread use of slave labour was almost the insurmountable obstacle to the initial pre-industrialisation of Brazil and sharply contrasted with various 'progressionist ideas' which became a kind of intellectual vogue among various elites' groups. Even in the second half of the nineteenth century, as Freyre noted,

> slaves took over the work not so much of horses or oxen, which were being suppressed in a number of their duties, but of machines, which the patriarchal and slave-based economy of the Empire continued to ignore. (Freyre 1986: 332).

In fact, modernisation oriented mostly towards the growth of prestigious, elitist consumption favouring conservation of the archaic order and slavery because an exploitation of slave labour with low costs was the simplest and cheapest mode that enabled increasing the primary goods' (commodities') exports for obtaining luxury goods from Britain, France or other West European countries.

The concrete specialisation of Brazil in the early capitalist world economy depended on demand for one or another commodity that was most profitable at a given time and allowed purchasing the maximal quantity of goods for prestigious consumption. Celso Furtado demonstrated four big cycles of Brazil's specialisation corresponding to provision of the biggest volume of manufactured imports for the oligarchic elites. These cycles had been (1) production of cane sugar ('*colónia açucareira*'), approximately from 1570 to 1660, and formation of the North-East economic complex with slavery; (2) cycle of gold, when the mines (extracting pre-industries) were beginning to develop (1680–1750); (3) cycle of sugar again and cotton, the main raw material for the rising textile industry in Britain (1780–the end of the nineteenth century); (4) cycle of coffee (from the mid-nineteenth century to 1929) (Baer 1989: 10–19 (Chap. 2); Furtado 1959: 36–44, 55–61, 70–82, 91–96, 111–113, 133–140, 207–216). But independently, on the concrete domination of one or other kind of outputs in the economy, the agrarian sector monopolised by oligarchic inheritors of the first colonisers had been the main source of wealth. The political independence from the Portuguese Crown proclaimed in 1822 changed nothing in this respect. (It is worth to note that Brazil was the only country in Latin America where the new, independent ruler, the emperor Dom Pedro I, came directly from the royal family—in contrast to the former Spanish colonies where representatives of the ruling monarchy were dismissed through the wars for independence.)

The monoculture's specialisation upon the base of slave labour impacted on the pace and peculiar path of urbanisation in Brazil. The specific process of urbanisation expressed, by itself, the conservative character of Brazilian modernisation. Cities in

Brazil emerged as the points or fortresses (*fortalezas*) for the political, military and administrative power, not being originally the centres for craftsmanship and early industry—in contrast to Western Europe where the growth of industry and the process of urbanisation conditioned each other. In the second half of the nineteenth century, several Brazilian cities transformed into settlements for the upper and middle classes, including representatives of the trade-agrarian oligarchy, top military officers and civil servants. In fact, there was a discrepancy between urbanisation and industrialisation in Brazil. Certainly, the rise of big cities meant the simultaneous growth of the middle classes, but, unlike their European contemporaries, these social groups were rarely linked to the development of industrial activities with corresponding demand for services in education, scientific research, engineering, management, etc. It led to the interesting phenomenon of the rise of *cities without citizens* when the urban population, primarily the urban middle class, did not make up a community of autonomous individuals, but depended on the dominating oligarchic groups (and later, on the state) (Cardoso 1972a: 50–51, 59).

Brazilian urbanisation, being apparently delinked from industrialisation, succeeded in the specific economic development of urban areas. In particular, while the service sector in North America and Western Europe began rising *after* the industrial growth or, sometimes, grew hand in hand with industry, the development of services in Brazilian cities, as a rule, preceded the growth of industry. The big cities, the future metropolises, such as São Paulo, Belo Horizonte, Pôrto Alegre and, not to mention the then capital, Rio de Janeiro, became the centres of attraction for trade and various services, including, of course, administrative ones. But their growth was weakly connected with the rise of industry as itself. For example, São Paulo developed as a city very rapidly, gravitating coffee traders, semi-aristocrats, semi-merchants, without significant growth of modern manufacturing industry until the beginning of the twentieth Century when industrialisation commenced swiftly developing (Martins 1976: 79–80; Schwartzman 2007: 53–54; Singer 1974: 19–58). This peculiar path of urbanisation conditioned the structure of urban employment. Most working people who lived in cities were employed in the service sector and at small semi-industrial/semi-artisanal enterprises with poor mechanisation, low productivity and, respectively, poor wages. The growth of such an employment had become particularly evident (as an undeniable fact of social life) in the second half of the nineteenth century, when the old, trade-agrarian social and economic system based on slavery had gradually been disintegrating under impact (rather external than rising 'from within') of the world capitalist market and institutionalisation of the state machine with its military and bureaucratic apparatus.

After the formal abolition of slavery in 1888, this process accelerated, stimulating migration of the former slaves and members of 'big families' (so to speak, members of 'secondary importance'—domestic servants, landless peasants, etc.) into growing cities. There these people made up settlements, 'streets' (*ruas*) as social space opposing to the rich, their former masters, who built up 'homes' (*casas*). Such migration spontaneously transplanted the old clientelistic-patrimonial relationships, though, of course, in modified forms, from the countryside to urban areas. Indeed, the newcomers who migrated from poor rural areas to growing cities became new urban pariahs, marginals who sought any form of support in an unknown, often unfriendly social environment. The establishment of interpersonal, familial relationships was often the only way for them to survive in the conditions of urban life.

At the same time, the old oligarchy did not tend to dismantle the material and political fundaments of its dominance after abolition of slavery. On the contrary, the oligarchy, including the part that moved to cities ('urbanised oligarchy'), tended to strengthen them by means of partial renovations, apparently integrating some features of the industrial capitalist system, often borrowed from abroad, into its proper universe (Fernandes 1981: 208–211). In fact, apart from the just mentioned patrimonialism of the poor, there was also 'patrimonialism of the rich who privatised, step by step, the enlarging public sphere (the sphere of publicity with rising and complicating political and judicial institutions, newspapers, education, and so on) in their hard opposition to disdained population of *ruas*; at best, they regarded the latter with suspicion. Habits inherited by the both social poles from slavery had been embodied in the transplantation of the country-side into urban areas (*o campo na cidade*)' (Souza 2017: 58–60).

On the one hand, one of the most peculiar features of this difficult Brazilian modernisation consisted in the long-time co-existence of the transplanted patrimonialism with archaic relationships, and on the other hand, disseminating liberal ideas with individualistic values borrowed from the advanced countries (Britain, France, United States, Italy or Germany), often—thanks to immigration from the Old World. This borrowing was a pattern of 'imitative', 'prestigious' consumption, which concerned not only material but also 'intangible' goods, such as, for example, philosophical and social doctrines. In particular, the positivism in its French version (Auguste Comte) and to a lesser degree in the British version (John Stuart Mill) played a big role in maturing the spiritual, intellectual premises for November Revolution of 1889 when the emperor Dom Pedro II was dismissed from the throne and the republic was proclaimed (Freyre 1962: 15–32). Nevertheless, as Freyre noted, 'the Republic in Brazil came into being (*nasceu*) as penetrated by Monarchy. Principally anti-monarchic in appearance, it was essentially continuer of Monarchy to a big degree' (Freyre 1959, T.2: 388). Thus, the long and difficult process of modernisation in Brazil appropriated a form of *selective modernisation* (Souza 2000: 254, 265–267), when the individualistic values and ideas diffused into the tissue of society much more rapidly than the economic achievements, and the social relationships and public institutions, to which these ideas should have been corresponding, developed.

The outward-looking economy of Brazil with domination of cotton and coffee as the main exportable goods favoured to economic activity in a sphere of circulation, trade and finances. The bourgeoisie that began rising in the nineteenth century was primarily speculative, mercantile bourgeoisie (Bresser-Pereira 1984: 37–38): it earned profits mainly from trading, often due to a poorly developed market with many natural and artificial restrictions, such, in particular, as hugely long distances between various seacoast cities and deep provinces in *sertãos* or Amazonia. Evidently, such types of bourgeoisie with *rent-seeking consciousness* were very far from the Weberian ideal of rational entrepreneur, the main social agent of the modern, capitalist production. Nevertheless, the first industrial (or, more exactly, pre-industrial) enterprises began emerging in Brazil still in the mid-century, about 1840–1855. A spontaneous growth of light industry began accelerating in the second half of the nineteenth Century, at least, at the technological level of manufactories (Cattapan-Reuter 1984: 51–65; Furtado 1972: 81–86; Soares 1984: 17–49). Often they were established by the immigrants, newcomers from Europe; respectively, their workers had been recruited mostly from immigrants, too, because, in many cases, they were the only people capable of working even at those poorly equipped, primitive manufactures, the "pre-factories" of modern industry. In 1850 there were a little bit more than 50 quasi-industrial enterprises that outputted simple goods for everyday consumption. At that time, textile industry began emerging, in spite of strong competition with the imported British goods; in 1866 there were... 9 textile factories with 768 workers. In addition, the imports of equipment, machines and tools rapidly increased—from 11 per cent of the total import in 1850 to 28 per cent—in 1868 (Gaulard 2019: 24–25). In 1881, the amount of manufacturing enterprises in Brazil exceeded 200; in particular, the number of factories that produced woven goods (*tecidos*) had grown to 44 with 3000 workers. Simultaneously, a diversification of industry began, and some enterprises of heavy industry (metallurgy, metal-processing, etc.) emerged. In 1920 there were already 13,336 industrial establishments which employed 275.5 thousand workers (Caio da Silva Prado Júnior 1959: 265, 267; Simonsen 1973: 14–15, 20–21). Then General Motors and Ford opened offices in Brazil, hoping to organise the assembly-line production of cars in the future (Caio da Silva Prado Júnior 1959: 272). However, the share of industry in Brazilian GDP did not exceed 20 per cent—the frontier that would evidence the steady industrial development of the country at that time—over the first three decades of the twentieth century. This share had grown from 11.6 per cent in 1900 to 13.1 per cent, in 1910, and to 15.7, in 1920.[2] It was much lower than in the then developed countries, whereas the growth of industrial output in the 1920s underwent slowdown after the initial rise in the late nineteenth to the early twentieth centuries: the average annual rate of this growth was 5.5 per cent in 1901–1910, 6.1 per cent, in 1911–1920, and 5.1, in 1921–1929 (Gaulard 2019: 28–29; IBGE 2006: 388; the author's calculations on: IPEA 2002).

Meanwhile, together with the initial industrialisation, very delayed in comparison to advanced countries, some important concomitant changes began occurring in a social consciousness of Brazilian elite. Namely, whereas modernity had previously been conceived as something exclusively imported and borrowed from the then developed countries, this attitude began changing while the local industry gradually augmented and urbanisation proceeded with the respective growth of modern social groups, mainly, the new urban middle class. There was a significant turn that commenced in the 1920s–1930s. Modernity, at least, in eyes of a part of Brazilian elite, should become also an effect of the proper efforts aimed at development of economy, techniques of production, education, sciences, etc. It meant the profound

[2]In constant 1949 prices (note of the IBGE—V.Kr.).

shift in consciousness from “the external modernity to the national modernity” (Claval 2004: 139–141). Respectively, already in the 1920s some developmentalist ideas began maturing in consciousness of some upper social groups, including even a part of the ‘coffee-elite’ of São Paulo and other Southern states of the country. These ideas were far from the liberal economic vision, glorifying a ‘free market’ as the best mechanism of resources allocation in economy, being oriented to use rather non-market tools and approaches to the country’s development (Perissinotto et al. 2014: 509–510). Really, it was the shift, though not completed, from modernity perceived only as a prestigious consumption ‘like in Europe’ to modernity produced and created domestically. Obviously, further steps on the way to industrialisation would hardly be possible without such shift.

An insistent necessity of such steps emerged in 1929–1930 when Brazil, as well as other Latin American countries, faced the effects of the Great Depression in the USA and Europe. The demand for coffee and cotton, sugar and wheat had dramatically fallen, by 30–60 per cent on various commodities groups. It restrained import of consumer goods, succeeding in crises in trade and payment balances, inflation and other economic difficulties with subsequent political cataclysms. The tide of mass discontents, revolutions and coups d’état had run on the continent, and Brazil was not excluded from this trend.

4.2 The Revolution from Above and the Spurt of Late Industrialisation

The Revolution of 1930, when the Old Republic (*República Velha)*, oligarchic and elitist, collapsed, gave us a bright example of conservative modernisation. It was the response of the most forward-looking part of the old elite to the rise of people’s outrage—preventing the uprising of masses and revolution from below by a steered revolution from above. As Antônio Carlos Ribeiro de Andrada, the Brazilian politician at that time, said, ‘we make the revolution till the people will make it’. The main vector of this revolution, with consequent modernisation of economy and political life, was directed towards a preponderance of ‘progress via order’ over ‘progress via liberty’ (Rogrigues 1965: 91, 183). Such an approach meant an inevitable search for ‘squaring of circle’—the compromise between reforms and anti-reforms, modernisation and partial conservation of the old social system, the balance between heterogenous political forces that were united together against the bankrupted regime but had different, often diametrically opposed views on the country’s future.

Was it possible to carry out modernisation without compromises with the bankrupted ‘forces of past’ that led the country to failure? Unfortunately, a further radicalisation of the Revolution 1930 would likely succeed in full economic collapse. ‘To break backbone of coffee-culture (*cafeicultura*)—the mother of all economic and political evils in the country—would mean to break the rising capitalism’ in Brazil because then it should be necessary to destroy the banking system (it continued remaining in hands of the old financiers and 'coffee-elites') with inevitable growth of unemployment, fall of incomes, inflation, subversion of the taxation system (Cano 2015: 447–448) and other 'delights' that accompanied, for example, the Russian Revolution in its first years.

Really, the old oligarchy was debilitated but held a big part of the economic resources, so it could maintain a pretence, though now not as fully as previously, to political power. Neither the urban middle class (being dependent on the old oligarchic system), nor the rising industrialists, owned resources sufficient for establishment of their socioeconomic and political order (Weffort 2003: 133–136). Therefore, the compromises between further modernisation and conservation of several relics of the past were economically inevitable. Really, it presupposed the continuation of conservative modernisation but with much bigger emphasis on 'modernisation' than previously. In particular, Getúlio Vargas, the president of Brazil in 1930–1945 and 1951–1954, did not risk to approach the agrarian reform that could dismantle the system of *latifundismo* inherited from the colonial times, the radical reforms in some other respects notwithstanding. At the same time, the regime of Getúlio Vargas (when he carried out the coup d'état' and established the autocratic regime of his personal authority in 1937) promoted an idea of the 'new man' (*homem novo*), who should be created and educated under guidance of the state—an 'ultra-modernist' idea that resembled, in essence, to goals of the social engineering attitudes of the Stalinist regime (Lippi et al. 1982: 154–156). The engineering, Taylorist principles of labour organisation should have to play a significant role in the process of the 'new man' creation. At the same time, under the first rule of Vargas (1937–1945), the influence of the clerical circles, particularly, in the sphere of education, apparently increased. In addition, as 'a cherry on the top of cake', Vargas and his nearest circle did not avoid expressing their admiration of the regime of Mussolini.

In economic respects, the Revolution 1930 incited the new stage of industrial development—the *import substitution industrialisation* (ISI) aimed at radical diminishing imports of consumer goods and substituting them by the products manufactured at national plants and factories.

The strategy of ISI presupposed an interference of the state in economy. The state, which, in essence, was *the developmental state (el Estado desarrollista)* (Cardoso and Faletto 1970: 123–129, 1978: 143–148),[3] regulated the internal market as well as the external trade and foreign investments, banking, and construction of infrastructure. It used the economic and administrative forms of protectionism. In particular, it established high import tariffs that protected the internal markets from external competition and delivered various subsidies, loans and banking preferences to private business, stimulating, thereby, the growth of new industrial branches. In addition, state authorities established direct or indirect control over natural resources extraction, which was affirmed by respective laws. In the 1950s the state began

[3]Strictly speaking, Cardoso and Faletto called it 'the populist developmental state', Francisco Weffort—as *the state of compromise* (Weffort 2003: 135).

practising indicative economic planning, creating, simultaneously, the public sector that embraced the capital-intensive branches of industry, such as steel production, heavy machinery building, energy power chemical and petrochemical plants. Heavy industry as a whole had been treated not only as the base of national economies but also as the symbol of well-being. For instance, Getúlio Vargas argued that ‘the age of iron’ had to mark ‘the time of economic affluence’ (Werneck 1964: 292–293), deifying heavy industry almost in the same manner as the Russian Bolsheviks did it.

Since there is a huge amount of publications about the results of ISI in Brazil and other Latin America countries, it is hardly relevant to list here the numerous statistical data that characterise the changes in Brazilian economy and society from 1930 to the mid-1950s. Maybe it is worth mentioning that the share of industry in GDP increased from 14.8 per cent in 1930 to 25.6 per cent—in 1950 and to 29.9 per cent—in 1960. The share of agriculture decreased from 35.8 per cent to 22.4 and 16.9 per cent, respectively (IBGE 2006: 388).[4] In particular, the share of *manufacturing* industry in GDP had grown from 18.7 per cent in 1950 to 25.6—in 1960 (IBGE 2006: 389).[5] All this allowed to assert that Brazil already in the 1950s had become industrial-agrarian country—in contrast to vast majority of the then developing countries classified as the Third World with obvious domination of agriculture in their economies.

The ISI essentially modified the path of modernisation in Brazil but did not abolish its conservative character altogether. In particular, it did not destroy the system of *latifundias* in rural areas and did not resolve the problem of socioeconomic backwardness in the countryside. Certainly, the growth of agricultural output in Brazil somewhat accelerated while ISI proceeded: in the period from 1953–1957 to 1961–1965, it increased annually in average by 4.5 per cent, whereas over the entire period from 1934–1938 to 1961–1965, the agricultural output grew only by 2.5 per cent per year. These rates of growth outpaced the pace of population growth but insignificantly (Bairoch 1969: 32–33).[6] The agrarian sector and rural areas of Brazil were locked in a vicious circle: its socioeconomic backwardness did not stimulate modernisation, whereas a lack of modernisation, or slow modernisation, prevented it from abolishing its backwardness. On the contrary, the differences and divergence between urban, industrial development and agrarian stagnation, or even decline of rural areas and small towns, widened the socioeconomic and cultural gap between large cities and countryside, between the South/South-East with rapidly growing industry and North/North-East with old agrarian production and archaic socioeconomic relationships. The rural population was factually excluded from modernisation and deprived of the social benefits and opportunities available to many urban workers and middle-class groups. At the same time, huge masses of migrants came

[4]In constant 1949 prices (note of the IBGE—V.K.).

[5]Measured at factor costs (note of the IBGE—V.K.).

[6]In practice it succeeded in accelerating food inflation, which was stronger than general inflation and inflicted mainly on the poorest people, because the demand for agricultural products increased faster than their supply, particularly, in relation to agricultural exports growth.

to big cities from rural areas searching for 'the good life' and fortune. This process, that had spanned many decades and notably accelerated after the abolition of slavery, in the years of ISI, appropriated features of avalanche. But these newcomers, except for a very few of them, migrated to big cities from backward rural areas and did not have the necessary education and skills for acquiring a 'good job'. They could hope there, at best, for a poorly paid job, living in *favelas*, which became the centres of new poverty and criminality. For example, only in Rio de Janeiro, the then Federal capital, did the number of favelas increase from 58 with 169,305 inhabitants in 1950 to 147 with 335,063 residents in 1960 (IBGE 1953: 27–28, 1968: VI, 2–3).

As a rule, the inhabitants of favelas were people who pertained to a specific social group, tremendously large but non-performed politically and voiceless—the under-proletariat (*subproletariado*). The vast majority of this stratum was composed of agricultural workers, often occupied seasonally, and domestic servants who earned their poor wages not from the capitalist production, but from incomes of the upper groups. Under-proletarians had an informal, precarious occupation without work record cards (*carteiras de trabalho*) and worried only about elementary subsistence (Singer 1981: 22–24, 85–94, 105–120, 131–133). According to estimations of Paul Singer, the Brazilian under-proletariat amounted to 72.5 per cent of the economically active population in 1960. Over the 1960s, its share did not change—72.4 per cent in 1970. Hence, the number of under-proletarians steadily increased in absolute terms while industrialisation proceeded and the total population grew.[7]

Obviously, these masses of newcomers to the industrial centres were not fit for intensive labour at modern plants (Fernandes 2008: 76–77). Moreover, urban industry had involuntarily been adjusting to the existing quality of the labour force, and a lot of small, poorly equipped 'business entities', mostly in the informal sector of low productivity, emerged together with a few advanced, often foreign- or state-owned enterprises.

At the same time, it would be erroneous to think that entrepreneurs who hired poorly trained or illiteral workers had been the far-seeing actors of modernisation. They originated either from the old trade-agrarian oligarchy or from immigrants. A big part of the latter came from the countries of Southern Europe, mostly from its rural areas. Their social consciousness was 'overloaded' by various pre-bourgeois, patrimonialistic prejudices and had a little common with 'the spirit of capitalism' in Weberian sense. Evidently, the ISI practice began changing their consciousness, but these changes proceeded very slowly. As Cardoso noted in his study of the entrepreneurial class in Brazil, the accelerated growth of industry in the ISI period did not succeed in the formation of an *innovative mentality* among capitalists (Cardoso 1972b: 133–134). Clearly, while there were sometimes fortunate businessmen in conditions of market competition, they remained unable to attain success through

[7]In 1960 the economically active population of Brazil was 23.3 million people, in 1970—30.2 million (CEPAL/ECLAC 1996: 712–713). Therefore, according to estimations of P .Singer, the number of under-proletarians in 1960 was about 16.9 million, in 1970—21.9 million; it increased by 5 millions (about 30 per cent) over 10 years.

making radical technological and managerial innovations. Many felt themselves to be patrons of their workers and as clients in relation to the state, asking the government to defend them from foreign competitors. In addition, a part of the entrepreneurial class, rooted socially and mentally in the old oligarchy, being not very numerous but socially and politically influential, determined the image and path of Brazilian modernisation to much greater degree than all of 'the foreigners', immigrants or their descendents imbued as they were with 'the spirit of capitalism' (Ibid.: 170–171).

According to the traditional approach many Brazilian workers and entrepreneurs considered industrial labour as a curse or at best, as an unpleasant obligation but not as a field for creative, innovative activity which would essentially correspond to the character of industrial system (Furtado 2008: 151–152).[8] Such an archaic approach was inherited from the epoch of slavery. Capitalists regarded their workers as a kind of property and treated them often as slaves, whereas the workers conceived of the entrepreneurs as masters, either good or bad. Evidently, both views were hardly compatible with the advanced principles of management which would be adequate to support the technical level and opportunities of borrowed and installed technologies. On the contrary, managerial decisions and the behaviour of entrepreneurs were often irrational and ineffective from the point of view of the long-term business strategy (Fernandes 2008: 79–81).

On the eve of the 1950s–1960s, the model of development upon the base of ISI had accomplished its 'historical mission' and struck on the proper barriers.

- The ISI model could not resolve the employment problem of the growing population in a framework of modern industrial kinds of labour activity. This problem had partly been resolved due to the large informal sector—the sphere of occupation for the under-proletariat with poor wages and, respectively, poor demand for consumer goods.
- A continuation of ISI did not spare Brazil (or other Latin American countries) from the necessity of importing capital goods, tools and equipment, for the newly emerging branches of heavy industry. It affected the trade balance and required it to attract additional resources for financing the development of this industry and infrastructure. As a result, loans and foreign investments began to be intensively used, and already by the second half of the 1950s (under the presidency of Juscelino Kubitschek who proclaimed to pass a path of 50 years of development for 5 years), the Brazilian market had become the most internationalised internal market in Latin America (Arend and Dutra Fonseca 2012: 41). Thus, the policy of ISI did not lead to diminishing dependence of Brazil on external factors of development but, on the contrary, aggravated the country's dependency on the centres of the world-system.
- ISI did not change the structure of Brazilian exports. The country continued exporting primary goods, including coffee, while the price of commodities and

[8] '. . .technology constitutes the final expression of human creativity in the industrial civilisation'—wrote Furtado (Furtado 2008: 151).

manufactured goods went in the opposite direction. The former decreased (in particular, there was the notable drop in coffee prices in the second half of the 1950s), the latter increased, mainly due to their technological complexity, and all this had a negative effect on the trade and payment balances (Baer 1989: 50–53; da Conceição Tavares 1964: 3, 1998: 216).
- The imports of machines and equipment required maintaining the overvalued exchange rate of the cruzeiro (the currency existed in 1942–1967). It was disadvantageous for exporters of commodities and lowered the general competitiveness of Brazilian industry (Hirschman 1968: 26–27). In fact, the high exchange rate of the cruzeiro squeezed the income of primary goods' exporters to the benefit of industrialists and urban strata. Hence, the policy of ISI succeeded in the growing discontentment among agricultural and raw materials' producers, inheritors of the old oligarchy.

In purely economic terms, the limits and self-exhaustion of ISI were expressed in an obvious slowdown of economic growth prior to the 1950s and 1960s. This slowdown was accompanied by intensifying inflation. Certainly, in the greater historical context, although these were understandable difficulties and costs associated with rapid development, they did however erode the previously existing broad alliance, the main social-political condition of ISI (Bresser-Pereira 1963: 20–25). The interests of its participants, the unionised industrial workers, industrialists, urban middle classes and the state bureaucracy (as one of the leading actors of the ISI policy)[9] diverged from each other to a greater degree, thus rousing the social conflicts. At the same time, the compromise of the so-called urban strata, with the old trade-agrarian oligarchy (whose incomes had been used, to a big degree, to engine the growth of industry since the early-1930s), also exhausted itself. In addition, the old antagonism between landlords and peasants, including those who were landless, appropriated a new dimension: the rising requirements of radical agrarian reform which led to direct clashes between two opposite classes.

In a large sense, all these social and economic tendencies led down the blind alley of conservative modernisation. In the beginning of the 1960s, Brazilian conservative modernisation and Brazil as a whole remained at *the point of bifurcation*. The country's development could have potentially followed the way of further modernisation without the adjective 'conservative', with a strong Leftist bias and elimination of the old oligarchy relics. However, the Lefts' variant of further modernisation would hardly be successful, taking into account how the then Left forces, primarily the Communist Party, were dogmatised by their naïve belief in superiority of the Soviet model which then came, ultimately, to its objective historical limit. The variant of ultra-conservative reaction was improbable, too, because it would be inappropriate for the new urban strata. Therefore, the compelling historical choice, given the correlation of various political forces, internal and external, was *the change*

[9]As the effect of reforms carried out in the years of the first Vargas' rule (1930–1945, particularly since 1937), 'in Brazil there was an economic bureaucracy, technically competent and stable' (Perissinotto et al. 2014: 513).

within paradigm of conservative modernisation itself. Indeed, the privileged groups that tolerated ‘social experiments’ after the collapse of liberal economic model during the oligarchic republic of 1930 felt a threat to their dominance, particularly in the context of Cold War diffusion into Latin America after the Cuban revolution. Consequently, their response was the *coup d’état* on the 1st of April 1964. This event actually opened the way to the new version of conservative modernisation in Brazil.

4.3 The New Authoritarianism and the Project of a Tropical Mass Consumption Society

A rhetoric concerning modernisation was one of the key elements in the ideological self-justification of the established *military-bureaucratic authoritarian* regime. It attempted to carry out conservative modernisation in its ‘pure form’—for the advantage of the upper class and rejecting the previous policy of social compromises. This new version of conservative modernisation was conceptually rooted in ideas that had been elaborated in the so-called *Sorbonne*—the *Escola Superior de Guerra (Higher War College)* in Brazil in the late 1930s (Comblin 1977: 18–37).[10] The leading idea of this military-political think tank was that national security should be adjusted according to the tasks of economic modernisation. The slogan ‘security and development’ (*‘segurança e desenvolvimento’*) was used by the Brazilian generals as the essence of the doctrine. The first part of this binomial, ‘security’, was interpreted as the specific ‘factor of production’, the most important condition of development, whereas the second one, ‘development’—was, in its turn, the indispensable premise of security. The coalition of conservative forces that seized power after the *coup d’état* was as heterogeneous as the Brazilian upper class. It served the differing interests of a section of industrial entrepreneurs, the old agrarian oligarchy (particularly from the North-East), financial capital and the old urban middle class, including the top bureaucrats and military figures. The configuration of these forces and interests was amorphous and changed according to the concrete situation inside of the country as well as in the world markets. In particular, there was a more conservative faction that represented the financial and trade-agrarian oligarchic groups, biased towards a more repressive policy in regard to the dismissed political forces. Also, there was a *neo*-conservative, technocratic movement supported by industrialists and connected with the industrial transnational capital. The representatives of this faction understood that it was insufficient to oppress the Leftist ‘subversive elements’ to prevent a ‘socialist revolution’ in the Cuban model. They thought that the best way to annihilate the threat of Leftism was to erode its social conditions—to build the national model of a mass consumption society and, thereby,

[10]The main author of this doctrine was general Pedro Aurélio de Góis Monteiro, who occupied the position of War Minister in the government of Vargas in 1934–1935, i.e. before establishment of ‘the New State’.

to abolish mass poverty in the population. Interpreting the *coup d'état* as a revolution (the Revolution!), the leaders and ideologues of the regime focused on the issue of the country's accelerated modernisation. '...Development is the axis of the Brazilian revolutionary process...—, wrote the general Carlos de Meira Mattos, ... the mission of the Revolution of March 31 consists in carrying Brazil to attain her place among the most developed nations of the globe by 2000' (de Meira Mattos 1975: 102, 103). Simultaneously, the regime promised a radical social transformation of the country through "a broad diffusion of the results of economic progress" (Simonsen and de Oliveira Campos 1974: 71). As it seemed to the regime's military leaders and allied civil technocrats, the proclaimed goals could be reached through the growth of investment. Indeed, the rate of gross investment in fixed capital as a percentage of GDP increased from 15.0 per cent in 1964 to 18.8 per cent in 1970, to 23.3 per cent in 1975 and, then, after a subsequent small decrease in 1976–1978, to 23.6 per cent in 1980 (counted on: IPEA 2019a). It was the effect of the regime's efforts aimed at stimulating the accumulation of capital by means of taxation policy, inflow of external loans, foreign investment and increased rates of profit. The latter rose because the real wages of the lower working classes were restrained due to oppression of the trade unions and Leftist political organisations.

At the same time, military-bureaucratic authoritarianism in Brazil sought support, not only from the old upper groups and industrialists, but also from the middle classes, stimulating the growth of their incomes and, simultaneously, the output of consumer durables for them (Carneiro Vieira 1976; Mathias and Salama 1985: 131–133). At the same time, it would be erroneous to think that the Brazilian authoritarianism worried solely about the increase of consumption and economic well-being of the middle class, particularly, its upper group. The regime strengthened also the *social positions* of this stratum, enlarging a sphere of its self-fulfillment and, thereby, attributing a sense of the proper significance to it. Namely, the regime, particularly under the presidency of the generals Emílio Garrastazú Médici (1969–1974) and Ernesto Geisel (1974–1979), created the new scientific-technological centres, opened universities and tended to stimulate scientific research.

In the years of military-bureaucratic rule, Brazil attained the fastest rate of economic growth in Latin America over the 1970s. The country's GDP increased annually by 8.7 per cent or by 6.1 per cent per capita (CEPAL/ECLAC 1993: 68–69). The regime, mainly in the 1970s under Médici and Geisel, enlarged the practice of strategic planning and attempted to carry out an industrial policy, not restrained by tariff regulation. As a result of these efforts, Brazil created new, technologically advanced branches of industry: aircraft, electronic, nuclear power, not to mention the manufacture of vehicles, tractors, machinery, etc. The structure of external trade had notably improved: the share of manufactured goods in exports increased from 2.2 per cent in 1960 to 41.4 per cent in 1984 (the last year of authoritarianism)—at that time, this was the best performing such indicator in Latin America (CEPAL/ECLAC 1987: 183–184). Finally, the regime, without essentially touching the system of *latifundismo,* nevertheless stimulated the start of modernisation in the agrarian sector of economy.

It cannot be said that Brazilian authoritarianism completely ignored the problem of poverty in the country. This problem had been recognised, but its solution was reliant on the mechanism of 'market forces' in combination with the technological progress and subsequent growth of economy. The military leaders and their allies among civilian technocrats believed, either sincerely or demagogically, that on its own, economic growth would sooner or later provide its fruits for the poor. Meanwhile, the regime recognised the importance of ordinary people's skills for economic development and applied some efforts though insufficient, for improving mass education. But the main efforts in the sphere of education were aimed at tertiary education for youngsters from privileged groups, according to the elitist approach to the problem of development as a whole.

The technocratic approach to modernisation did not allow it to eliminate the wide social disparities in Brazil. On the contrary, the rapid growth of GDP was accompanied by the 'tortoise' pace of poverty reduction: the share of poor households only decreased from 49 per cent in 1970 to 4[illegible] per cent in 1979 (CEPAL/ECLAC 1993: 45), whereas the total volume of the economy increased almost twofold over the same period.

The elitist modernisation did not lessen but, on the contrary, aggravated the brutal contrasts between rich and poor, capitalists and workers, *latifundistas* and peasants, as well as the divergence between economic and social development. It not only widened social differentiation but also directly reduced the incomes of the poorest groups. The real minimal wage in Brazil declined from December 1959 to December 1980 by 25.7 per cent. Its fall in the municipality of São Paulo (as the most industrialised area in Brazil) measured in ratio against the cost of a basic consumer basket was even bigger than in the country as a whole. It had shrunk by 35 per cent from December 1959 to December 1966, then, after relative stabilisation in 1967–1970, it continued decreasing, though by the slower pace: from December 1971 to December 1980, it had fallen by [illegible]7 per cent (counted on: IPEA 2019c, d; Salário Mínimo Brasileiro). Thus, the real minimal wage in the biggest and most economically developed city in Brazil, more than halved over 20 years. The Gini coefficient, which had always been very high in Brazil (the country was among the world 'leaders" in this respect), had increased from 0.565 in 1970 to 0.580 in 1980, and the decile coefficient (the ratio of incomes of the richest 10 per cent of population to those of the poorest 10 per cent) augmented from 40.1 to 44.3 times (Malan and Bonelli 1983: 66–73 and my calculations). The apparent (and temporary) decrease of inequality in the late 1970s–the early 1980s was conditioned by the numerical growth of the middle class (mostly because of realisation of the development plans and augmentation of the number of qualified specialists) and its incomes until 1981–1982 when these real incomes began falling due to a growing crisis. But the nominal decrease of inequality did not result in any improvement in the conditions of the poorest groups. Their incomes in ratio to the income of the rich, in the absolute terms continued to diminish (Mathias and Salama 1985: 135).[11] Moreover, the system of taxation in Brazil had a regressive character; it did not lessen but increased the income inequality. For example, those people whose income did not exceed 1 minimal wage had to pay 36 per cent as taxes; the people with incomes between 10 and 15 minimal wages were paying 22.4 per cent, and, finally, the rate of taxes for the richest whose incomes exceeded 100 minimal wages was equal to 14.1 per cent. In addition, there was the sales tax (*imposto sobre circulação de mercadorias*) which spread to all goods, including ones for consumption by the poorest (Serra 1983: 9–13). By degree of income inequality in the 1980s, Brazil occupied the second place in the world, just beyond of such poor and underdeveloped country as Sierra Leone (Gaulard 2019: 122).

The elitist character of the regime's modernisational policy spread to the sphere of social security, healthcare and education. Still in 1964–1967, the regime began carrying out large-scale privatisation of this sphere. As a result of this measure, medical services, education and social insurance became less accessible to lower socioeconomic groups despite the fascinating growth of their formal indicators (Fagnani 1997: 188–193, 200–202).

As a result of conservative modernisation under aegis of the authoritarian regime, Brazil was nearing the developed countries in the size of its economy and the technological level of some industries, but despite this a major part of the country's population still pertained to the Third World from the perspective of social development indicators and living conditions. In total, from 60 to 67 per cent of the Brazilian population existed outside the economic 'miracle' (Jaguaribe et al. 1986: 18, 21, 69; Jaguaribe 1993: 11–13). The yields of accelerated growth promised by the ruling generals and their supporters among the civil technocrats did not reach the majority of Brazilians. This fact was not the only expression of the limits of conservative modernisation; these limits also were expressed in the deep crisis of the 1980s, at least, beginning from 1982, when the Brazilian economy met external challenges and could not respond to them. The main cause of this inability to adequately respond was the deepening imbalance between selective economic and social development.

In spite of the many achievements in the economy and infrastructure, the Brazilian economy remained an economy of 'cheap labourer', and capital hired mainly unskilled, poorly paid workers. Brazilian private capital, as a whole, did not move towards the exploitation of a skilled labour force as the developed countries did after the Second World War. Conversely, the exploitation of 'cheap labourer' in the 1960s–1980s was a kind of self-deception; it could provide the short-term advantages but the long-term losses. One of such losses consisted in the decline of the general effectiveness of industrial capital in Brazil since the mid-1970s. The rate of profit fell, too, not being countervailed by the increasing total factor productivity or

[11]The named authors noted that their data were incomplete and did not fully reflect real inequality in Brazil.

Table 4.1 The average rates of growth of the fixed capital's stock (machines and equipment only!), value added in manufacturing industry and GDP as a whole in Brazil, 1965–1985, by quinquennial (1965 as the base year)

Indicators	1965–1970	1970–1975	1975–1980	1980–1985
Stock of fixed capital (machines and equipment)	7.5	11.3	9.4	4.2
Value added in manufacturing industry	10.2	10.7	7.2	−0.6
GDP as a whole	8.1	10.1	7.2	1.3

Counted on: IPEA (2009b, 2019b), IBGE (2019)

labour productivity. This decline lasted until 1994–1995 (Gaulard 2011: 178–185, 2019: 39–40, 122–123), when it stabilised for some time.

Indeed, the widening inequality and falling real incomes of most ordinary people restricted the effective demand. In its turn it led to relative overproduction. A sign of industry's adjustment to this situation was the growth of idle productive capacities. A large (and extending) part of machinery, tools and equipment had not been completely used. It could be illustrated by the growing gross capital stock embodied in machines and equipment. The pace of its growth in comparison with the average rates of the growth of value added in industry and GDP as a whole signifies the rapid increase of capital-intensity of industry and, respectively, the decrease of industry's effectiveness (Table 4.1).[12]

The falling efficiency of capital lowered stimuli to invest in industry. Consequently, in the years of industrial boom under the authoritarianism, the premises for deindustrialisation in Brazil matured latently in a shadow of the economic 'miracle' (Bruno 2007: 67–72; Gaulard 2015: 230–232, 235–239, 242–243). In other words, the 'miracle' of the first half of the 1970s put up fundaments for the subsequent debacle of the 1980s. Attempts, partly spontaneous, partly deliberate, to compensate for diminishing effectiveness of industrial capital by a further increase of investment did not resolve the problem but aggravated it, requiring it to attract additional resources. Behind the domestic resources redistributable at the cost of the working people, there were such sources as foreign investments and loans which had been used for attaining 'the future prosperity' since the mid-1950s, still under the presidency of JK (Kubitschek). In the years of 'miracle' and onwards the loans pours into Brazilian economy at a steady stream. The growth of credit(s) had been the main props of the 'miracle', and when the regime, particularly under the presidency of general Geisel, intensified its industrial policy with an emphasis on megaprojects (hydroelectric power plants, gigantic petrochemical enterprises, etc.), the debts of all kinds, internal or external, had grown hugely (da Conceição Tavares and de Assis 1986: 33–37, 57–60). As a whole, the total debt of the country, including its foreign

[12]Certainly, it is also necessary to take into account the shares of capital embodied in machines and equipment distinctively in agriculture, industry and services. The effectiveness of fixed capital, including equipment, is different in each of these big sectors of economy. However, the study of such details spills far beyond the boundaries of our subject of research.

part, private, public and corporate as well, rose much faster than economy increased. The external debt's dynamics can be performed as the following: 1960–3462 million US$, 1965–3644, 1970–5295, 1975–21,171, 1980–53,847, 1985–95,857, 1987–107,514 millions (IPEA 2009a). According to Fernando Henrique Cardoso, the skyrocketing growth of indebtedness, not the regime's 'wise economic policy', was the main engine of the country's economic 'miracle', particularly, in 1967–1974 (Cardoso 2004: 9), although this assessment is somewhat exaggerated.

In the 1980s Brazil entered a period of deep economic crisis, the growth of economy in some of those years notwithstanding. Still earlier, in the late-1970s, the social alliance that was the main base for conservative modernisation since 1964—the local capital, the state technobureaucracy oriented to multinational corporations, and the top military (historically connected with the old oligarchy and its inheritors)—began disintegrating under impact of rising difficulties (Bresser-Pereira 1978: partes 2, 3). Foreign indebtedness, self-sustaining and poorly regulated inflation, the rise of mass social and democratic movements protesting against dictatorship (requirements of the direct presidential elections under the slogan 'Direct elections now!' ('*Diretas já!*')—all these and many other phenomena confluenced into one powerful tide that conditioned a transition to democracy and, as it seemed to many actors of the events, to the new model of development. Really, this transition lasted 10 years, from March 15, 1985 when the last president in military uniform, João Batista Figueiredo handed over the presidential band to his civil successor, José Sarney, to January 1, 1995, when the well-known sociologist, formerly the president of the International Sociological Association and campaigner for democratisation in the years of dictatorship, professor Fernando Henrique Cardoso, entered the palace Planalto as the 34th president of Brazil.

Over this difficult and painful transitional period Brazil rejected the state-led developmental model and approached the neoliberal, pro-market reforms based on the Washington Consensus model. They appeared as a new version of conservative modernisation, primarily advantageous for the upper class. Nevertheless, it could not be said that these reforms, as well as the previous versions of conservative modernisation, contained only negative, destructive tendencies, although the positive changes as a whole were difficult to see beyond a batch of the old problems inherited from the past.

References

Abramovitz, M., & David, P. A. (1973). Reinterpreting economic growth: Parables and realities. *The American Economic Review*, *63*(2). In Papers and Proceedings of the eighty-fifth annual meeting of the American Economic Association, pp. 428–439.

Arend, M., & Dutra Fonseca, P. C. (2012). Brasil (1955-2005): 25 anos de catching up, 25 anos de falling behind. *Revista de Economia Política, 32*(1), 33–54.

Baer, W. (1989). The Brazilian economy: Growth and development. In *3rd*. New York.: Praeger.

Bairoch, P. (1969). *Diagnostic de l'évolution économique du Tiers-monde. 3-ème édition. Revue et augmentée*. Paris: Gauthier-Villars.

Bresser-Pereira, L. C. (1963). O empresário industrial e a Revolução Brasileira. *Revista de Administração de Empresas, 3*(8), 11–27.

Bresser-Pereira, L. C. (1978). *O colapso de uma aliança de classes*. São Paulo: Editora Brasiliense.

Bresser-Pereira, L. C. (1984). Six interpretations of the Brazilian social formation. *Latin American Perspectives, 11*(1), 35–72.

Bruno, M. (2007). Financiarisation et accumulation du capital productif au Brésil : Les obstacles macro-économiques à une croissance soutenue. *Revue Tiers Monde, 189*, 65–92.

Caio da Silva Prado Júnior. (1959). *Historia Econômica do Brasil* (5-a ed.). São Paulo: Editora Brasiliense (1-ra edição – 1945).

Cano, W. (2015). Crise e industrialização no Brasil entre 1929 e 1954: a reconstrução do Estado Nacional e a política nacional de desenvolvimento. *Revista de Economia Política, 35*(3), 444–460.

Cardoso, F. H. (1972a). A Cidade e a Política. In P. I. Singer & F. H. Cardoso (Eds.), *A Cidade e o Campo. (CEBRAP. Caderno 7)* (pp. 31–63). São Paulo: CEBRAP.

Cardoso, F. H. (1972b). *Empresário Industrial e Desenvolvimento Econômico no Brasil* (2-a ed.). São Paulo: Difusão Européia do Livro (1-a edição – 1964).

Cardoso, F. H. (2004). Más allá de la economía: Interacciones de la política y desarrollo económico. *Revista de la CEPAL, 83*, 7–12.

Cardoso, F. H. (2010). "To be stable, democracy needs to be effective in reducing mass poverty and social inequality" (interview). *Svobodnaya Mysl' (Free Thought), 1*, 29–38. (in Russian).

Cardoso, F. H., & Faletto, E. (1970). *Dependencia y desarrollo en América Latina. Ensayo de interpretación sociológica*. México: Siglo XXI (1-ra edición – 1969).

Cardoso, F. H., & Faletto, E. (1978). *Dependency and development in Latin America* (Translated by Marjory Mattingly Urguidi). Berkeley, Los Angeles: University of California Press.

Carneiro Vieira, J. P. (1976). Le «citoyen-consommateur» en échec: Industrialisation monopoliste périphérique et ascension des nouvelles couches moyennes au Brésil. *Revue Tiers-Monde, 17* (68), 846–854.

Cattapan-Reuter, E. (1984). L'industrie à l'époque de 'l'Encilhamento'. In: F. Mauro (dir.), *La préindustrialisation du Brésil: Essais sur une économie en transition, 1830/50–1930/50*. Paris: Éditions du CNRS, 51–65.

CEPAL/ECLAC (Comisión Económica para América Latina y el Caribe/Economic Commission for Latin America and the Caribbean). (1987). *Anuario Estadístico de América Latina y el Caribe /Statistical Yearbook for Latin America and the Caribbean*. New York: UN.

CEPAL/ECLAC. (1993). *Anuario Estadístico de América Latina y el Caribe/Statistical yearbook for Latin America and the Caribbean 1992*. NU: Santiago de Chile.

CEPAL/ECLAC. (1996). *Anuario Estadístico de América Latina y el Caribe/Statistical yearbook for Latin America and the Caribbean*. Santiago de Chile: Naciones Unidas.

Claval, P. (2004). *La fabrication du Brésil: Une grande puissance en devenir*. Paris: Belin.

Comblin, J. (1977). *Le pouvoir militaire en Amérique Latine. L'idéologie de la Securité Nationale*. Paris: Jean-Pierre Delarge/Éditions universitaires.

da Conceição Tavares, M. (1964). The growth and decline of import substitution in Brazil. *The Economic Bulletin for Latin America, IX*(1), 1–59.

da Conceição Tavares, M. (1998). El proceso de sustitución de las importaciones como modelo de desarrollo reciente en América Latina. In *Cincuenta años de pensamiento en la CEPAL. Textos seleccionados* (Vol. 1, pp. 209–227). Santiago de Chile, México, D.F.: Fondo de cultura económica, NU.

da Conceição Tavares, M., & de Assis, J. C. (1986). *O Grande Salto para o Caos*. (2-da ed.). Rio de Janeiro: Zahar (1-ra edição – 1985).

de Meira Mattos, C. (1975). *Brasil – Geopolítica e Destino*. Rio de Janeiro: Olympio.

de Oliveira, F. (2011). *Crítica á razão dualista. O Ornitorinco. Préfacio Roberto Schwarz*. São Paulo: Boitempo (1-ra edição – 2003).

Fagnani, E. (1997). Política social e pactos conservadores no Brasil: 1964/92. *Economia e Sociedade, 8*, 183–238.

Fernandes, F. (1981). *A Revolução Burguesa no Brasil. Ensaio de Interpretação Sociológica* (3-ra ed.). Rio de Janeiro: Zahar (1-ra edição – 1974).

Fernandes, F. (2008). *Mudanças sociais no Brasil. Aspectos do desenvolvimento da sociedade brasileira*. São Paulo: Global Editora (1-a edição – 1960).

Ferraz F. 1990. A construção da modernidade. In J. P. dos Reis Velloso (coord.), *Modernização Política e Desenvolvimento*. Rio de Janeiro: José Olympio. 7–19.

Fiori, J. L. (2001). Pour un diagnostic de la « modernisation » brésilienne. *Revue Tiers-Monde, 42* (167), 493–513.

Freyre, G. (1959). *Ordem e Progresso. Processo de Desintegração das Sociedades Patriarcal e Semipatriarcal no Brasil sob o Regime do Trabalho Livre: Aspectos de Um Quasi Meio Século de Transição do Trabalho Escravo para o Trabalho Livre; e de Monarquia para a República. Tomo 2*. Rio de Janeiro: José Olympio.

Freyre, G. (1962). *Obras reunidas de Gilberto Freyre. T. 3. Ordem e Progresso. Processo de Desintegração das Sociedades Patriarcal e Semipatriarcal no Brasil sob o Regime do Trabalho Livre: Aspectos de Um Quasi Meio Século de Transição do Trabalho Escravo para o Trabalho Livre; e de Monarquia para a República*. Tomo 1. 2-a Rio de Janeiro: José Olympio.

Freyre, G. (1978). *The master and the slaves (Casa-Grande & Senzala). A study in the development of Brazilian civilization* (Translated from the Portuguese by Samuel Putnam). 2nd English language edition, revised. New York: Alfred A. Knopf

Freyre, G. (1986). *The mansions and the shanties (Sobrados e Mucambos). Making of modern Brazil* (Translated from the Portuguese and edited by Harriet de Onís. Berkeley). Los Angeles: University of California Press.

Furtado, C. (1959). *Formação Econômica do Brasil* (2-a ed.). Rio de Janeiro: Fundo de Cultura (1-ra edição – 1959).

Furtado, C. (1972). *Analise do "Modelo" Brasileiro* (3-ra ed.). Rio de Janeiro: Paz e Terra.

Furtado, C. (2008). *Criatividade e dependência na civilização industrial. Edição definitiva*. São Paulo: Companhia das Letras (1-ra edição – 1978).

Gaulard, M. (2011). Les causes de la désindustrialisation brésilienne. *Revue Tiers Monde, 52*(205), 171–190.

Gaulard, M. (2015). The Brazilian deindustrialization: Financialization is not guilty. *Brazilian Journal of Political Economy, 35*(2), 227–246.

Gaulard, M. (2019). *L'économie du Brésil* (2-e ed.). Paris: Bréal.

Hirschman, A. O. (1968). The political economy of import-substituting industrialization in Latin America. *The Quarterly Journal of Economics, LXXXII*(1), 1–32.

IBGE (Instituto Brasileiro de Geografia e Estatística). (1953). *As Favelas do Distrito Federal e o Censo Demográfico de 1950*. Rio de Janeiro: IBGE.

IBGE (Fundação IBGE – Instituto Brasileiro de Estatística). (1968). *Censo Demográfico de 1960. Favelas do estado da Guanabara*. Rio de Janeiro: IBGE.

IBGE. (2006). *Estatísticas do Século XX*. Rio de Janeiro: IBGE. Archive of the author (versão eletrônica http://www.ibge.gov.br/seculoxx/seculoxx.pdf).

IBGE. (2019). *Sistema de Contas Nacionais: Brasil: 2017. Tabelas. Crescimento do PIB em volume acumulado entre dois anos – Brasil – 1947-2017*. Retrieved February 07, 2020, from ftp://ftp.ibge.gov.br/Contas_Nacionais/Sistema_de_Contas_Nacionais/2017/tabelas_xls/PIBReal_1947_2017.xls

IPEA (Instituto de Pesquisa Econômica Aplicada). (2002). *IPEAdata. Produto interno bruto (PIB) – indústria: variação real anual, 1901–1947*. Atualizado em 29.10.2002. Retrieved May 24, 2019, from http://www.ipeadata.gov.br/Default.aspx

IPEA. (2009a). *IPEAdata. Dívida externa registrada, 1899-2008*. Atualizado em 26.06.2009. Retrieved May 30, 2019.

IPEA. (2009b). *IPEAdata. Estoque bruto de capital fixo – máquinas e equipamentos a preços constantes de 2000, 1950-2008*. Atualizado em 09.03.2009. Retrieved June 01, 2019.

IPEA. (2019a). *IPEAdata. Contas nacionais. Formação bruta de capital fixo, 1947-2018*. Atualizado em 14.01.2019. Retrieved May 30, 2019.

IPEA. (2019b). *IPEAdata. Contas nacionais. Produto interno bruto (PIB) – indústria de transformação: variação real anual, 1948–2018.* Atualizado em 14.01.2019. Retrieved June 01, 2019.

IPEA. (2019c). *IPEAdata. Preços. Cesta básica no municipio de São Paulo.* Atualizado em 08.05.2019. Retrieved May 31, 2019 http://www.ipeadata.gov.br/Default.aspx

IPEA. (2019d). *IPEAdata. Salário mínumo real.* Atualizado em 08.05.2019. Retrieved May 31, 2019 http://www.ipeadata.gov.br/Default.aspx

Jaguaribe, H. (1993). *Crise na República: 100 anos depois. Primeiro ou Quarto Mundo?* Rio de Janeiro: Thex.

Jaguaribe, H., Guilherme dos Santos, W., Paiva Abreu, M., de Fritsch, W., & Bastos de Ávila, F. (1986). *Brasil, 2000. Para um novo Pacto Social* (3-a ed.). Rio de Janeiro: Paz e Terra (1-a edição – 1985).

Lippi, O. L., Pimenta, V. M., & de Castro Gomes, A. M. (1982). *Estado Novo: Ideología e Poder.* Rio de Janeiro: Zahar.

Malan, P. S., & Bonelli, R. (1983). *Crescimento Econômico, Industrialização e Balanço de Pagamentos: o Brasil dos Anos 70 aos Anos 80. (Textos para Discussão Interna No 60.).* Rio de Janeiro: IPEA – Instituto de Planejamento Econômico e Social.

Martins, L. (1976). *Pouvoir et développement économique: Formation et évolution des structures politiques au Brésil.* Paris: Anthropos.

Mathias, G., & Salama, P. (1985). Heurs et malheurs des couches moyennes au Brésil. *Revue Tiers-Monde, 26*(101), 129–142.

Moore, B. (1967). *Social origins of dictatorship and democracy. Lord and peasant in the making of the Modern World.* Boston: Beacon Press (1-st published – 1966).

Mota, A., & Delanty, G. (2015). Eisenstadt, Brazil and the mutiple modernities framework: Revisions and reconsiderations. *Journal of Classical Sociology, 15*(N1), 39–57.

Perissinotto, R., Neves Costa, P. R., Nunes, W., & Dantas, A. (2014). Elites estatais e industrialização: ensaio de comparação entre Brasil, Argentina e México (1920-1970). *Revista de Economia Política, 34*(3), 503–519.

Rogrigues, J. H. (1965). *Conciliação e Reforma no Brasil: Um desafio histórico-cultural.* Rio de Janeiro: Cilização Brasileira.

Salário Mínimo Brasileiro. *The constantly renovated resource.* Retrieved February 11, 2020, from http://portalbrasil.net/salariominimo.htm

Schwartzman, S. (2007). *Bases do Autoritarismo Brasileiro* (4-a ed.). Rio de Janeiro: Publit Soluções Editoriais (1-ra edição – 1982).

Serra, J. (1983). O sistema tributário: diagnóstico e reforma. *Revista de Economia Política, III*(1), 5–29.

Simonsen, R. (1973). *Evolução Industrial do Brasil e Outros Estudos.* São Paulo: Companhia Editora Nacional, Editora da Universidade de São Paulo.

Simonsen, M. H., & de Oliveira Campos, R. (1974). *A Nova Economia Brasileira.* Rio de Janeiro: Olympio.

Singer, P. (1974). *Desenvolvimento Econômico e Evolução Urbana (análise da evolução econômia de São Paulo, Blumenau, Pôrto Alegre, Belo Horizonte e Recife).* São Paulo: Companhia Editora Nacional.

Singer, P. (1981). *Dominação e Desigualdade: Estrutura de classes e repartição da renda no Brasil.* Rio de Janeiro: Paz e Terra.

Singer, A. (2018). *O lulismo em crise: Um quebra-cabeça do periodo Dilma (2011-2016).* São Paulo: Companhia das Letras.

Soares, L.C. (1984). A Manufatura na Sociedade Escravista: O Surto Manufatureiro no Rio de Janeiro e nas suas Circunvizinhanças (1840-1870). In: F. Mauro (dir.). *La préindustrialisation du Brésil: Essais sur une économie en transition, 1830/50–1930/50.* Paris: Éditions du CNRS, 13–49.

Souza, J. (2000). *A Modernização Seletiva: Uma interpretação do dilema brasileiro.* Brasília, DF: Editora Universidade de Brasília.

Souza, J. (2017). *A Elite do Atraso: Da Escravidão à Lava Jato*. Rio de Janeiro: LeYa.
Weffort, F. (2003). *O populismo na política brasileira* (5-a ed.). Rio de Janeiro: Paz e Terra (1-ra edição – 1978).
Werneck, S. N. (1964). *Historia da Burguesia Brasileira*. Rio de Janeiro: Cilização Brasileira.

Chapter 5
The New Model of Development or Conservative Modernisation in the Left-Centrist Arrangements (1995–2015)?

In his speech pronounced in the Senate on December 14, 1994, the president-elect Fernando Henrique Cardoso underlined the end of the Era of Vargas: the end of the model of autarchic development with an interventionist state. That model enabled rapid industrialisation and profoundly changed Brazilian society in many respects. However it also became an obstacle to further development as conditions changed. Cardoso repeated his thought about the end of Vargas' Era in his inaugural speech on the 1st of January, 1995 (Cardoso 1995a: 9–11, b: 10–11). However, as it turned out, it was not easy to divert Brazil's direction from the previous 50 years, nor to find efficient responses to the new external and internal challenges. The reality was much harder than it seemed initially, and the process of deliverance from the past was no less contradictory and painful than the past itself.

5.1 The *Plano Real* and Neoliberal Reforms

One of the main strategic tasks in the 1990s was the control of destructive inflation. All previous attempts to counter it were unsuccessful and failed for one reason or another. Neither the introduction of the new currency (the cruzado instead of the rapidly devaluating cruzeiro) in 1986, nor the emergency plan of 1987, nor 'the shock therapy' proclaimed by the president Collor de Mello in 1990–1991 could stop inflation, which ran out of control and began destroying the national economy and society.

Being the Minister of Finance before his presidency, Cardoso approached the inflation problem not as an economist-technocrat but as a sociologist. He presupposed that inflation, as with any other socioeconomic phenomenon, was not a depersonalised process but had its own actors who derived benefits from it. These

V. Krasilshchikov, *Brazil - Emerging Forever?*, Societies and Political Orders in Transition, https://doi.org/10.1007/978-3-030-50208-9_5

were (1) politicians at all levels of authorities and with various ideological views who gave irresponsible promises, particularly before elections, that could not be kept without additional monetary costs; (2) financial players and speculators who gained due to fluctuations of the national currency under conditions of permanent inflation; (3) entrepreneurs who increased prices for their goods according to the 'inflation expectations' and, thereby, instigated their own growth; (4) trade-unions that saw wage rises linked to the rate of inflation, whereas entrepreneurs, referring to 'greedy workers', justified the elevation of prices. Only the poorest social strata, with no levers to influence prices or monetary circulation, were doomed to suffer from inflation in full measure (Cardoso 2006: 18[illegible]–184, Cardoso 2013: 225–228). Taking into account the interests of all these beneficiaries of inflation, it was necessary to elaborate the economic mechanisms that would make inflation disadvantageous not only for a majority of the population but also for some groupings that could influence the economic processes. It was also necessary to dismantle, firstly, monopolism at all levels of the economy, whether in the country as a whole or at the regional level, and, secondly, the system of patrimonialism/clientelism profoundly rooted not only in the developmental state of the 1930s–1970s but mainly inherited from the slavery and oligarchic structures with *latifundismo*. The *Plano Real* launched by Cardoso in December 1993, when he was the Minister of Finances, had to resolve a set of economic, financial, social and institutional problems that had remained unresolved since the start of democratic transition in 1985 (Cardoso and Graeff 2012: 16–23).

The *Plano Real,* realised in 1994–1995, aimed to suppress inflation and stabilise the financial system of Brazil. But this plan, in contrast to all preceding stabilisation programmes, was not restrained by solely economic measures. It embraced a broad spectrum of reforms: fiscal reform with reduction of the number of taxes; redistribution of incomes and expenditures between the federal, states and municipal authorities; reform of the social security system; reform of the state-owned monopolies, particularly in a sphere of infrastructure; reform of the electoral and party system; and reform concerning civil servants and their job stability aimed at notable improvement of governance.

While Cardoso, initially as the Minister of Finances under Itomar Franco and later as the President, announced and realised his plan, he proceeded from a set of the following premises: (1) the well-known negative, even destructive effects of dependency for such a country as Brazil can be neutralised by means of adequate social policy; (2) a contradictory character of dependent capitalist accumulation now does not principally differ from that in developed countries where some similarities with unfolding processes at the semi-periphery have risen in the conditions of globalisation after the decade of neoliberalism. In other words, 'sectors of the central countries are now facing situations that make them closer to what occurs in less developed countries and vice versa' (Cardoso 2009: 301); (3) the associated-dependent development of semi-peripheral countries can be combined with liberal-democratic political regimes because one of the main factors of authoritarianism in Latin America, Cold War, has disappeared and, therefore, various revolutionaries and guerrillas sent from the USSR or Cuba did not cause horror among the upper and middle classes; (4) the military-bureaucratic authoritarian regimes established in the

Southern Cone in the 1960s–1970s were peacefully displaced due to civil society activity, therefore, a deep non-violent transformation of society is also possible (Cardoso 2009: 304–307; Santos 1998: 60–61).

Nevertheless, attempts to implement the *Plano Real* had been facing resistance from various 'groups of pressure' with local vested interests already at the stage of consideration in the Congress. And Cardoso constantly had to overcome this resistance, often agreeing to arrange compromises as 'lesser evils' (Bacha 1997: 177–193; Baumann and Mussi 1999: 13–48; Flynn 1996: 402–404, 408–413, 416–420; Montero 2005: 33–49; Saad-Filho and Morais 2018: 60–66).

According to the plan, the budget expenditures were partly cut and partly rationalised, the financial discipline strengthened, and the budget had a primary surplus. At the same time, the government established, largely using the information technologies in finances, a strong control for tax evasion, which had been a kind of national sport, no less popular than soccer (football). Under the presidency of Cardoso, Brazil became one of the most computerised countries in the world in the banking-financial sphere. The plan provided access to bank accounts for poorly paid people, too, whereas the old rules provided such opportunities only for those whose monthly salary or another income was not beneath six minimal salaries.[1] Such measures allowed to decrease a monetary mass in cash and curbed inflation expectations. Henceforth the poor might not spend all their salaries immediately but expend money over time.

The largest (but not the main) social stratum that felt advantages of the plan's implementation was the under-proletariat (*subproletariado*), the stratum that could not defend its interests in the conditions of permanent inflation and suffered from the latter to a bigger degree than other social groups. Over 3 years, from 1993 to 1996, the number of poor decreased by 9 million, from 60.9 million people to 51.8 million, or from 43.0 per cent of the total population to 34.7 per cent, respectively (IPEA 2019). The people who previously could not buy food products such as milk or chicken, began purchasing these alimentary goods. Actually, perhaps, the anti-inflationist plan in Brazil took into account the problems of the poor for the first time in decades, whereas all preceding programmes of the fight against inflation succeeded in worsening conditions for the numerous Brazilian underclass.

However, apart from the large masses of poor, there were also, of course, other and more influential beneficiaries of the *Plano Real* implementation. And the main beneficiaries of the Plano Real were neither the poorest groups, nor the urban middle class, nor industrialists but financiers, money-men who gained primarily from equalisation of the new currency unit, real, to the US dollar with a concomitant increase of the interest rate. They gained from a partial deliverance of Brazil from the excessive external indebtedness because a part of the external debt turned into an internal one nominated in reals (*reais*—R$), the process that began still under the military regime (Gaulard 2019: 95–97). Really, therefore, the process of financialisation of the Brazilian economy that started on the eve of the 1970s–

[1]In 1990 only 31.6 per cent of Brazilians had a bank account (Berthelot 1991: 15).

1980s (when it became more profitable to invest into financial tools than into industry) had achieved its maturity. Indeed, when the average annual rate of interest reached 20–25 and even 45 per cent in 1999, under the impact of financial speculators' attacks on real) (BCB 2019) being one of the highest in the world, it was hardly reasonable to invest in industry where the rate of profit reached a maximum 10–15 per cent. In fact, oppression of inflation and financial stabilisation had been paid for by further redistribution of resources from the productive sectors of economy to the financial sector.

Regarding financial stabilisation, Cardoso and his economic team understood that the sphere of finances and monetary circulation was indistinguishable from the processes in production and regulation of the economy as a whole. They did not reduce the macroeconomic stabilisation to monetary measures only but also presupposed profound structural changes. One of such changes should be the large-scale privatisation of state-owned enterprises, particularly in the sector of infrastructure and public services. In this connection, it is worth noting that privatisation in Brazil under the presidency of Cardoso was much more effective than, for example, in neighbouring Argentina where it had been carried out by the 'Bolshevist' methods, not speaking about Russia and most other post-Soviet countries where the millionaires and even billionaires emerged from nothing, being 'appointed' by the corrupted bureaucrats' assignments. The total amount of proceeds from privatisation in Brazil in 1995–2000 was equal to 91.6 billion US$, including debts of the formerly state-owned and now privatised enterprises (Pinheiro 2000: 22).

Factually, the Plano Real fitted in with the Washington Consensus principles of neoliberalism, dominating in the Western economic discourse since the late 1970s. But was Brazil ready for neoliberal reforms? (Obviously, the same question could be put in regard to all other Latin American and East European countries in the 1990s.)

Before answering this question, not as easy as it seems at a first glance, we have to consider why neoliberalism appeared an attractive doctrine and policy in many peripheral and (particularly) semi-peripheral countries. Certainly, it had partly occurred because of the deep crisis of preceding statist models of development that were unable to respond to the new challenges. However, there were also undeniable achievements of the microelectronic/information technologies revolution, which coincided with the rise of market fundamentalism. This revolution widened the gap between the world economic and technological leaders, a gap that had begun narrowing in the 1970s. It inspired not only the influential groups which were always interested in lesser state regulation of the market (prima facie, the commodities exporters and financiers) but also a significant part of society to pick up the 'new' (actually well-forgotten old!) economic model as the alternative to the collapsed one. Fabio Erber sarcastically remarked on this occasion: 'Public opinion, as expressed by consumers, wanted Miami, not the Silicon Valley' (Erber 1995: 221). And not all people understood that Miami existed for weekends whereas the Silicon Valley achievements required hard intensive work from Monday to Friday.

As it is well known, in 1971 'Intel' introduced a microprocessor that opened the way to the microelectronic and IT era. Simultaneously, due to the preceding policy of the welfare state, a large, well-educated new middle class had arisen as an actor within the new technological revolution. This social stratum, particularly, its upper and most active part, tended towards free creative activity, being freed from excessive state regulation, strong corporate hierarchy and other attributes of the declining late industrial, Fordist-Keynesian system. It had the proper purposes and pretensions for a peculiar, even elitist role in society. In addition, this social stratum endeavoured to self-fulfilment, including its own business in new branches of economy.

These endeavours had a solid background: the immense volume of accumulated human capital embodied in the intellectual, creative capacities of this social group. This capital enabled its 'owners' to be sure in an unpredictable environment of markets and new businesses. Meanwhile, a big part of this capital had been created in households and was partly funded due to the social expenditures of the welfare state and/or public foundations (for education, healthcare, etc.). Hence, the so-called market renaissance in the USA and UK had been based, to a large degree, on a non-market premise.

The interests of the new middle class coincided with those of big business, including transnational corporations, and banking capital. They all tended to restrain the trade unions for increasing profitability of production on the national and global scale, to weaken the state regulation of economy, to make a labour market more flexible. It is necessary to note that the strategic counter-offensive of Big Capital to the positions of labour conquered in the 1930s–1970s would be much less successful without the help of new technological achievements.

Unfortunately, the new 'pro-market' actors, who promoted 'market renaissance' in the West, did not exist in Brazil or any other Latin American country, at least, in a full degree, to the beginning of the 1990s. There were old 'pro-market' actors, and they could not be agents of the same implementation of neoliberalism as in the 'pattern' Anglo-Saxonian countries.

Therefore, Brazil was insufficiently ready to adopt neoliberal economic policies similar to those of the USA and UK. It meant that the results of neoliberalism in Brazil should have been differing from the results attained in highly developed countries (where they were not positive in all respects). However, at the same time, it was impossible to save the obsolete, statist model that could yield nothing except the new versions of clintelism with corruption, inflation, ineffective regulation and, in the end, aggravating backwardness.

Indeed, the implementation of the Plano Real operated as Janus, in twofold directions. On the one hand, it made any economic activity more predictable and favoured long-term investment. Because of the resumed investment (as well as on the cause of the increased consumers' demand), the rate of growth increased, though it did not attain the pace of the 'miracle' years (1967–1974) (Table 5.1).

As a result of the attained stabilisation and resumed investment, the partial modernisation of production took place in manufacturing industries outputting consumer durable goods. It was the so-called short cycle of technological modernisation in industry that allowed the elevation of productivity in several manufacturing sectors of the Brazilian economy. The share of gross investments in fixed capital as a percentage of GDP increased from 14.4 per cent in 1993 to 15.2 per cent in 1995

Table 5.1 The rate of growth of Brazilian economy, 1990–2005, as percentage to the preceding period

1990	1992	1994	Average over 1990–1994	1995	Average over 1996–2000	Average over 2001–2005
−4.4	−0.5	5.9	1.3	4.2	2.1	2.9

Sources and the author's calculations: CEPAL/ECLAC 2017: cuadro 2.1.1.1.xls

and to 18.1 in 1997 (Bielschowsky 1999: 19–34; Bielschowsky et al. 2002: 25–30, 34–41).

On the other hand, these moderate achievements were combined with inevitable liberalisation of external trade, mainly by means of decreased custom tariffs. It opened the internal market for importation of qualitative and relatively cheap manufactured goods. The high exchange ratio of the new currency, *real*, to US dollar (1 real = 1 dollar) was obviously favourable to the increased imports. In the new conditions, many industrial enterprises could not compete and had to lock out their workers or to change an assortment of their output to lower technological complexity. In fact, the implementation of the *Plano Real* accelerated the process of deindustrialisation in Brazil. In addition, trade liberalisation with the corresponding growth of imports led to an increased trade deficit and, hence, aggravated the problem of the total payment balance. This problem had to be solved by the inflow of not just direct, but mostly speculative investments ('hot capitals').

Later, during his second presidential term in 2000, Cardoso, overcoming the resistance of various groups in Congress, promoted a voting bill about fiscal responsibility (*A Lei de Responsibilidade Fiscal*). The law had an undoubtful significance, not only for managing finances at all levels of authority but also for restraining corruption. It contributed to dismantling the clientelistic practices when the patrimonial relationships had been transplanted from an archaic *fazenda* to modern urban life, whereas the costs of these 'transfers' were covered by taxpayers.

It was almost inevitable that the Brazilian *real,* with its high parity to US dollar, should have been undergoing speculative attacks. In January 1999, when the second term of Cardoso had just begun, the government was obliged to abandon one of the pivotal principles of its original plan: it agreed to currency devaluation with its 'free floating' on the waves of financial globalisation. The *real* had lost half of its previous value but internal inflation remained under control. In 1999 the monetary authorities of Brazil headed by the Central Bank moved to target inflation mostly by means of monetary tools, regulating the rate of interest and monetary aggregates. Later, in the long-term prospect this measure drew the Brazilian economy into the funnel of specific crisis, but it appeared effective in the short-term.

Because of the *real* devaluation, poverty began increasing again as it had been in the situation of crises. The share of poor had grown from 35.8 per cent of the total population in 1996 to 37.5 per cent in 1999 (CEPAL 2002: 211). The initial positive effect of financial stabilisation for industry disappeared, and the economy turned to deindustrialisation again. The devaluation of *real* slowed but did not stop this process, although, at the same time, the passenger aircrafts for regional lines,

'Embraer', had become the main goods export in 2000–2001. Brazil exported them for 6.3 billion dollars in 2000 and for 5.8, in 2001, or 11.4 and 10.0 per cent of the total exports of goods, respectively (CEPAL/ECLAC 2003: 122–123 and the author's calculations).

Under the presidency of Cardoso the reforms of social policy had started. They were aimed at de-bureaucratisation of the system of social assistance, primarily in the spheres of healthcare and education The local authorities at the municipal level got more rights and more responsibility for distribution of social aid among the needy. Since 1995 the main social indicators, whether it concerned the infantile/maternal mortality, common disease incidence or attendance of school by children from poor families, improved (Tavares de Almeida 2003: 104–107). There were launched and implemented important social programmes aimed directly at reduction of poverty, in particular, the programme *Bolsa Escola.* This programme conditioned a social assistance, though, in essence, very moderate, to those poor families whose children attended school. It was an attempt to disrupt the vicious circle of 'illiteracy–poverty–illiteracy' when the children from poor families were obliged to abandon school and to work, remaining illiterate or, at best, poorly educated; hence, they could get only poorly paid jobs, etc. Also, it is necessary to mention the Programme of Eradication of Infantile Labour (*Programa de Erradicação do Trabalho Infantil—PETI*) aimed at deliverance of children and adolescents up to 16 years from necessity to work for survival of them and their families. This programme tightly correlated with the *Bolsa Escola* and presupposed a provision of benefits to poor families whose children were obliged to work: 25 reals for each kid in municipalities with 250,000 and less inhabitants, 40 reals in municipalities with a population of more than 250,000. A realisation of this programme decreased the number of children and teenagers at the age between 5 and 17 years who were involved into a hired work: from 9.5 million (22.3 per cent of all children of this age) in 1995 to 5.1 million in 2003, although this amount augmented a little to 5.9 million in 2005 with subsequent diminution to 4.4 million in 2009 (Pereira Alberto et al. 2016: 460).

What concerns the relations between the state and unionised labour, the reformers' attempts to attribute flexibility to the labour market succeeded in relative stagnation of the real wage. After the notable increase in the first years of the *Plano Real* implementation, 1994–1997, by 41 per cent in December 1997 in ratio to the level of July 1994, they fell to the end of the second term of the Cardoso presidency and exceeded that level only by 7 per cent (IPEA 2003). The rate of open unemployment rose from 6.7 per cent in 1995 to 9.9 per cent in 2002 (10.4—in the difficult year 1999 after the devaluation of real (IPEA 2016). Simultaneously informal employment increased. Some enterprises in manufacturing industry, even big ones, apart from numerous small business entities in service sector, used informal labour, hiring temporarily low-skilled workers. Such practices meant that neither these labourers nor their employers paid taxes and contributions into social security/assistance system; hence the growth of informal employment actually restricted opportunities for financing of social programmes and reduction of poverty (Lautier 2003: 535–536).

The serious difficulties Brazil faced in 1998–2002, from devaluation of real to evident slowdown of the economic growth, allowed some critics of Cardoso to accuse him and his socioeconomic policy of following the military regime's elitist modernisation to the advantage of the upper 20 per cent of population (Souza 2015: 246), although such assertions are obvious exaggerations.

Summing up the results of Fernando Henrique Cardoso rule, it can be said that his government was originally constrained in the choice of one or another tactics for achieving the proclaimed strategic goal: to transform Brazil into an open, highly developed country without mass poverty in the conditions of globalisation, financial and technological as well. In this respect, the concrete situation in Brazil of the mid-1990s resembled that which existed in the 1930s when Vargas had to take into account the interests of the coffee-oligarchy, which controlled the financial system. (Thus, the shadow of 'the Era of Vargas' hung over the new reformers, who were obliged to act according to the principle 'little is better than nothing', i.e., restricted, even truncated reforms are better than a lack of reforms at all.)[2] Liberalising the external trade and financial operations, the reformers under the leadership of Cardoso hoped to dismantle the obsolete practice of state-protected entrepreneurship with clientelism and economic irresponsibility of the capitalist class. They attempted to compel this class to become 'a cat that catches mice instead of stealing sausages in the state-protected kitchen' (like Pinochet in Chile with assistance of 'Chicago boys' did, carrying out enforced economic liberalisation under the umbrella of the military dictatorship, often through a technological simplification of many enterprises). But really it was often necessary to choose between 'bad' and 'very bad'. As a result, to the end of the Cardoso presidency, the public debt of Brazil doubled and the current account deficit was hanging over the financial system.

However, the reformers who performed themselves in the 1980s as the Left-centrist (and originally were the sincere Left-centrists in a depth of their souls) acted as the Right-centrists, propping upon the heterogeneous coalition of different groups, including regional oligarchies, which demonstrated a miraculous capacity to mimicry, saving themselves from a genuine transformation. In particular, liberalisation of the economy and privatisation of the large state-controlled sector of big and medium enterprises did not fully dismantle the old ties between the state's economic bureaucracy and private firms, but rather modified them. In some cases, whether it concerned several entire branches as a whole or only the regional and local levels, privatisation opened the way to oligopolies with restricted, imperfect competition and strengthened ties between private business and the state authorities (Abu-El-Haj 2007: 100–103; Kröger 2012: 891–892). Thus, a deliverance from the heritage of the Vargas Era appeared not as easy as previously assumed. In other words, the old, conservative structures and segments of Brazilian society that

[2] Some authors compare Cardoso-president to Cardoso-sociologist, who was known as a Left-centrist, social-democratic critic of Brazilian reality (de Oliveira 2011: 132; Pastoret 2006). As Theotônio dos Santos, the distinguished theoretician of dependency, said about Cardoso, he was "a man from the left with the language of the right" (Santos dos 1998: 67).

hindered further modernisation (in a broad sense) appeared super-survivable in the new situation (Fiori 2001: 507–509). As Cardoso recognised later, "neoliberalism had won. But, in contrast to what people think, against my will" (Quoted on: Anderson 2011: 44, note 38).

The intention to combine neoliberal economic policy with a moderate social-democratic attitude in regard to social affairs, very contradictory in itself, could hardly continue for a long time, particularly in the concrete conditions of Brazil. The endeavour, which might have been sincere, to drift from the pattern of conservative modernisation by attack on the patrimonial-clientelistic relationships and practices (through liberalisation of economy and its opening to the global competition), did not succeed in the principal shift in the country's development path. The reforms, prima facie privatisation, subverted monopolism of the state-owned enterprises in some branches of the economy, mainly in infrastructure and public services, but did not abolish it completely. The private monopolies, particularly at the regional level, existed as previously together with oligarchic structures.

Thus, the real changes were rather superficial and did not deconstruct the profound imbalances and disparities of society. But the reforms initiated by the government of Cardoso bore new hopes and even steep aspirations for further improvement of life after the victory over inflation.

5.2 The Left Turn: Combining Incompatibles?

As it was said above, the main beneficiary of the neoliberal economic policy was, and has been, financial capital. It acquired the biggest 'yields' of neoliberal transformation and gained from the reforms to a much bigger degree than other actors did. However, this big beneficiary has not been interested in dismantling the old pattern of conservative modernisation. The path of conservative modernisation (with emphasis on *conservative* instead of one on *modernisation*) did not become the route to/through deep transformation of the country, but the public demand for changes already existed. The electoral victory of Luiz Inácio Lula da Silva and his presidential inauguration on the 1st of January of 2003 were the responses to arisen aspirations for changes.

Box 5.1 The Presidential Campaign of 2002: A Competition Between the Left-Centrist Candidates?

At a first glance it was paradoxical that the principal competitors who ran for the presidency in October 2002 came from the Left-centrist wing of the political spectrum. On the one hand, there was José Serra, the candidate of the PSDB (Party of Brazilian Social Democracy), the former Minister of Healthcare in the government of Cardoso, Professor of Economics, who

(continued)

Box 5.1 (continued)
wrote Marxist papers about Brazilian economy when working at the University of Campinas, a fortress of the Left Brazilian intellectuals, and in the past, the leader of left-biased Brazilian Union of Students before the coup of 1964, the political emigrant. Later he was adviser to Fernando Flores, the Minister of Finances of the Allende government in Chile in the last months of its existence before the bloody coup headed by Pinochet in 1973. On the other hand, there was Luis Inácio Lula da Silva, 'companheiro Lula', the leader of the Workers' Party (Partido dos Trabalhadores—PT), the former trade-union leader, ally of Cardoso and other Left-liberal intellectuals in the fight for democratisation in the years of authoritarianism. The Brazilian voters had chosen Lula, 'the people's president' who originated from the under-proletariat of the North-East.

Perhaps it is relevant to remark that when Lula ran for presidency in 1994, competing with Cardoso, many ordinary people, including inhabitants of favelas, said: 'Let the known Professor rule, may be, then our life will become better a little'. In 2002 many of them said: 'Professors already ruled over us, now let the president from common people, the former worker rule'. Nevertheless, it did not hinder Lula from forming his team, inviting no less known Professors than those who worked with Cardoso. It is sufficient to call such names as Guido Mantega, Cristovam Buarque, José Graziano or Nilcéia Freire (the first woman who was the rector of the University of the State Rio de Janeiro).

Meanwhile, the electoral victory of Lula and the PT did not mean radical change of socioeconomic policy in the country. Indecision, in which many Leftists accused Lula, was conditioned not only by his endeavour to avoid a negative reaction of the financial circles to possible ultra-Leftist measures, such as the total de-privatisation of the formerly state-owned enterprises, while the external dependency of Brazil on the global financial market was very strong. The new government had to take into account the specific character of the political system in Brazil, which has been inconsistent with whatever radical reforms (Cheibub 2009: 11–17). Namely, any reformers were remembering the actual, concrete state of the political spectrum in the National Congress, so the compromises and fluctuations should be inevitable. The PT and Lula, like Cardoso before him, were compelled by a set of circumstances to act with caution. In practice, the changes of socioeconomic policy during the PT rule meant rather correction, 'little adjustment' of this policy according to the voters' aspirations for the more effective solution of social problems.

Lula continued the financial-economic policy of his predecessor. The Left-centrist government together with the Central Bank of Brazil maintained financial stability by means of monetarist tools, regulating the interest rate and monetary mass in circulation, the budget surplus, and open markets. Neither Lula nor the PT as a whole did not initially proclaim the long-term task of the new developmental strategy and policy which would somewhat resemble the plans of Joscelino Kubitschek (to pass the 50 years historical distance in 5 years!) or the Plans of National Development elaborated under the presidents-generals Médici and Geisel. Lula and the PT emphasized the reduction of poverty, radical improvement of access to healthcare and education for the poor and the raising of minimal salaries as their main goals. In other words, they put the social problems in the focus of their policy as a whole. In this respect, the PT (as well as some other Latin American Left and Left-centrist parties and movements in the beginning of the century) differed not only from its old Right and Right-centrist opponents but also from the old Left. The latter, recognising, of course, a necessity to redistribute incomes to the advantage of poor groups, treated nationalisation/de-privatisation, enlargement of the state-owned sector and public investments as indispensable conditions for successful social policy. Thus, there was a conversion of priorities of the social and technical-economic aspects of development, and Patrus Ananias, the Minister for Social Development and Hunger Alleviation in the PT government from 2004 to 2010, criticised the economists' fallacy that growth itself promotes social inclusion and justice (Ananias 2007).

Strictly speaking, such an approach looked new in relation to the old, dogmatic Left visions, but was not novel as a whole and corresponded with an influential current within a framework of the mainstream economics. The declared shift in policy to the problems of excessive inequality, poverty and deprivation of elementary social services for most ordinary people in Brazil did not deviate from the strategic modifications of neoliberalism reflected in the World Bank approach to the growth issues in the late 1990s. After a set of *more than modest* successes of the Bretton Woods institutions' recommendations (let's remember the crisis on the eve of 1994–1995 in Mexico which had been treated as 'the pattern country' by the Washington Consensus' admirers), the World Bank (the 'awful enemy' and 'bugbear' for all Leftists across the world!) began calling to take into account social and environmental problems (Pender 2001: 402–408). In particular, this institution underlined in one of its Development Reports that excessive and 'unfair' inequality is not only bad from the moral and political points of view but also succeeds in ineffective allocation of resources, conserves market imperfections, impedes required investment and deteriorates a quality of public institutions which should provide effective functioning markets. Therefore, as authors of the report concluded, the dichotomy between pro-growth policies and policies aimed at more equity is false (World Bank 2005: 7–10, 89–106).[3] Later a little, in the special publication about the Mexican problems, it was focused on numerous steadfast inequalities as the main obstacles to stable economic growth in the country (Bourguignon and Dessus 2009: 48–50; Guerrero et al. 2009: 142–152). At last, the World Bank noted the ineffectiveness of inequality for growth in 2018 in the report about East Asia

[3] '…the impact of (the same amount of) growth on poverty reduction is significantly greater when initial income inequality is lower' (World Bank 2005: 9).

Table 5.2 Public expenditures in Brazil for education, healthcare and social needs as a whole, 1993–2014, in constant US$ of 2010 and as percentage of GDP (the average annual for respective biannual period)

Types of public expenditures	1993–1994	1997–1998	2001–2002	2005–2006	2009–2010	2013–2014
All public expenditures for social needs per capita, US$ 2010	1464	1751	1886	2176	2749	3141
– As percentage of GDP	17.9	20.1	21.2	22.5	25.1	26.3
– As percentage of all public expenditures	57.5	50.5	64.3	72.3	71.7	74.8
Public expenditures for education per capita, US$ 2010	345	408	406	445	611	692
– As percentage of GDP	4.2	4.7	4.6	4.6	5.6	5.8
Public expenditures for healthcare per capita, US$ 2010	245	327	368	449	573	622
– As percentage of GDP	3.0	3.7	4.1	4.6	5.2	5.2

Source: CEPAL (2016a: 78–84)

(World Bank 2018: 29–45) where tendencies to the rise of some 'Brazilian' features have been observable in the last 15–20 years.

Hence, the proclaimed emphasis on social policy and social issues did not exceed boundaries of the contemporary reformist paradigm and did not put an existence of capitalism in Brazil under question. On the contrary, it has been an attempt to improve it, eliminating the centurial disparities between the economic and social aspects of Brazilian modernisation, between the declarable political progressism and practical conservatism.

What was really done over thirteen and a half years of the PT rule, from the first inauguration of Lula on January 1, 2003, and August 31, 2016, when the Senate impeached Dilma Rousseff?

According to the pre-electoral promises and PT programme, the expenditures for social needs, including ones for healthcare and education, grew at an accelerated pace. The dynamics of such expenditures in the years of Cardoso's and Lula's rule are presented in the Table 5.2.

It is notable that in 2013–2014, to the end of the PT rule's *success story*, 70 and more per cent (73.0, in 2011–2012, and 74.8 in 2013–2014) of all public expenditures were targeted at social needs. By this indicator Brazil exceeded almost all countries in Latin America (the average indicators in the continent were 65.8 and 66.4 per cent, respectively) and began catching up with Western European countries. The only country in Latin America that overtook Brazil on this indicator a little, by 1 per cent point, was Uruguay, with 74.2 per cent of the total budget in 2011–2012 (CEPAL 2016a: 78). Lula's programme *Fome Zero* (Hunger Zero) abolished such scandalous and intolerable phenomenon as hunger among the poor (in the country which has been the third manufacturer of civil aircrafts in the world!). Concerning the share of poor people in the total population of Brazil, it diminished from 37.8 per cent in 2002 to 16.5 per cent in 2014 by 34 million people. The main drivers for this

Table 5.3 Indicators of poverty and income inequality in Brazil, 2002–2017

Indicators	2002	2005	2008	2011	2014	2017
The share of poor in the total population, %%	37.8	34.4	25.3	21.0	16.5	19.9
The number of poor, millions people	68.0	68.3	49.5	41.9	34.0	42.0
Gini coefficient on the total population	0.570	0.552	0.536	0.526	0.514	0.539

Sources and the author's calculations on CEPAL/ECLAC (2002: 173); CEPAL/ECLAC (2007: 23); CEPAL/ECLAC (2010: 23); CEPAL/ECLAC (2015: 19); CEPAL (2019), cuadros 5 y 14

reduction in poverty were the raise of minimal wages from year to year (see Chap. 7), the enlargement of formal employment with work record cards (*carteiras de trabalho*), and transfer of wages to banking cards. In other words, economic growth in Brazil under the PT rule had apparently become pro-poor. It was not only accelerating but also outpacing the annual rate of inflation in 2006 for the first time in over 50 years and 'The Economist' underlined this fact with unconcealed admiration (Economist 2009: 4). In addition, the economic growth had been accompanied by reducing income inequality, although this inequality remained very high even by Latin American standards. The general dynamics of these changes as a whole are presented in the Table 5.3.

One of the main social programmes launched by the Lula government in November 2003 (and not revoked completely even after the displacement of Dilma Rousseff in 2016) has been the *Bolsa Família* (Family Allowance), the conditional cash transfer programme later recognised by the World Bank and International Monetary Fund as one of the largest and most successful programmes of such kind in the world. (Similar programmes have existed in other Latin American countries, for example, in Mexico (*Progresa/Oportunidades*), Chile (*Chile Solidario*), Argentina (*Jefes de Hogar*), Uruguay (*Plan de Equidad*), Colombia (*Familias en Acción*), but they all were of lesser volume.) The *Bolsa Família* combined a fight against poverty with an inducement of poor families to send their children to school instead of working. It united and perfected such programmes initiated by the Cardoso administration as the *Bolsa Escola*, PETI, *Cartão Alimentação* (Food Card) and *Auxílio Gás* (subsidies for consumption of gas by poor families).[4] The *Bolsa Família* presupposed a payment of benefits to poor families if their children attend, at least, 85 per cent of all lessons in school and pass a procedure of necessary vaccination. At the start of this programme in January 2004, the size of benefit was not too big. If, for example, the monthly family income per capita did not exceed 50 R$ (the threshold of extreme poverty), a family got 50 R $ as an allowance for each person. If the monthly income was higher than 50 R$ but lower than 100 R$, the then line of 'ordinary' poverty, the allowance was 15 R$ per child for families with a maximum of three children up to 15 years old. Later the

[4]Antony W. Pereira noted in his paper about the *Bolsa Família*: 'There has been strong continuity across the Cardoso, Lula and Rousseff administrations with regard to anti-poverty programmes' (Pereira 2015: 1687).

concrete size of these benefits augmented while the minimal level of wage and the poverty line lifted according to inflation, and the programme was spread to the poor families with adolescents of 16–17 years conditionally on their attendance of school (Guerreiro and Fereira da Souza 2012: 2–3; Hall 2006: 696–706; Soares et al. 2006: 3–5).

Initially *Bolsa Família* supported 3.5 million families, but over time it proliferated to 13.8 million families, about 50 million people or 25 per cent of the total population. In 2007 and 2014, the programme was enlarged: the amount of payments was augmented because the minimal monthly threshold of poverty beyond which the benefits should have been assigned increased to 89 reals per capita. In 2011, under the presidency of Dilma Rousseff, *Bolsa Família* had become a component part of the general strategic plan 'Brazil Without Misery' (*Brasil Sem Miséria*) aimed at full eradication of the extreme poverty in which 16.2 million people, (around 8 per cent of the country's population) survived on a monthly income of 70 reals or less. At last, in 2012 the *Bolsa Família* incorporated the programme 'Tender Brazil' (*Brasil Carinhoso*) and henceforth embraced poor families with children aged up to 6, too.

According to various estimations, a contribution of the *Bolsa Família* with all concomitant programmes into the general decrease of inequality (measured by the Gini coefficient) was between 12 and 21 per cent (Paiva et al. 2013: 35) among all factors of the inequality and poverty diminution [the main of them was the stable raise of minimal wage (Saboia 2009: especially pp. 579–588)]. Certainly, such contribution into the total reduction of poverty looks very modest. However, the programme's significance has been much bigger for the decrease of extreme poverty: the share of the population living in the conditions of poverty had fallen from 13.2 per cent in 2001 to 4.6 per cent in 2014 (2.9 times), whereas the share of all poor diminished from 37.5 to 16.5 per cent (2.3 times), respectively (CEPAL 2016b: cuadro 10 and my calculations—V.Kr.). In addition, the *Bolsa Família* as a whole had the positive multiplicative effect for the country's GDP and final consumption growth already in the first years of its implementation. Then each real (1 R$) invested into this programme elevated the GDP by 1.78 R$ (Neri et al. 2013: 200–203). Meanwhile, it would be erroneous to exaggerate the 'weight' of the programme for the country's economy and budget: it has been about only 0.4–0.5 per cent of GDP, or 2.9–3.0 per cent of the total expenditures for social needs. Even under the Lula rule, this magnitude was 6–7 times less than the sum expended by the government for debt servicing. The latter expenditures went to the government creditors, namely, to the people who could hardly be called poor: various financial institutions, rich persons holding treasury bonds, foreign investors, etc. In the opinion of many observers, the *Bolsa Família* had a limited impact on the improvement of incomes distribution, although it would be impossible to say that its realisation was useless at all (Amann and Baer 2009: 36–39; Haddad 2009; Gaulard 2019: 129–130). It not only alleviated the old Brazilian social disease (extreme poverty) but also improved feeling among the poorest families. The *Bolsa Família* elevated their 'sense of optimism', inducing them to believe in the proper efforts aimed at abandoning poverty (due to conditionality of the programme) (Neri 2014: 44–45).

Nevertheless, the *Bolsa Família* did not essentially impact on the profound causes of poverty in Brazil. It did not principally change the structure of occupations in the adult population nor their educational attainment. In the opinion of some observers (and this opinion merits consideration), the programme favoured a 'culture of dependence', creating a habit of state-protected paternalism among the poor where 'to be poor' became a preferable and even advantageous state for some part of them (Hall 2008: 814–816; Lautier 2003: 181–184). The *Bolsa Família* could be, at best, *one of the programmes* aimed at inclusion of poor, previously excluded from the 'community of citizens', into full social life; in other words, it could become a starting point for further deepening of social policy but not as a goal itself.

The period of Left-centrist rule since 2003 has been marked by the diminution of profound interregional disparities, too, though this process started still under the military regime. Then industrialisation commenced gradually spreading from the region of São Paulo to the North-East (Krasilshchikov 2017; Maracci 2017: 9–20). The gap between the relatively developed South and South-East, on the one hand, and the backward North and North-East, on the other, began slowly though steadily shrinking. The decreased interregional disparities can be expressed as the diminishing coefficient of statistical variation on the average gross regional product per capita across the states. This coefficient fell from 55.6 per cent in 2005 to 54.1 per cent in 2010 and to 46.8 per cent in 2014 but increased to 48.3 per cent in 2016 [counted on: (CEPAL 2016b: cuadro 2; IBGE 2007, tables 2, 4; IBGE 2016a: table 1; IBGE 2018b: 3, 9)].

Box 5.2 Calculation of the Statistical Variation Coefficient on Gross Regional Product (GRP) per Capita

The coefficient of statistical variation V has been calculated according to the formula $V = \sigma{:}X$, where σ is the square root of statistical dispersion, which, in turn, is the average squared deviation from X—the average magnitude. The latter in the given case is not the simple average of all gross regional products per capita of all 26 states plus the Federal District Brasilia; it is the weighted average. This magnitude is the quotient of division of the total sum of all GRPs by the total population. It is necessary to take into account that the total sum of all gross regional products may differ from the gross domestic and/or national product. The latter is somewhat bigger than the nominal sum of all regional products. For example, the GDP per capita in Brazil was 30,411 reals (R$) in 2016, whereas the average GRP per capita in that year was 29,917 R$.

The gap between the states, units of Federation (*Unidades da Federação*), with the highest and lowest GRP per capita (in current prices) diminished from 9.23 times in 1995 to 8.85 times in 2000, increased to 9.33 in 2005 with subsequent reduction to 8.49 in 2010 and to 6.4 in 2016 [counted on (IBGE 1999, 50–51; IBGE 2002a, 57; IBGE 2007, table 4 (p.40); IBGE 2012, table 4 (p. 16); IBGE 2018b, 9)]. Of course, the interregional gap by the GRP per capita in Brazil remains still excessive;

nevertheless, it is impossible to ignore the positive changes that took place in this respect in the last 20–25 years. It occurred mostly thanks to more rapid economic growth in the North and North-East, the regions with the poorest, least developed states of Brazil, than the growth in the developed South and South-East. This unevenness of economic development can be assessed as positive, aimed at diminishing huge interregional disparities in the country. The regional development policy carried out by the PT government favoured such *positively uneven* development, although it was modestly proceeding within boundaries of ordinary credit, tax and investment stimulation (Cavalcante and Uderman 2009: 270–277).

Besides the diminishing interregional disparities, there has also been the observable narrowing gap of income per capita between urban and rural areas. For the first time in the modern history of Brazil, the incomes of rural households grew faster than those in urban areas. In particular, average household incomes (*rendimentos de domicílios*) in urban areas exceeded the average rural areas' incomes 2.7 times in 1995, 2.5 times in 2001 and 2.1 times in 2007, with a subsequent slow decrease to 1.9 in 2013–2015 [counted on (IBGE 1997, 60; IBGE 2002b, table 7.1; IBGE 2008, table 7.1; IBGE 2014, table 7.1; IBGE 2016b, table 7.1)]. Such a convergence between the urban and rural areas, particularly at the level of households whose monthly incomes were within two minimal wages per month, succeeded in a notable improvement of access of the rural families to durable goods and other contemporary conveniences. Table 5.4 and Figure 5.1 illustrate this convergence between urban and rural households in a sphere of consumption over the years of the Cardoso, Lula and Dilma Rousseff governments' rule

It may have seem that the reduction of poverty and positive changes in the disparities between the urban and rural areas signified the beginning of a mass consumption society in Brazil, the implementation of the old romantic dreams of the 1960s. However, this *recent* version of a mass consumption society constructed under the auspices of PT has resembled a project completely dislocated from that vision. *That* project should have been developed upon the Fordist-Keynesian foundation: the mass production of consumer goods, including technically complicated durables (with a domination of capital-function over capital-property, manager over proprietor) and the welfare state with numerous social benefits. The *recent* project began to be realised in the conditions of globalisation and dominance of the financial sphere over productive sectors of the economy. The main tool of its implementation has been not the growth of production (as it was in the case of late industrialisation in Japan or South Korea), but the enlargement of access of the poor strata to financial resources, primarily the growth of credit for consumption. Thus, an inclusion of *those previously excluded from development* into the contemporary process of globalisation proceeded through private consumption by means of their inclusion into the banking system. For many of them, it has been the only way of such an inclusion into the globalised world, in contrast to the Fordist-Keynesian period when the main way to 'a happiness from possession' of material goods lay through intensive work, and consumer credits were only *the supplemental tools* for acquiring desired goods.

Table 5.4 Shares of households with permanent residence, possessing consumption durable goods and monthly incomes up to two minimal wages in urban and rural areas, as a percentage of all respective households, 1995–2015

	Urban households					Rural households[a]				
Types of durable goods	1995	2001	2007	2013	2015	1995	2001	2007	2013	2015
TV sets	69.31	83.71	93.26	96.15	96.40	31.76	54.08	73.84	89.26	89.89
Refrigerators	54.52	74.05	86.29	96.38	97.21	21.17	41.31	60.61	86.33	89.39
Laundering machines	5.95	10.82	18.18	37.83	43.78	1.73	3.64	4.64	12.52	16.15

[a]For 1995, not taking into account the rural population of the North region states: Acre, Amapá, Amazonas, Pará, Rondônia and Roraima (note of the IBGE)
Counted on IBGE 1997, 61–63 (table 8.2); IBGE 2002b, table 7.2; IBGE 2008, table 7.2; IBGE 2014, tables 7.2a–7.2c; IBGE 2016b, tables 7.2a–7.2c

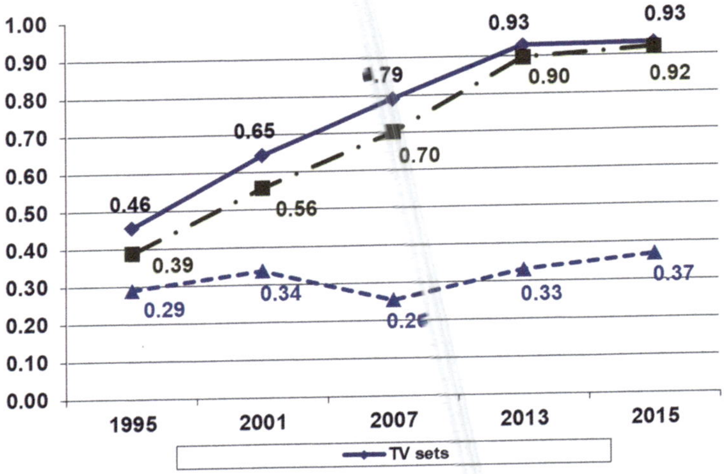

Fig. 5.1 Ratio of possessions of some durable consumer goods by rural households* to the level of urban households, 1995–2015 (the level of urban households = 1.00 in each respective year). *Only households with incomes within the limit of two minimal monthly wages. Composed on, see note to the Table 5.4

Indeed, the total volume of all credits in the Brazilian economy increased from 22 per cent of GDP in 2001 to almost 60 per cent by the end of 2014. 47 per cent of the latter were offered to private consumers, and the volume of personal credits grew faster than the real minimal salary raised: by 140 and 80 per cent, respectively, over 2001–2015. Two thirds of all personal credits, or 32 per cent of the total volume of credits in the economy, were lent for purchasing consumer goods, whereas the biggest increment of credits for purchasing expensive, technically complicated durables took place among the poor social groups. As a result of the credits' growth, an indebtedness of the Brazilian families to the end of the PT rule, in 2015, amounted 48 per cent of their incomes, whereas it was equal only to 22 per cent in 2006 (Lavinas 2015a: 35–37, 45–48, b: 32–35). It meant that an ascendance of the large masses of poor to 'heights of happiness' was paid for by the augmented credit bubble.

The notable growth of social expenditures went hand in hand with the monetisation of some benefits and services. For instance, about 60 per cent of all expenditures for social needs in 2013–2015 took the form of monetary transfers via banking accounts. And this process fully corresponded to the neoliberal principles of socioeconomic policy. As Lena Lavinas wittily remarked, the slogan 'finances for all' has become a new neoliberal mantra (Lavinas 2015a: 42–44, 49), although, I should like to specify, in the Left-centrist arrangement, too. By the way, it is worth noting that the PT's *enlargement of credit policy* anticipated the G-20 global recommendations aimed at restraining the financial turbulence of 2008–2009 by involving the large masses of 'ordinary customers' into financial operations. Such practice was fully fitted to the dominating neoliberal attitude (Soederberg 2013: esp. 598–599, 606–608), the apparent Keynesian mask notwithstanding.

Considering the social policy of the PT, it is impossible to neglect the attained positive changes in education and healthcare. Firstly, the level of education of economically active Brazilians (15–64 years) elevated very rapidly, and the World Bank experts noted that Brazil progressed in education even faster than China in the period from 1990 to 2010 (Bruns et al. 2012: 3). The improvement of the education indicators occurred, to some degree, due to the abovementioned programme *Bolsa Família* which reduced the share of children (at the age of 6–16 years) who did not attend school from 8.4 to 5.4 per cent. The number of boys of 6–16 years who did not attend school fell by 40 per cent, the number of girls of the same age, by 30 per cent from 2003 to 2011 (Craveiro and de Ximenes 2013: 114). Though the share of illiterate persons at age 15 and more years remained relatively high, 10.0 per cent in 2007, 8.0 in 2015, and 7.0 in 2017 (IBGE 2016b: table 4.15, 2018a: table 3.3), it was conditioned mostly by illiteracy of elders. For example, the share of illiterates among the people whose age exceeded 65 years reached 25.7 per cent in 2015. The share of those persons who studied 9 or more years increased from 22.5 per cent in 1995[5] to 52.4 per cent of all people aged 10 or more years in 2015 (counted on IBGE 1997, 11 (table 3.2), 2016b, table 3.2). The share of Brazilians at age from 25 to 59 years who studied 10 and more years increased from 33.1 per cent in 1999 to 55.5 per cent in 2013 in urban areas and from 7.2 per cent to 20.4 per cent in rural areas, respectively. Among youngsters between 15 and 24 years, the share of those who studied 10 and more years increased in urban areas from 30.4 per cent in 1999 to 53.1 per cent in 2013, in rural areas from 10.0 per cent to 32.8 per cent, respectively. At the same time, the average number of years spent by all Brazilians of 25 years and more in various educational institutions lifted from 6.5 in 2005 to 7.9 years in 2015. Nevertheless, Brazil lagged behind Chile on this indicator for almost a quarter of century (CEPAL 2014, cuadros 26, 27; IBGE 2016b, gráfico 4.12 (p. 64), tables 4.13, 4.15).

One of the goals of the PT's social policy was the improvement of the access of poor youngsters to higher education. Firstly, the number of federal universities, mostly in the North and North-East, increased from 43 in 2002 to 59 in 2011 (Sicsú 2013: 24). Secondly, the launched programmes of the Fund for Financing of the Higher Education Students (*Fundo de Financiamento ao Estudante do Ensino Superior*) and University for All (*Universidade para Todos*—ProUni) allowed notably to elevate the rate of youth enrolment into higher education. In 2005, 11.4 per cent of all Brazilians at the age between 18 and 24 years studied at universities and higher colleges. This indicator had jumped up to 18.4 per cent in 2015. At the same time, the *gross* enrolment ratio in the tertiary education of Brazil attained 50.5 per cent in 2016. (For comparison: in Chile it was 87 per cent, in Argentina 80 per cent, in France 64 per cent, in Uruguay 63 per cent, in the UK 56 per cent, in

[5]The figure from 1995 not taking into account the rural population of the North region states: Acre, Amapá, Amazonas, Pará, Rondônia and Roraima (note of the IBGE).

Table 5.5 Indicators of infant mortality in Brazil and the world (average), 1990–2016 (per mille, ‰, live births)

The indicators		1990	2000	2010	2015	2016
The infant mortality (under 1 year)	Brazil	60	32	17	14.6	13.5
	The world (average)	67	56	40	31.6	29.9
The infancy mortality (at the age from 1 to 5 years[a]	Brazil	23	6	2	1.8	1.6
	The world (average)	34	25	15	10.1	9.4

[a]Counted as difference between infant mortality and total infant mortality (aged under 5 years)
Source: For 1990—UNDP 1992: 148–149; for 2000—UNDP 2002: 175, 177; for 2010—UNDP 2013: 167, 169; for 2015—UNDP 2016: 227, 229; for 2016—UNDP 2018: 49, 51

Switzerland 57 per cent and in China 39 per cent of the population of 'university students age', [i.e. from 18 to 24 years) in 2010–2015, whereas the average ratio of gross enrolment into tertiary education in the world was then 35 per cent (UNDP 2016: 230–233)]. In absolute terms, the number of students (independent of their age) at the tertiary level of education in Brazil increased from 4.9 million in 2005 to 7.3 million in 2015 (IBGE 2016b: table 4.6). In this regard it is worth attending to the fact that in public educational institutions the share and number of the tertiary level's students who came from families pertaining by their incomes to the two lower quintiles had grown from 8.1 per cent in 2005 to 22.3 per cent in 2015. Among the tertiary level's students of the private institutions this share raised over the same time from 2.9 to 14.8 per cent, respectively (IBGE 2016b: gráficos 4.8, 4.9 (p. 61)). These data mean an obvious enlargement of the vertical social mobility for youth in Brazil due to the Left-centrist social policy, though such mobility has still been very far from the desirable level.

With concerns to the situation in public healthcare, it has clearly been illustrated by dynamics of such indicators as the expectancy of life at birth and infant mortality.

The expectancy of life at birth increased from 66.9 years in 1991 to 69.8 in 2000, to 73.9 in 2010 and to 76.0 in 2017 (72.5 for men and 79.6 for women).[6] It was higher than the average indicator in the world (72.2) and corresponded to the level of Hungary (76.1) (UNDP 2018: 22–23, 25). Since 1990 this indicator has been improved in Brazil to a bigger degree than in many other countries with life expectancy at birth in Brazil increasing by 8.8 years from 1990 to 2017 (on the UNDP data, or by 9.1 from 1991 to 2017—according to the IBGE). The average increase of this indicator in the world has been only 7.5 years (from 1990 to 2017) (UNDP 1992:130–131; UNDP 2018: 25).

The improvements in healthcare of children have been no less significant. In particular, Brazil experienced the fascinating decrease of the mortality of children (live births). The country's achievements in this aspect of social development are displayed in Table 5.5.

[6]On the data of the IBGE, 75.7 years—according to the data of the United Nations Development Programme (UNDP 2018: 23)

Thus the progress in social development of Brazil was undeniable. As it seemed to many observers, this progress began attributing a new quality to Brazilian society and allowed, at last, to hope that Brazil would cease being 'a country with permanently promissory future' or, on the contrary at the same time, *a country with permanently losing opportunities*. However, the obvious social achievements appeared actually not as stable as they initially looked. The social revanche of conservative forces in 2015–2018 turned positive trends in social development back to the 'historically proven' path of elitist development to the advantage of the upper strata. Why could this revanche take place? The answer to this question is indistinguishable from ones to other questions. The first of them is about the economic *base and costs* of the social achievements under the PT rule. The second question is about how the social changes in Brazil were profound. In other words, did the social policy of the Left-centrist governments change the social structure of the gigantic country, and if yes, to what degree did it change Brazilian society?

Meanwhile, it is necessary to take into account that the PT had to permanently compromise with the political forces, which were not interested in changing the previous trajectory of development and wanted to conserve it as long as possible. As Lula said in one of his interviews, the difference between a desire to do something and a real opportunity to do it is like the Atlantic Ocean by its size (Gómez Bruera 2015: 216). Inevitability of the compromises constrained the 'field of opportunities' for the Left/Left-centrist policy and increased the costs of reforms, not necessarily in the quantitative sense but rather, qualitatively. In fact, they led to a qualitative degradation of the country's economic structure and, prima facie, its premature deindustrialisation, which accompanied its decline into the middle-income trap. This slippage went hand in hand with an erosion of the original social base of the PT, thereby modifying the party itself and influencing its policies.

References

Abu-El-Haj, J. (2007). From interdependence to neo-mercantilism: Brazilian capitalism in the age of globalization. *Latin American Perspectives, 34*(5), 92–114.

Amann, E., & Baer, W. (2009). The macroeconomic record of the Lula Administration, the roots of Brazil's inequality and attempts to overcome them. In J. L. Love & W. Baer (Eds.), *Brazil under Lula. Economy, politics and soceity under the worker-president* (pp. 27–43). Houndmills, Basingstoke: Palgrave Macmillan.

Ananias, P. (2007). Patrus critica 'visão economicista' e defende ação do ministério. *O Globo*, 12.04.2007. Retrieved June 07, 2019, from https://extra.globo.com/noticias/brasil/patrus-critica-visao-economicista-defende-acao-do-ministerio-662783.html

Anderson, P. (2011). O Brasil de Lula. *Novos Estudos, 91*, 23–52.

Bacha E. 1997. Plano Real: Uma Segunda Avaliação. In L.S. Pinheiro (coord.), *O Plano Real e Outras Experiências de Establização* (pp. 177–204). Brasilia: IPEA – CEPAL.

Baumann, R., & Mussi, C. (1999). *Algunas características de la economía brasileña desde la adopción del Plan Real. CEPAL. Serie temas de coyuntura, N 5*. Santiago de Chile: NU.

BCB (Banco Central do Brasil). (2019). Retrieved July 18, 2019, from http://www.bcb.gov.br/Pec/Copom/Ingl/taxaSelic-i.asp#notas

Berthelot, J. (1991). Politique industrielle et politique économique au Brésil. *Caravelle, 57*. Numéro consacré au Brésil, pp. 5–51. Retrieved June 21, 2019, from https://doi.org/10.3406/carav.1991.2466, https://www.persee.fr/doc/carav_1147-6753_1991_num_57_1_2466

Bielschowsky, R. (1999). *Investimentos na indústria brasileira depois da abertura e do real: o mini-ciclo de modernizações, 1995-1997. (Serie Reformas Económicas, 44)*. Santiago de Chile: CEPAL. La versión electrónica. Retrieved July 02, 2019, from http://repositorio.cepal.org/handle/11362/7507

Bielschowsky, R., Clemente de Oliveira, J., Wohlers, M., Thadeu Abicalil, M., Oliva, R., Fonseca, R., & Soares, S. (2002). *Investimento e reformas no Brasil: Indústria e infra-estrutura nos anos 1990*. Brasilia: IPEA – CEPAL.

Bourguignon, F., & Dessus, S. (2009). Equity and development: Political economy considerations. In S. Levy & M. Walton (Eds.), *No growth without equity? Inequality, interests, and competition in Mexico* (pp. 45–69). Washington, DC, Houndmills, Basingstoke: World Bank, Palgrave Macmillan.

Bruns, B., Evans, D., & Luque, J. (2012). *Achieving world-class education in Brazil: The next agenda*. Washington, DC: World Bank.

Cardoso, F. H. (1995a). *Discurso de Despedida do Senado Federal: Filosofia e Diretrizes de Governo, 14 de dezembro de 1994*. Brasilia: Presidência da República Federal do Brasil.

Cardoso, F. H. (1995b). *Discurso de Posse do Presidente da República Fernando Henrique Cardoso no Congresso Nacional, 1 de janeiro de 1995*. Brasilia: Presidência da República Federal do Brasil.

Cardoso, F. H. (with Brian Winter). (2006) *The accidental president of Brazil. A memoir*. New York: Public Affairs.

Cardoso, F. H. (2009). New paths: Globalization in historical perspective. *Studies in Comparative International Development, 44*, 296–317.

Cardoso, F. H. (com Brain Winter). (2013). *O improvável Presidente do Brasil – recordações* (2-a edição). Rio de Janeiro: Civilização Brasileira.

Cardoso, F. H., & Graeff, E. (2012). Political leadership and economic reform: The Brazilian experience in the context of Latin America. In J. Santiso & J. Dayton-Johnson (Eds.), *The Oxford handbook of Latin Amerucan Political Economy* (pp. 13–42). Oxford: Oxford University Press.

Cavalcante, L. R., & Uderman, S. (2009). Regional development policies, 2003-2006. In J. L. Love & W. Baer (Eds.), *Brazil under Lula...* (pp. 263–281). New York: Springer.

CEPAL. (2002). *Panorama Social de América Latina 2001-2002*. NU (Naciones Unidas): Santiago de Chile.

CEPAL. (2014). *Panorama Social de América Latina 2014*. Santiago de Chile: NU. Anexo estadístico – la versión electrónica. Retrieved June 15, 2019, from http://repositorio.cepal.org/bitstream/handle/11362/37626/5/anexo_estadistico2014_es.zip

CEPAL. (2016a). *Panorama Social de América Latina 2015*. NU: Santiago de Chile.

CEPAL. (2016b). *Panorama Social de América Latina 2015*. Santiago de Chile: NU. Anexo estadístico – la versión electrónica. Retrieved June 11, 2019, from http://interwp.cepal.org/anuario_estadistico/anuario _2015/es/index.asp

CEPAL. (2019). *Panorama Social de América Latina 2018*. Santiago de Chile: NU. Anexo estadístico – la versión electrónica. Retrieved June 10, 2019, from http://repositorio.cepal.org/bitstream/handle/11362/44395/14/AnexoPS2018_es.xlsx

CEPAL/ECLAC. (2002). *Anuario estadístico de América Latina y el Caribe/Statistical yearbook for Latin America and the Caribbean 2001*. NU: Santiago de Chile.

CEPAL/ECLAC. (2003). *Anuario estadístico de América Latina y el Caribe/Statistical yearbook for Latin America and the Caribbean 2002*. NU: Santiago de Chile.

CEPAL/ECLAC. (2007). *Anuario estadístico de América Latina y el Caribe/Statistical yearbook for Latin America and the Caribbean 2006*. NU: Santiago de Chile.

CEPAL/ECLAC. (2010). *Anuario estadístico de América Latina y el Caribe/Statistical yearbook for Latin America and the Caribbean 2010*. NU: Santiago de Chile.

CEPAL/ECLAC. (2015). *Anuario estadístico de América Latina y el Caribe/Statistical yearbook for Latin America and the Caribbean 2015*. NU: Santiago de Chile.
CEPAL/ECLAC. (2017). *Anuario estadístico de América Latina y el Caribe/Statistical Yearbook for Latin America and the Caribbean 2016*. Santiago de Chile: NU. La versión electrónica. Cuentas nacionales/National counts. Retrieved February17, 2020, from http://interwp.cepal.org/anuario_estadistico/Anuario_2016/es/index.asp
Cheibub, J. A. (2009). Political reform in Brazil: Recent proposals, diagnosis, and a suggestion. In J. L. Love & W. Baer (Eds.), *Brazil under Lula. Economy, politics and society under the worker-president* (pp. 9–25). Houndmills, Basingstoke: Palgrave Macmillan.
Craveiro, C. B. A., & de Ximenes, A. (2013). Dez Anos do Programa Bolsa Família: Desafios e Perspectivas para a Universalização da Educação Básica no Brasil. In T. Campello & M. C. Neri (Eds.), *Programa Bolsa Família: Uma década de inclusão e cidadania* (pp. 109–123). Rio de Janeiro: IPEA.
de Oliveira, F. (2011). *Crítica á razão dualista. O Ornitorinco. Préfacio Roberto Schwarz*. São Paulo: Boitempo (1-ra edição – 2003).
Economist. (2009). "Getting it together at last". A special report on business and finance in Brazil. *The Economist, 8657*, 14–20.
Erber, F. S. (1995). The political economy of technology development: The case of the Brazilian informatics policy. In M. I. Bastos & C. Cooper (Eds.), *Politics and technology in Latin America* (pp. 173–199). New York: Routledge.
Fiori, J. L. (2001). Pour un diagnostic de la « modernisation » brésilienne. *Revue Tiers-Monde, 42* (167), 493–513.
Flynn, P. (1996). Brazil: The politics of the 'Plano Real'. *Third World Quarterly, 17*(3), 401–426.
Gaulard, M. (2019). L'économie du Brésil, 2e édition, Levallois-Perret, Éditions Bréal, coll. « Thèmes & débats ».
Gómez Bruera, H. F. (2015). *Lula, el Partido de los Trabajadores y el dilema de gobernalidad en Brasil. Traducción de Ana Inés Fernández*. México: Fondo de Cultura Económica, Centro de Investigación y Docencia Económica.
Guerreiro, O. R., & Fereira da Souza, P. H. G. (2012). *O Bolsa Família depois do Brasil Carinhoso: uma análise do potencial de redução da pobreza extrema. IPEA. Nota Técnica N 14*. Brasilia: IPEA.
Guerrero, I., López-Calva, L. F., & Walton, M. (2009). The inequality trap and its links to low growth in Mexico. In S. Levy & M. Walton (Eds.), *No growth without equity? Inequality, interests, and competition in Mexico* (pp. 111–156). Washington, DC, Houndmills, Basingstoke: World Bank, Palgrave Macmillan.
Haddad, M. A. (2009). A spatial analysis of Bolsa Família: Is allocation targeting the needy? In J. L. Love & W. Baer (Eds.), *Brazil under Lula...* (pp. 187–203). New York: Springer.
Hall, A. (2006). From Fome zero to Bolsa Família: social policies and poverty alleviation under Lula. *Journal of Latin American Studies, 38*(4), 689–709.
Hall, A. (2008). Brazil's Bolsa Família: A double-edged sword? *Development and Change, 39*(5), 799–822.
IBGE (Instituto Brasileiro de Geografia e Estatística) 1997. PNAD (Pesquisa Nacional por Amostra de Domicílios) 1995. 17, 1. Rio de Janeiro: IBGE
IBGE. (1999). *Contas Regionais do Brasil, 1985-1997 (Contas Nacionais N 3)*. Rio de Janeiro: IBGE.
IBGE. (2002a). *Contas Regionais do Brasil 2000 (Contas Nacionais N 8)*. Rio de Janeiro: IBGE.
IBGE. (2002b). *PNAD 2001* (Vol. 22). Rio de Janeiro: IBGE.
IBGE. (2007). *Contas Regionais do Brasil: 2002-2005 (Contas Nacionais N 21)*. Rio de Janeiro: IBGE.
IBGE. (2008). *PNAD 2007* (Vol. 28). Rio de Janeiro: IBGE.
IBGE. (2012). *Contas Regionais do Brasil 2010 (Contas Nacionais N 38)*. Rio de Janeiro: IBGE.
IBGE. (2014). *PNAD 2013* (Vol. 33). Brasil.Rio de Janeiro: IBGE. Tabelas em Excel, versão eletrônica. Retrieved June 14, 2019, from ftp://ftp.ibge.gov.br/Trabalho_e_Rendimento/

Pesquisa_Nacional_por_ Amostra_de_Domicilios_anual/2013/Volume_Brasil/Brasil/brasil_tc_brasil_domicilio_xls.zip

IBGE. (2016a). *Contas Regionais do Brasil: 2010-2014 (Contas Nacionais N 53)*. Rio de Janeiro: IBGE.

IBGE. (2016b). *PNAD 2015* (Vol. 35 (Volume Brasil)). Rio de Janeiro: IBGE. Tabelas em Excel, versão eletrônica. Retrieved June 14, 2019, from ftp://ftp.ibge.gov.br/Trabalho_e_Rendimento/Pesquisa_Nacional_por_Amostra_de_Domicilios_anual/2015/Volume_Brasil/Brasil/Brasil_xls.zip

IBGE. (2018a). Síntese de indicadores sociais Uma análise das condições de vida da população brasileira 2018. Rio de Janeiro: IBGE. Tabelas em Excel, versão eletrônica. Educação. Retrieved June 14, 2019, from ftp://ftp.ibge.gov.br/ Indicadores_Sociais/Sintese_de_Indicadores_Sociais/Sintese_de_Indicadores_Sociais_ 2018/xls/3_Educacao_xls.zip,

IBGE. (2018b). *Sistema de Contas Regionais: Brasil 2016*. Rio de Janeiro: IBGE.

IPEA (Instituto de Pesquisa Econômica Aplicada). (2003). *IPEAdata. Rendimento médio real do trabalho principal nas RMs: índice (jul. 1994 = 100), mensal de 1993.01 até 2002.11.* Atualizado em 18.02.2003. Retrieved June 6, 2019, from http://www.ipeadata.gov.br

IPEA. (2016). *IPEAdata. Taxa de desemprego 1992-2014*. Atualizado em 06.01.2016. Retrieved June 6, 2019, from http://www.ipeaddata.gov br

IPEA. (2019). *IPEAdata. Indicadores sociais. Número de indivíduos pobres – Linha de Pobreza Baseada em Necessidades Calóricas, 1976-2014*. Retrieved June 4, 2019, from http://www.ipeadata.gov.br

Krasilshchikov, V. (2017). Cambios de las disparidades interregionales en Brasil. *Iberoamérica, 2*, 54–79. Retrieved from http://iberoamericajournal.ru/es/ iberoamerica-2017-no-2.html

Kröger, M. (2012). Neo-mercantilist capitalism and post-2008 cleavages in economic decision-making power in Brazil. *Third World Quarterly, 33*(5), 887–991. https://doi.org/10.1080/01436597.2012.674703.

Lautier, B. (2003). La protection sociale dans le Brésil de Lula : Trop de dépenses, ou trop peu de recettes ? *Revue Tiers Monde, 175*, 527–554.

Lavinas, L. (2015a). A financeirização da política social: O caso brasileiro. *PolítiKa, 2*, 35–51.

Lavinas, L. (2015b). Modelo social em crise. *Revista Política Social e Desenvolvimento, 18*, 31–38.

Maracci, G. D. (2017). *Política social e desequilíbrios regionais no Brasil em tempos de crise. Texto para Discussão n 301*. Campinas: Instituto de Economia de UniCamp.

Montero, A. (2005). *Brazilian politics: Reforming a democratic state in a changing world*. Cambridge, UK: Polity Press.

Neri, M. (2014). *Inequality in Brazil: Measurement, trends, impacts and policies (The opening keynote presentation at the WIDER (World Institute of Development Research of the UN) International Conference "inequality – measurement, trends, impacts, and policies"*, Helsinki, September 5–6, 2014. Retrieved June 13, 2019, from https://www.wider.unu.edu/sites/default/files/Events/PDF/Slides/Neri.pdf and archive of the author.

Neri, M., Vaz, F. M., & Fereira da Souza, P. H. G. (2013). Effeitos Macroeconômicos do Programa Bolsa Família: Uma Análise Comparativa das Trasferências Sociais. In T. Campello & M. C. Neri (Eds.), *Programa Bolsa Família: Uma década de inclusão e cidadania* (pp. 193–206). Rio de Janeiro: IPEA.

Paiva, L. H., Falcão, T., & Bartholo, L. (2013). Do Bolsa Família ao Brasil sem Miséria: Um Resumo do Percurso Brasilero Recente na Busca da Superação da Pobreza Extrema. In T. Campello & M. C. Neri (Eds.), *Programa Bolsa Família: Uma década de inclusão e cidadania* (pp. 25–46). Rio de Janeiro: IPEA.

Pastoret, C. (2006). Cardoso el opositor académico vs. Cardoso político: ¿Continuidad o ruptura? *Revista de Economía Institucional, 8*(15), 79–95.

Pender, J. (2001). From 'structural adjustment' to 'comprehensive development framework': Conditionality transformed? *Third World Quarterly, 22*(3), 397–411. https://doi.org/10.1080/01436590120061679.

Pereira, A. W. (2015). *Bolsa Família* and democracy in Brazil. *Third World Quarterly, 36*(9), 1682–1699. https://doi.org/10.1080/01436597.2015.1059730.

Pereira Alberto, M. F., Rocha da Costa, R., Branco Pessoa, M. C., Grangeiro Belém, K. K., & Silva, S. L. G. (2016). Programa de Erradicação do Tranalho Infantil: Concepções de Educandos e Famílias. *Psicologia: Ciência e Profissão, 36*(2), 458–470.

Pinheiro, A. C. (2000). *A Experiência Brasileira de Privatização: O Que Vem a Seguir? (Textos para Discussão).* Rio de Janeiro: BNDES.

Saad-Filho, A., & Morais, L. (2018). *Brazil: Neoliberalism versus democracy*. London: Pluto Press.

Saboia, J. (2009). Salaire minimum et distribution de revenu au Brésil sur la pérode 195-2005. Évolutions et résultats de simulations. *Revue Tiers Monde, 199*, 567–589.

Santos, T. D. (1998). The theoretical foundations of the Cardoso government: A new stage of the dependency-theory debate. *Latin American Perspectives, 25*(1), 53–70.

Sicsú, J. (2013). *Dez Anos que Aabalaram o Brasil e o Futuro?* São Paulo: Geração Editorial.

Soares, F. V., Soares, S., Medeiros, M., & Guerreiro, O. R. (2006). *Cash transfer Programmes in Brazil: Impacts on inequality and poverty*. UNDP – International Poverty Centre. Working paper 21. Brasilia, D.F.: international poverty Centre.

Soederberg, S. (2013). Universalising financial inclusion and the securitisation of development. *Third World Quarterly, 34*(4), 593–612. https://doi.org/10.1080/01436597.2013.786285.

Souza, J. (2015). *A tolice da inteligência brasileira, ou como o país se deixa manipular pela elite.* Rio de Janeiro: LeYa.

Tavares de Almeida, M. H. (2003). Los desafíos de la reforma social en Brasil: Continuando con el cambio. *Nueva Sociedad, 187*, 101–113.

UNDP. (2002). *Human development report 2002: Deepening democracy in a fragmented world.* Oxford: Oxford University Press.

UNDP. (2013). *Human Development Report 2013. The rise of the south: Human Progress in a diverse world.* New York: UNDP.

UNDP. (2016). *Human development report 2016: Human development for everyone.* New York: UNDP.

UNDP. (2018). *Human development indices and indicators. 2018 Statistical update.* New York: UNDP.

UNDP (United Nations Development Programme). (1992). *Human Development Report 1992.* Oxford: Oxford University Press.

World Bank. (2005). *World development report 2006: Equity and development.* Washington, DC, New York: World Bank, Oxford University Press.

World Bank. (2018). *Riding the wave: An east Asian miracle for the 21st century. World Bank East Asia and Pacific regional report.* Washington, DC: World Bank. https://doi.org/10.1596/978-1-4648-1145-6.

Chapter 6
The Costs of Success and Return to the Past

The obvious achievements of the PT social policy were paid for by high costs, and this payment had far-reaching effects for the Brazilian economy and political fortunes of the country's Left-centrist forces as a whole. Considering these costs and their effects, it is necessary to distinguish the globally conditioned processes of economy and society from those which were a result of the political compromises with conservatives and the mistakes of the PT, though even the subjective and 'purely' timeserving political decisions had real objective foundations.

The two main concomitant tendencies accompanying the rule of the Left-centrist forces in Brazil have been *deindustrialisation of the economy* and *reprimarisation* of the country's external trade, i.e. the rapid growth of agrarian and raw materials exports at the cost of manufactured goods exports. And these tendencies have not only had economic impacts but also serious political consequences.

6.1 Deindustrialisation and Its Types

Apparently, deindustrialisation means a diminution of the shares of industry (particularly its manufacturing branches) in GDP and the total employment of population over a long period of time, as this diminution becomes the stable tendency in economy. Nevertheless, the diminishing share of industry's output in the economy does not exclude a growth of industrial output in physical volume and in value as well. The manufacturing industry may continue growing (except, of course, during periods of recession), but it grows at a slower pace than the service sector. The latter may grow as a result of two main factors: (1) diversifying consumer demand that shifts from consumption of goods to consumption of services and (2) because of the new needs of industry itself (an enlargement of R&D, technical services,

V. Krasilshchikov, *Brazil - Emerging Forever?*, Societies and Political Orders in Transition, https://doi.org/10.1007/978-3-030-50208-9_6

maintenance of equipment, development of necessary infrastructure, training of engineers and skilled workers, etc.).

Before considering the concrete process of deindustrialisation in Brazil, the country of late industrialisation, it is relevant to scrutinise deindustrialisation in those developed countries where it began earlier and evolved on the proper premises for itself.

The first economist who foresaw the tendency to deindustrialisation was Karl Marx. He based his forecasting not upon an intention of 'good people' to abolish all negative aspects of factory labour but upon his analysis of industrial development. Marx deduced this trend from the increasing 'science intensity' of the capitalist (i.e. industrial) production, while the contribution of manual labour decreased. In particular, Marx wrote:

> The entire production process then appears no longer as subsumed under the immediate skill of the worker, but as technological application of science. Capital thus tends to impart a scientific character to production, and immediate labour is reduced to a mere moment of this process. (Marx 1987: 85)

He predicted a displacement of people from the production process with their profoundly changing functions:

> Labour no longer appears so much as included in the production process, but rather man relates himself to that process as its overseer and regulator. . . . . . .No longer does the worker interpose a modified natural object as an intermediate element between the object and himself; now he interposes the natural process, which he transforms into an industrial one, as an intermediary between himself and inorganic nature, which he makes himself master of. He stands besides the production process, rather than being its main agent. . . . . . .This process is simultaneously. . . application, experimental science, material creative and self-objectifying science, with respect to the developed man, whose mind is the repository of the accumulated knowledge of society. (Ibid.: 97)

Factually, Marx forecasted that the growth of productivity and complication of the production process under industrial capitalism would lead to transformation of scientific knowledge into productive force. In this respect he anticipated the late twentieth century conceptions of post-industrial or knowledge-based society, although there were still very weak premises for such a transformation in his time.

The real premises for deindustrialisation on the fundament of industrial development arose in the twentieth century in a framework of the Fordist-Keynesian economic model, with mass production for mass consumption and radical changes in demand. One of the first scholars who focused on the gradually maturing process of deindustrialisation was British-Australian economist Colin Clark (1940). Although Clark did not use the term 'deindustrialisation', he underlined that while the total income of a national economy increases, the services sector grows faster than the agrarian and industrial outputs grow. Indeed, the problem that worried Clark concerned the inner connection between the structural changes and the growth of economy:

> As real income per head increases, it is quite clear that the *relative* demand for agricultural products falls all the time, and that the relative demand for manufacture first rises, and then falls in favour of services." . . . "Given these changes in demand, we also have to take into

> account the efficiency with which the different industries will work to supply them. Real product per man-hour in manufacture, for example, nearly always advances at a greater rate than real product per man-hour in other sectors of the economy. For that reason, a *stationary* relative demand for manufactures would lead to a *decreasing* proportion of the labour force employed therein. Even when the relative demand for manufactures is increasing, we still generally expect, in the long run, a decreasing proportion of the labour force to be employed therein. (Clark 1957: 493, 493–494)

According to Clark's calculations, the share of those employed in services, including government services, army and police, in the USA and Great Britain was higher than the shares of people occupied in agriculture or the manufacturing industry[1] in 1920–1921. Sweden crossed this frontier before 1930 and France in the mid-1930s [counted on: (Ibid: 512–520)]. In the USA, the *share of incomes* in services, such as transport, communications, commerce and finances (43.7 per cent), notably exceeded the share of manufacturing industry (25.7 per cent) before the Great Depression. Later, in the first post-war years, French sociologist, economist and one of the first futurologists, Jean Fourastié, underlined the structural shift in economic output and labour force employment from agriculture and industry to services compared to the fast-growing industrial productivity (Fourastié 1949: 55–72). While post-war Europe still lay in ruins, Fourastié questioned the objective limits to consumption. He wrote, in fact, about the absolute saturation of consumers (the inelasticity of demand in regard to supply—'l'*inelasticité* de la demande en regard à l'offre') (Fourastié 1949: 2), although then many people still suffered from a shortage of elementary goods. Meanwhile, the Fordist-Keynesian economic system operated in both directions, not only from the demand side but also from the supply side. Thereby, it hugely accelerated demand in conditions when demand for elementary goods ceased growing and industry offered a rapidly expanding assortment of non-food consumer goods.

The process of structural changes with the prospect of deindustrialisation started in the motherland of modern industry, Great Britain, and with lag for 2–3 years in the USA, gradually spreading later to other industrially developed countries. In particular, the share of manufacturing industry in the UK GDP peaked in 1951 (37.67 per cent) and in GDP of the USA in 1953 (26.47 per cent). The share of the same branch of the UK economy in employment reached its historical maximum in 1954 (41.83 per cent of all employed), and in the USA this share in employment peaked in 1953 (27.83 per cent of all occupied) [the author's calculations on: (UK Central Statistical Office 1961: 105–107, 130, 239, 243, 1965: 107, 1970: 118, 279, 285; US Bureau of the Census 1956: 296, 1959: 304, 307, 1961: 203, 207, 301, 304, 1965: 326)]. In the 1960s and the first half of the 1970s, these two indicators, characterising the manufacturing industry's development, reached their maximum in other developed countries (see below Table 6.1). Moreover, employment in the manufacturing industry began falling in the absolute terms, too. For example, according to some estimates, the maximal level of employment in manufacturing industry of the Great

[1]Electricity- and gas-supply industries are included, but mining and construction are excluded.

Table 6.1 Levels of GDP per capita (in US dollars of 1990 on PPP) at the start of deindustrialisation in some 'old' OECD countries and countries of East Asia and Latin America, 1950–2011

Countries	Maximal share of manufacturing industry in GDP			Maximal share of employed in manufacturing industry		
	Share (% %)	Year	GDP per capita	Share (% %)	Year	GDP per capita
Developed countries of OECD						
Canada	23.29	1961	88[illegible]	22.73[a]	1970	12,050
France	25.40[b]	1961	77[illegible]	27.89	1974	13,113
Germany (Fed. Rep.)	40.65	1961	79[illegible]	39.39[a]	1970	10,839
Japan	32.63	1970	971[illegible]	27.44	1973	11,434
Spain	23.33	1972	709[illegible]	27.47	1971	6618
Sweden	26.94	1974	13,885	28.29	1974	13,885
UK	36.90	1955	786[illegible]	41.83	1954	7619
USA	26.47	1953	10,613	27.83	1953	10,613
Countries of Latin America						
Argentina	34.85	1976	796[illegible]	24.69[c]	1984	7426
Brazil	32.47	1985	491[illegible]	17.08	1978	4678
Chile	19.57	1974	499[illegible]	16.80	1976	4347
Colombia	20.05	1976	371[illegible]	25.95[d]	1978	4042
Mexico	23.34	1988	577[illegible]	19.56	2000	7275
Perú	21.51	1988	376[illegible]	23.24[e]	1986	3946
Uruguay	23.42	1986	601[illegible]	30.57	1974	5123
Venezuela	30.85	1986	872[illegible]	17.18	1987	8805
Asian NICs of the first generation						
Hong Kong	19.81	1984	12,8[illegible]6	71.04	1972	6473
Korea, Rep. of	30.73	2011	21,7[illegible]1[f]	27.80	1989	8027
Singapore	26.44	1980	9058	30.37	1981	9450
Taiwan, province	43.10	1986	7477	46.60[g]	1993	11,950
Asian NICs of the second generation						
Indonesia	29.86	1997	3684	13.31	2001	3299
Malaysia	28.72	2000	7874	24.88	1994	6622
Philippines	28.51	1973	1964	11.50	1978	2262
Thailand	31.29	2010	9372	15.26	2004	7824

[a]Approved data before 1970 is not available
[b]Data borrowed from *Institut national de la statistique et des études économique. Bases des données. Les comptes nationaux annuels base 20*[illegible]
[c]Gran Buenos Aires
[d]Seven main cities in the country
[e]Lima and its suburbs
[f]2010
[g]Paid employment
Source: The author's calculations on databases of UNCTAD and ILO (for 1970–2011); for UK and US in the 1950s–1960s: UK Central Statistical Office 1961: 105–107, 130, 239, 243; 1965: 107; 1970: 118, 279, 285; US Bureau of the Census 1956: 296, 1959: 304, 307, 1961: 203, 207, 301, 304, 1965: 326; OECD/OCDE 1979: 7–8, 103–104, 195–196; MoF 1998, Table 6.1; GGDC 2013

Britain was reached in 1966 at 8.58 million people. After that year it steadily decreased (Thatcher 1979: 32–33).

As with every social-economic process, deindustrialisation had not only the quantifiable aspect expressed in the shares of GDP and employment but also qualitative aspects, too.

It was notable that Colin Clark, considering this observed shift towards the service sector dominating the economy, used the well-known Cobb-Douglas production function which calculates the ratio between inputs of capital and labour, on the one hand, and output, on the other.

As is well known, this function has the following form:

$$f(L, C) = bL^k\, C^{1-k},$$

where L and C are inputs of labour and capital, respectively, and b coefficient calculable empirically. Experimenting with many data sets, Cobb and Douglas obtained for the US economy over the period between 1890 and 1922 the relationship

$$P = 1.01\, L^{0.75}\, C^{0.25}.$$

This relationship reflected the actual state of the industrialised US economy at that time, but after 1922 it ceased corresponding to the empirically obtained data (Clark 1957: 586–589). It meant that something 'enigmatic' began occurring in the US industry. Then Robert Solow introduced the parameter of technical progress A into the Cobb-Douglas production function as

> *any kind of shift* (italics of Solow—V.K.) in the production function. Thus slowdowns, speedups, *improvements in the education of the labor force* (my italics—V.K.), and all sorts of things will appear as 'technical change'. (Solow 1957: 312)

In the first approximation, this parameter was presupposed to be *neutral*[2] and could be performed as

$$A(t) = e^{at}, \text{where } t \text{ signifies time.}$$

Thereby, the modified production function took on the following form:

$$P = AL^k\, C^{1-k} e^{at}.$$

Restricting his calculations 'to private non-farm economic activity' (i.e. to private industry and services sectors), Solow tried to estimate the technical change's contribution to the growth of American GDP over 1909–1949. He came to the important

[2] '...I have defined neutrality to mean that the shifts were pure scale changes, leaving marginal rates of substitution unchanged at given capital/labor ratios' (Solow 1957: 316).

conclusion, directly concerning the topic of our research, that 'the average rate of progress' in 1930–1949 was higher than in the preceding period, 1909–1929 (Ibid: 316). According to Solow's calculations about 87.5 per cent of the total increase of the US non-agricultural GNP (gross national product) over the period of 40 years (1909–1949) was contributed by increased productivity (Ibid: 316, 320), due to 'intangible inputs'. Thus, the technical/technological progress notably accelerated following the Great Depression.

The contribution of the mentioned 'technical change' to the increased output and productivity was called 'Solow residual'. Certainly, the quantitative aspect (the concrete magnitude) of the latter is debatable, and many other economists reported their own results of its calculations, but nobody ignored the emerging dependence of material production on non-material factors such as organisation, applied scientific knowledge and the education of labourers. In particular, Edward Denison compared the rates of economic growth in nine Western countries (the USA, the UK, West Germany, France, Italy, Belgium, Denmark, Netherlands and Sweden) to each other (mainly in 1950–1962 but in some cases he took the larger period, from 1909 to 1957). He convincingly demonstrated how the raised educational level of the US labour force led to the general acceleration of output growth (Denison 1967: 78–108). Thus, the development of industrial production succeeded in diminishing the role of mechanical industrial tools and equipment ('irons') in the production process whereas the role of non-mechanical and even non-material, intangible components began increasing. In essence, it was the self-negation of industrialism and meant *technological deindustrialisation*.

However, techniques and production technologies are indistinguishable from the humans who create and use them. The social side of beginning deindustrialisation consisted not only in the peculiar role of professional management but mostly in the changed image of a large proportion of labourers. A number of employed engineers, technicians, architects and scientists occupied in applied research, etc. (not to mention school teachers and university professors who trained the future labourers) increased much faster than a number of manual workers, and still Fourastié in the early-1950s treated this phenomenon as a steady long-term trend (Fourastié 1953: 34–35). With the lapse of time, this trend continued to evolve. As experts of the World Bank underline, the growth and development of industry cannot today proceed without the growth of services necessary for industry itself: maintenance and repair of equipment, enlargement of the R&D sphere, marketing, personnel management, etc. (Hallward-Driemeier and Nayyar 2018: 145–166).

The tendency towards deindustrialisation (in the name of industrial development) succeeded in the rise of post-industrial economies, which have primarily been associated with the increasing significance of services in the sphere of scientific, theoretical knowledge and education for economic and technological development. As Daniel Bell, one of the most prominent scholars to note the substantial shift towards the significance of science for production, wrote:

> [I]n the post-industrial society, the chief problem is the organization of science, and the primary institution the university or the research institute where such work is carried out. (Bell 1973: 116)

Respectively, a new social agent (actor) of the production process has been emerging while the service sector begins prevailing in the economy.

> The central person is the professional, for he is equipped, by his education and training, to provide the kinds of skill which are increasingly demanded in the post-industrial society. (Ibid: 127)

The general conclusion Bell made from his considerations focused on the emerging dependency of society on the *production of theoretical knowledge* (Ibid: 212–242).[3]

Such a dependency has been the effect of previous highly developed industrial production and signified a definite frontier in the process of deindustrialisation. In this regard, it is worth noting that all significant technological breakthroughs in the framework of industrial paradigms (such as production of artificial materials (plastics, synthetics, etc.), nuclear power stations, aircraft and aerospace industries, gigantic hydroelectric power plants and so on) took place only due to a decisive application of scientific knowledge in the production process. They all happened before the beginning of the 1970s. Since that time (1971, the year when the 'Intel' microprocessor was made) and afterwards, the main directions of technological innovations have somewhat been linked to information technologies (IT) and digitalisation, though, of course, building upon the foundation of microelectronics, this genuine 'cherry on top' of the late-industrial production system.

The growth of transnational companies (TNC) in the 1960s additionally accelerated deindustrialisation. They split up the entire production processes into several 'sub-processes' and transferred parts of them to less developed countries. The latter stimulated their proper industrialisation and competed with the 'old' industrial powers. However, it would be mistaken to explain deindustrialisation in developed countries by the rising competition with newly industrialising countries of the former Third World. As Robert Rowthorn and Ramana Ramaswami estimated, the importation of manufactured goods from industrialising countries of the South *together* with the relative decrease of investment in manufacturing industries of the developed countries conditioned the pace of their deindustrialisation to a small degree (Rowthorn and Ramaswamy 1998: 22). The internal processes in the developed countries have been more significant for their deindustrialisation than the influence of external factors, such as trade competition with newcomers in manufacturing industries. In particular, the economic policies carried out by the neoconservatives in power favoured this process. This policy was a social revenge to trade unions, Leftist political organisations and the welfare-state, which all became excessively influential actors and 'tormented' capital, challenging its domination. Moreover it was global in dimension and proceeded together with the processes that were evolving

---

[3]"The post-industrial society, it is clear, is a knowledge society in a double sense: first, the sources of innovation are increasingly derivative from research and development (and more directly, there is a new relation between science and technology because of the centrality of *theoretical* knowledge); second, the weight of the society—measured by a larger proportion of Gross National Product and a larger share of employment—is increasingly in the knowledge field" (Bell 1973: 212).

in some non-Western, formerly backward countries. Meanwhile, since 1973–1974, when the crisis of the Fordist-Keynesian system of mass production for mass consumption and corresponding institutions (particularly the welfare-state) became evident, deindustrialisation in the industrially advanced countries was accompanied by the growth of labour and total factor productivity. This growth was somewhat slower than in the golden years of 1950–1973, but much faster than in 1870–1950, when the manufacturing industry grew in both the share of value added and absolute terms, except, of course, during times of crises and wars (Maddison 1987: 649–651, 665). Manufacturing industry in the 'old' industrialised countries remained the technologically complicated branch of their economies, whereas the simplest branches moved to the newly industrialising countries. In other words, deindustrialisation in the West (and later in Japan) correlated with the accelerated industrialisation in the South and East.

However, over time the process of deindustrialisation spread to the 'new comers' of industrial development, too. It became the character feature of all 'tiger' economies (Hong Kong, the Asian pioneer and leader in deindustrialisation, Korea, Singapore, Taiwan, Malaysia, Thailand, Indonesia and the Philippines) and had clearly appeared in Latin America. This process embraced the biggest Asian countries, India and China, though in the latter it started only some years ago after 'super-industrialisation'.[4] Thus, deindustrialisation had become the global, worldwide trend. According to the UNCTAD data, the share of manufacturing industry in the global product (measured as the sum of all national GDPs) diminished from 24.6 per cent in 1970 to 14.9 per cent in 2003 and henceforth oscillated around 15.5–16.0 per cent. Will it change in the middle- or long-term future? This question remains to be answered.

However, deindustrialisation in most of the 'old' industrialised countries differs from deindustrialisation in the countries of late industrialisation. In the latter case it began before its proper premises matured in economy, so it is worth distinguishing mature and *premature (precocious)* deindustrialisation from each other.[5] Certainly, each of them has definite social effects, but those of premature deindustrialisation are notably worse than when deindustrialisation evolves as the result of high industrial development.

[4]Here I do not consider the cases of some East and Central European countries, the post-Soviet space, Africa and the Middle East. There either deindustrialisation did not take place at all because of a lack of whatever significant industry or it had been the result of deliberate economic policy of the local elites, although not without 'the external aid' in some cases.

[5]As D. Rodrik notes, the concept of premature deindustrialisation relating to developing countries was introduced for the first time by Dasgupta and Singh (2006, esp. 5–6, 15–17); Rodrik (2016: 2, note 4).

Box 6.1 Four Negative 'Ds': The 'Satellites' of Premature Deindustrialisation

Premature deindustrialisation, particularly in its extreme, most acute forms, may be accompanied by four other 'Ds'. These are (1) disorganisation, i.e. a decrease in the level and quality of production process organisation and management; (2) degradation of the technological level of production and declining processing complexity; (3) a decrease in the qualification of labourers, whether they are engineers, managers or ordinary executives (workers); and (4) a decrease in the complexity (i.e. simplification and primitivising) of the final output products.

The concrete studies of all these effects and, simultaneously, external appearances of premature deindustrialisation make up a distinctive field of research which spills over beyond the framework of this book. However, it is necessary to remember that the third 'D', concerning skills of labourers, may be universal in character: it may take place in the conditions of *mature* deindustrialisation, too, because of automation and robotisation of labour operation when the sole duty of labourers consists in pressing buttons.

For better comprehension of premature deindustrialisation, it is useful to compare the levels of income or GDP per capita at which deindustrialisation began in each group of countries under scrutiny. The results are presented in the Table 6.1.As Table 6.1 shows, the turning point at which deindustrialisation started in different countries has been GDP per capita (measured in US dollars of 1990 on PPP) equal to 8–10 thousands.[6]

It is notable that the first-tier NICs of East Asia began undergoing that process at almost the same level of incomes as the 'old' industrial nations. Among the second-tier Asian NICs and Latin American countries, only Malaysia, Argentina and Venezuela stayed closely to such level of incomes when their deindustrialisation had become an irreversible trend. The other Asian 'tigers' of the second generation and most countries of Latin America, not to mention the Asian giants China and India, entered their period of deindustrialisation at lower levels of income per capita (and, in addition, much more inequitably distributed) than the industrially developed countries of the West and East Asia. With regard to deindustrialisation in Brazil, it not only differs from the similar processes in the 'elderly' industrialised countries but also has appropriated more acute and destructive forms than premature deindustrialisation in some other emerging countries.

[6]R. Rowthorn and R. Ramaswamy performed approximately the same data while counted the level of incomes per capita at which deindustrialisation began in the western countries (Rowthorn and Ramaswamy 1998: 14–18).

Table 6.2 Change of the share of manufacturing industry in GDP of Brazil and Latin-Caribbean American countries (LCA) as a whole, 1970–2017, as percentage (upon the base of prices in US$)

	1970	1980	1990	2000	2010	2015	2017
Indicators upon the base of current prices							
Brazil	24.6	30.5	25.2	13.9	12.7	10.5	10.5
LCA as a whole[a]	22.3	22.7	22.1	16.1	14.4	13.3	12.7
LCA without Brazil	21.8	20.1	20.4	17.0	12.7	14.7	14.0
The share of Brazil in manufacturing industry of LCA	21.5	32.8	40.0	25.1	39.3	26.5	30.0
Indicators upon the base of constant (2010) prices							
Brazil	15.1	17.1	15.0	14.0	12.7	10.8	9.9
LCA as a whole[a]	16.4	16.8	15.9	15.3	13.7	12.5	12.2
LCA without Brazil	16.5	16.6	16.5	16.2	14.4	13.6	13.7
The share of Brazil in manufacturing industry of LCA	32.9	42.7	40.3	37.1	39.3	34.7	31.9

Source: UNCTAD 2020

[a]Including Brazil as a part of the continent

6.2 Deindustrialisation in Brazil

Today many scholars underline that Brazil, as well as many other countries in Latin America and Africa, experiences just premature deindustrialisation (Arendt 2015: 28 et ff.; Bresser-Pereira 2012: 13; Bresser-Pereira et al. 2016: 494–502; Dávila-Fernández 2015: 577, 581, 585, 595–597; Feijó et al. 2005: 1–3, 5, 13, 16; Gaulard 2016: 69–76; Marconi and Rocha 2012; Oreiro and Feijó 2010: 223; Palma 2005: 105–109; Rodrik 2015: 15–26, 2016: esp. 2–4, 20–21; Salama 2012a: 224–225, 242–246, b: 66–68, 2014a: 26–29, b: 98–100, 2019: 74–76). It began later than in the USA, Canada or Western Europe (the maximal share of manufacturing industry in Brazil, as we see from the table above, was reached in 1985–1986, at about 32 per cent of GDP) and coincided with the start of transition from authoritarianism to democracy.

Deindustrialisation in Brazil can be evidenced, at first, by the declining share of manufacturing industry in the country's GDP and in the total manufacturing industry of Latin-Caribbean America as a whole. In this regard, it is worth comparing the shares of manufacturing industry between the economies of Brazil and Latin-Caribbean America as a whole to each other over the period of more 40 years (Table 6.2).

Recalculation of this data on Brazil upon the base of current prices in reals does not significantly change the observable trend. In particular, in this case the share of manufacturing industry in GDP was 15.3 per cent in 2000, 15.0 per cent in 2010 and declined to 12.0 per cent in 2014. The elevation of this indicator to 12.5 per cent was the effect of a fall in commodity prices and does not mean the principal alteration of the considerable tendency [counted on (IBGE 2016b: table 10.1)]. As we see, the

Table 6.3 Average annual rates of decrease (−) or increase (+) in the shares of manufacturing industries in GDP of some "elderly" industrialised countries, Latin-Caribbean America (LCA) and Brazil, as percentage between 1970 and 2015

	1980/1970	1990/1980	2000/1990	2010/2000	2015/2010	2015/1980
Canada	−1.42	−1.06	−1.01	−5.33	−1.11	−1.65
France	−0.98	−1.31	−1.19	−3.32	+1.01	−1.60
Germany[a]	−1.50	−0.46[b]	−0.33	−0.30	+1.01	−0.24[c]
Japan	−2.21	−0.36	−1.95	−0.73	−0.29	−0.91
Spain	−0.90	−1.66	−1.01	−2.87	+1.01	−1.40
UK	−2.34	−1.42	−1.80	−3.81	+1.00	−1.96
USA	−1.30	−1.55	−1.45	−2.00	−0.32	−1.48
LCA countries	−0.26	−0.22	−2.34	−1.46	−0.67	−1.25
Brazil	+1.01	−2.03	−4.44	−0.77	−4.69	−2.75

[a]1970–1989—within borders of the then Federal Republic of Germany
[b]As ratio of 1989 to 1980
[c]As ratio to the share of manufacturing industry of the then existed FRG (in 1980)
Counted on UNCTAD 2020

share of manufacturing industry in GDP of Brazil fell faster than in the Latin American continent as a whole (either including or excluding Brazil as a part of the continent). Respectively, the share of Brazilian manufacturing industry in manufacturing industry of Latin America (together with the Caribbean) declined, too. The maximum of this share was reached in 1989 when Brazil outputted 45.4 per cent of all manufactured goods of the continent (measuring this output at current prices, whereas being measured in constant US dollars of 2010, this maximum was held in 1986, at 44.1 per cent). In addition, it is interesting to scrutinise 'the speed of deindustrialisation' in Brazil, comparing it with other countries, or, in other words, to measure how *the share* of manufacturing industry in GDP (not the output of this branch of economy in absolute terms) changed over the long period, 45 years (Table 6.3).

As Table 6.3 demonstrates, Brazil, particularly in the last years, exceeded even the 'old' industrially developed countries, which were 'pioneers' of deindustrialisation, in the pace of this process.[7] Since 1980 the share of manufacturing industry in Brazilian GDP shrank faster than in Great Britain where the process of deindustrialisation started earlier than in all other countries. Moreover, Brazil began undergoing the decrease of manufactured output in absolute terms whereas deindustrialisation in many other countries means only relative but not absolute falls of manufacturing output by its value. According to the data of UNCTAD and IBGE, the country attained the maximal volume of its production in 2013, just before the subsequent crisis and recession, 288.9 billion US$ (in constant prices of 2010). Beginning from that year the volume of manufactured output declined by 17.3 per

[7]Marcelo Arendt has come to similar conclusions, comparing the pace of deindustrialisation in Brazil to that in other countries (Arendt 2015: 40–48, 52–53).

cent to 2016 (approximately by 6.1 per cent per year),[8] and today it is almost impossible to imagine whether it will resume to grow at a significant rate, continuing to stagnate, at best, at the level of 2016–2017.

Another worrying aspect of Brazilian deindustrialisation concerns the dynamics of employment in the country's manufacturing industry. As it is known, a decrease of the share of people occupied in this branch of economy in the total employment has been one of the main forms of deindustrialisation as a whole. In industrially developed countries this process is the direct effect of growing productivity and coincides, as a rule, with an increased volume/value of manufactured output. In the case of premature deindustrialisation, the observable situation can be another; in particular, the employment in manufacturing industry of Brazil diminished to a lesser degree than the output. From the end of 2000 to the end of 2015 (December to December), the employment in manufacturing industry had fallen only by 11.0 per cent, whereas the share of the latter in GDP fell by 24.5 per cent, from 13.9 to 10.5 per cent of GDP measured in current prices in US$, or by 22.9 per cent, from 14.0 to 10.8 per cent of GDP measured in constant (2010) prices in US$ [counted on: (IBGE 2016a)]. It means that the share of manufacturing industry in Brazilian GDP fell faster than its share in the employment. This is testimony to the negative trend in productivity of this branch of the economy.

Indeed, calculations that take into account the absolute number of employed people demonstrate the fall in productivity of the Brazilian manufacturing industry. In 2000 each labourer produced manufactured goods on average valued at 24,256 US$ (measured in constant US$ of 2010), in 2010 at 24,214 US$ and in 2016 only at 22,250 US$ [counted on: (UNCTAD 20[illegible]; IBGE 2016b, table 15.1)]. Such dynamics of productivity leads to the conclusion that deindustrialisation in Brazil means the qualitative degradation and simplification ('de-sophistication') of the productive system. Beginning from 1997–1998, when the positive impulse of financial stabilisation exhausted itself, the branches of industry with intensive use of natural resources and unskilled or semi-skilled labour began prevailing over the branches with sophisticated, high technological intensity (Arend and Dutra Fonseca 2012: 43–47; Bruno et al. 2011: 96–98; Gaulard 2019: 115). The achievements of aircraft industry or production of various vehicles do not make up for the observed downward trend in the national economy.

The French economic geographers and sociologists Olivier Dabène and Frédéric Louault compared the lists of the biggest ten companies of Brazil in 1969 (the time of industrial boom) and 2012. In the both cases, 'Petrobras', the state-owned petroleum company, occupied first position. However the next nine positions pertained in 1969 to five electro-power companies, one to an iron-mining company ('Vale de Rio Doce'), one to a metallurgical company, one to a telecommunications company and one to a tobacco company. In 2012, the companies ('business entities') following in the list behind 'Petrobras' were three banks ('Itaú', 'Bradesco' and 'Banco do Brasil'), 'Vale de Rio Doce', financial investment holding ('Itaúsa'), two

[8]Counted on the data of UNCTAD.

electro-power companies, one metallurgical and one telecommunications company (Dabène and Louault 2013: 33). This comparison of the lists of the biggest companies in Brazil in 1969 and 2012 illustrates deindustrialisation from the point of view of the dominating business interests, the profound shift from industry to financial services.

Finally deindustrialisation in Brazil has been expressed, too, in the long-term deterioration of the external trade structure, and this process proceeds together with the general trend in Latin American development as a whole. In the 1990s the share of manufactured goods steadily exceeded 50 per cent in Brazilian exports (not including services). In 1993, a poor year for the country's economy, this share reached 58.9 per cent. In 2000, after some decline, it returned to this level (58.4 per cent of the total export of goods). In 2009, the export of manufactured goods was lesser than that of primary goods (commodities) for the first time in the preceding 30 years. In 2011–2015 this export fluctuated near 35–38 per cent and even began diminishing in absolute value from 88.3 billion US$ in 2008 to 77.5 billion in 2014 and to 71.9 billion in 2015. It grew again only once, in 2011, but remained below the 2008 level of 86.6 billion US$ (CEPAL/ECLAC 2017: cuadros 2.2.2.2, 2.2.2.4). Soya beans and iron ore had become the main exports of Brazil. Together they made up 21.2 per cent of the total Brazilian exports (including goods and services) on average for 2010–2015 (counted on: CEPAL/ECLAC 2017: cuadro 2.2.2.20). Thus, Brazil, like many other countries of Latin America, had undergone a *re-primarisation* of economy, i.e. returned to the situation when the production and trade of primary goods (agricultural products, raw materials, petroleum or, at best, semi-manufactured articles) prevailed in the economy.

Many Brazilian economists explain the premature deindustrialisation in their country, referring to the synergetic effect of the following factors' operation:

1. High exchange rates of local currencies, in particular, those of Argentine peso and Brazilian real, established in the first half of the 1990s and aimed at oppressing inflation.
2. Liberalisation of foreign trade, which succeeded in a loss of competitiveness of local manufacturing industries at internal markets.
3. Excessively high banking interest restrained inflation but detracted investment resources from industry and hampered credits for the latter.
4. The growth of foreign direct investment in the service sector (in particular, telecommunications) was faster than in the manufacturing industry.
5. The strong competition with China which displaced Latin American countries from the previously conquered markets in North America and Europe, not to mention the inflow of Chinese manufactured goods into the internal markets of Latin America (Cano 2012: 834–836; Jenkins 2015: esp. 51–59).

The 'main' reason for premature deindustrialisation in Brazil and other Latin American countries as well was the excessive financialisation of economy which, in turn, was the direct result of liberalisation started in the early 1990s. Indeed, this liberalisation aggravated the problem of trade and payment balances, particularly in conditions of external indebtedness, and the government offered bonds to plug the fiscal gap. The high rate of bond interest distracted a big part of resources that could have been used for productive investments in industry. This financialisation combined with the 'Dutch disease' ('*a doença holandesa*'). The latter has risen because of high prices for commodities, in particular, for soya beans and iron ore, augmented in large part due to the increased demands of China. It favoured the appreciation of the real with the consequent increase of imports and making the exports of manufactured goods disadvantageous. Thereby, the competitiveness of local manufacturing industry was undermined, and deindustrialisation was accelerated.

The efficient alternative to premature deindustrialisation, as it seems to many economists, consists in (1) the state regulated, active industrial policy like the developmental policy of Korea or Taiwan in the years of East Asian 'miracle's' blossom and (2) maintenance of a low exchange ratio of national currency for deliverance from 'Dutch disease' (Bresser-Pereira 2013: 384–386; Cano 2012: 847–850). Implicitly, it presupposes the increased rate of investment, although such an increase does not yet mean the active industrial policy. An efficiency of the latter depends also on the direction of investment: whether capitals are invested either in new equipment or in construction of new enterprises but with obsolete productive technologies, or in prestigious, luxurious dwellings, or in building of new schools and universities, etc. Obviously, the effects of increased investment can be different in each case.

However, may manipulations with the rate of interest and exchange ratio alternate the negative trend to premature deindustrialisation? Can these traditional and well-known measures from the arsenal of Keynesian policy be sufficient in the concrete Brazilian conditions? Instead, all the abovementioned factors influence the structure of the economy and favour its deindustrialisation. But they have been *factors*, not causes. When these factors began to operate in full measure at the end of the 1980s to the first years of the 1990s, the Brazilian economy had already made decisive steps along the path towards its precocious deindustrialisation.

As discussed in Chap. 4, the actual sources of premature deindustrialisation in Brazil are rooted in the model of Brazilian modernisation of the 1960s–1970s for the advantage of the upper 25, maximum 30 per cent of the population. Then the rapid growth of industry, instigated in large part by foreign investments and loans, excited the transnational corporations and the local entrepreneurs as well as the state economic bureaucracy for extending investment in industry and concomitant infrastructure whereas the effective demand lagged from the increased stock of fixed capital. This overinvestment led to falling effectiveness of capital and made further investment disadvantageous. The reverse side of the extended investment (with its diminishing effectiveness) was the increased weight of indebtedness, internal either external and public and private as well. This indebtedness began growing quickly while the external trade and payment deficits notably augmented, particularly after the first petroleum shock in 1973–1974. It led to the fiscal crisis of the government, accelerating inflation and restraining investment with a long payback period. In contrast to the 'tiger' economies of East Asia, the Brazilian industry, like manufacturing industries of other Latin American countries, suffered from the started microelectronic revolution, being incapable of using its advantages for maintaining competitiveness in the new international division of labour. The liberalisation of the economy in the 1990s not only affected the local industry through mechanism of competition but also aggravated the problem of trade and payment balances, and the government was obliged to offer bonds for plugging the fiscal gap. The high bond interest distracted a part of the resources that could potentially have been used as productive investments in industry.

Hence, the financialisation observed in the 1990s and afterwards has been the effect rather than the cause of complicated processes that evolved in the economy as a whole in the 1980s–2000s. With the lapse of time, the indebtedness had become a relatively autonomous, endogenous factor in the country's economic life (Berthelot 1991: 17–19). Its autonomy strengthened in the 1980s when operations with debts and bonds became a distinct branch in the economy and financial markets with increased interest rates became more and more attractive for investors. Thus, the Brazilian economy fell into a vicious circle: the diminishing effectiveness of industry made industrial investments less and less advantageous, succeeding in their decrease, whereas the latter led to a slowdown of industrial growth with inevitable deindustrialisation. The external factors, such as the intensifying competition because of trade's liberalisation in the 1990s and the advantages of financial operations with the high interest rates, attributed an additional acuteness to this process but were not its causes. Therefore, neither regulation of the interest rate nor search for 'the optimal exchange currency rate' (Bresser-Pereira 2012, esp. 10–11, 22–24, 2016: 335–343; Nassif et al. 2017) can fully alternate the recent negative trend, the undoubtful significance of such measures notwithstanding. The problem of premature deindustrialisation is, prima facie, the structural problem, and it is hardly possible to resolve it by 'a prompt attack', without deep changes in the structure of economy and distribution of incomes. In other words, it should be indispensable not only to use the monetary and taxation levers for stimulating investments in industry but to eliminate such factors of low effectiveness of these investments as the restricted effective demand because of mass poverty, i.e. to make the growth really pro-poor and socially oriented.

Did the Left/Left-centrist governments in Latin America, in particular, the PT government as their continental 'load-star', conceive an acuteness of the problem of deindustrialisation? Yes, they did, and even applied some efforts to change the situation and to reverse the tendency to deindustrialisation.

As a rule, the start of deliberate industrial policy in Brazil after the restoration of democracy in 1985 has been linked to the PT governments' activity. However, as far back as in the mid-1990s the administration of Cardoso elaborated some measures for stimulating technological development of the Brazilian economy for better and more effective inclusion of Brazil into the global economy (the Brazilian Programme of Quality and Productivity (PBQP) in Portuguese abbreviation). In particular, it supported the national software industry and used fiscal instruments to motivate firms to innovate (the Programme of Technological Development in Industry and also the similar programme for agriculture) (Laplante and Laplante 2017: 135–138). Later, the PT government deepened and enlarged a set of measures introduced by its predecessor, launching programmes of industrial and technological modernisation. Moreover, in the beginning of the century as Ilán Bizberg argues:

> Brazil was the only Latin American country that implemented a significant industrial (vertical) policy since the beginning of the years 2000 (actually, since the arrival of Lula in 2003); it was the only country where a more oriented, targeted industrial policy was applied. (Bizberg 2019: 141; see also: Santarcángelo et al. 2018: 23)

One of the first programmes of industrial policy under the PT rule was announced in 2004.[9] It was the so-called 'Industrial, Technological and External Trade Policy' aimed at stimulating four sectors of high knowledge-intensity: semi-conductors, software, pharmaceuticals and medicines and capital goods. At the same time, the government organised the Brazilian Agency of Industrial Development (*Agência Brasileira de Desenvolvimento Industrial*), which had to coordinate the efforts of different ministries and other authorities' bodies to realise the intended policy. The National Council for Industrial Development under the aegis of the president of Brazil began working, too, uniting representatives of the state, entrepreneurial circles and the academic community. However, the efforts applied to implementing this programme were assessed as ineffective, so in 2007 the government presented another programme designed to accelerate economic growth (PAC—*Programa de Aceleração ao Crescimento*).

Meanwhile, still before the PAC was launched, a peculiar part in the PT government's attempts to revitalise the industrial policy was assigned to the state-controlled petroleum concern 'Petrobras'. The government treated this company as a driver of technological modernisation not only in the oil and gas industry but also in related branches, such as shipbuilding. Since 'Petrobras' approached to deep-sea, pre-salt shelf exploration, it required a profound renovation of the respective vessels and platforms; indeed, the concern's demand allowed to revive the shipbuilding yards that began declining since the 1980s under the impact of the global competition. Unfortunately, the attempt to use 'Petrobras' as the main locomotive of new industrial development had a limited impact because of (1) weak cohesiveness of oil and gas sector with other branches of economy in the conditions of intensive competition and (2) institutional, managerial shortcomings in regard to the latter's development (Massi and Nem Singh 2018: 1138–1143). In addition, the practice of the state-led rent-seeking, as the scandal Lava Jato later showed (see also below, Chap. 8), when 'Petrobras' was the main actor in the widespread network of bribery, did not favour perfect competition and, therefore, neither profound managerial and technological modernisation of the company itself and related enterprises.

With regard to the PAC itself, this programme suggested a stimulation of private investment in industry and non-financial services, an increase of the public investment in infrastructure and removal of various administrative and juridical barriers to economic growth. An increase of investment should be attained due to a complement of some standard measures of the monetary, taxation and credit policies. The

[9]The PT programmes of industrial policy are observed in the CEPAL/ECLAC publication (Laplante and Laplante 2017: 138–155).

concrete branches of industry and services were simultaneously selected as the prioritised directions of the programme's accomplishment: development of digital TV, production of semi-conductors for electronic industry and output of microcomputers. Later the pharmaceutical industry was added to this list as one of the programme's priorities, too. Nonetheless, the main feature of the given programme consisted in emphasising investment in infrastructure. Thus, authors of the programme involuntarily followed their past social-political antagonists, the generals-presidents of the 1960s–1970s, presupposing—in a purely technocratic manner—that a development of infrastructure could almost automatically succeed in the growth of investment in modernisation of manufacturing industry. A question about the social actors capable of realising the programme as well as about the potential beneficiaries of its realisation was not even put for consideration.

The first attempts to accelerate industrial development by means of increased public investment in infrastructure showed an insufficiency of this measure for accelerating the industrial growth and for resolving the over-matured problem of premature deindustrialisation (let readers excuse me for this pun). One year later, just before the global Great Recession, the PT government supplemented the operating programme by 'the policy of productive development' (Política de Desenvolvimento Produtivo). It embraced 24 industrial branches of different technological intensities and proclaimed genuinely 'Napoleonic' goals: to augment the rate of investment from 18 to 21 per cent of GDP, to increase the private expenditures for R&D from 0.51 per cent of GDP in 2007 to 0.65 per cent in 2010 and to conquer the new world markets, elevating the share of Brazilian exports from 1.18 per cent of the world in 2007 to 1.25 per cent—in 2010 (ABDI 2008: 19–20), certainly, with emphasis on the exportation of manufactured goods with a great amount of value added.

As Brazilian economists marked, this updated programme was more or less successful only in regard to the low- and middle-tech sectors of industry but did not lead to notable progress in high-tech production (Coronel et al. 2014: 113–116). The announced strategic goals were not attained. The process of deindustrialisation went on as previously; the competitiveness of Brazilian manufactured goods (except aircrafts) declined, the 'brain-intensity' of the national industry did not increase, and Brazil continued losing positions in the continental and world markets. All these facts confirmed that the PT industrial policy failed to a large extent.

Why did it happen? There was not a single factor in the lack of success but a set of different unfavourable factors of the institutional, socioeconomic and political character (let us do not forget the great advice of Gerschenkron—see above Chap. 3). Summing up them, we can say that the Lula's government approached its industrial policy almost in the same manner as generals train their armies in past wars. At first, the industrial policy's priorities ('favourite branches') were not clearly defined; hence, the government's efforts were dispersed among many sectors of industry instead of being concentrated on two or three leading directions. They were mostly directed to support big firms ('Petrobras', for instance) which did not actually need state assistance. Secondly, the plans of industrial policy were linked to the electoral cycles: the government searched for immediate success 'here and now' instead of treating it as a laborious task for the long-term prospect. However, as is often the case, rapidly achieved results cannot be sustainable and contradict to the future strategic success. Thirdly, the PT industrial policy was not coordinated with the policy of taxation, scientific-technological research and development; it did not contain institutional instruments to prevent corruption or any other rent-seeking practice. Fourthly, the PT industrial policy suffered from a series of institutional shortfalls, in particular, from a lack of sufficient authority in the established state bodies responsible for the realisation of the launched policy. (On the contrary, for example, the Economic Planning Board in South Korea or the Economic Development Board in Singapore had the widest powers, while these countries carried out their miraculous transformation from 'small kittens' into strong industrial 'tigers'.) Thus, a bureaucratic mismatch impeded the effective coordination of different authoritative bodies' activity for implementation of the proclaimed policy. Fifthly, the PT government neglected the role of civil society (entrepreneurial and professional associations, NGOs, etc.) in the attainment of the announced goals.

The identified shortfalls of the PT industrial policy under Lula can be reduced to three points: (a) a discordance between the economic theory and practice; (b) an administrative, institutional disorder and poor governance; and (c) a lack of broad political support to the launched project (Gonçalves et al. 2019: 742–743, 747–751). As a response to the preceding unsuccessful (or, at best, semi-successful) industrial policy, the government of President Dilma Rousseff launched the Plan of Big Brazil (*Plano Brasil Maior*) in 2011. This plan again emphasised the problem of innovations and had the themed subtitle: 'To innovate to compete, to compete to grow' ('*Inovar para Competir. Competir para Crescer*'). The main direction of this plan was an improvement in national industry's competitiveness by means of diminishing the material and labour costs of production. The list of industry's branches that had to be in focus of the state industrial policy was notably enlarged in comparison to the previous programme of growth acceleration. This list comprised petroleum and gas extraction on the ocean shelf with use of underwater technologies, pharmaceutics and production of medical equipment, electric power industry with renewable sources of energy, bio-ethanol, telecommunications and information technologies, aircraft industry and development of new materials for it, defence of environment and 'green technologies' (ABDI 2014: [illegible]).

At a first glance, *Plano Brasil Maior* looked more solid and more detailed than the preceding programmes of industrial policy. At the same time, the three 'sacred cows' of the financial-economic policy (inflation targeting through the regulation of interest rates, fiscal policy aimed at maintenance of the primary budget surplus with only small corrections of taxation and the free floating of exchange rate) (Nassif 2015) were untouched, detracting potential investment resources from achieving the proclaimed goals. Moreover, the *Plano* had the same technocratic bias as the preceding plans launched under Lula in that: it made emphasis mainly on the development of the material elements of capital and production technologies. Though the plan stipulated a development of human resources, it treated such development as the training of skilled professionals, i.e. it approached this issue in technocratic manner also. In 2014, when the first yields of the plan's implementation should have emerged and matured, the Brazilian economy grew only by 0.5 per cent, entering the longest period of recession in its recorded history.

Box 6.2 The Old and New Developmentalism: Was There the Theoretical Basis for the PT Industrial Policy?

Was there any theoretical underpinning for the programmes of industrial policies of the PT when it was implemented? Or, did the PT elaborate those programmes without a theoretical basis, acting rather intuitively and being guided by its political principles? The latter looks likely than searching for a profound theory that can explain one or another measure of the Lula and Dilma Rousseff administrations for stimulating industrial modernisation in Brazil. (Perhaps, curiously, the policy of Jair Bolsonaro is more 'theoretically funded' than the policies of the PT: this is 'pure neoliberalism' in its radical, vulgar form, even more vulgar than the 'shock therapy' experiments under Collor de Mello or 'the economic liberalisation' under Pinochet whose policy has been a pattern for imitation from the point of view of the 38th president of Brazil.) A clear elaboration of the explanation for the PT programmes of industrial development is provided in the process of practical activity, while the demand for such an explanation rose and the problem of deindustrialisation was aggravated. It became possible to speak about any clearly composed conception that could be used as an explanation of the PT industrial policy only to the end of the first decade, in 2008–2010. This conception might be assessed as *the new developmentalism*—'the developmentalism of the epoch of neoliberal capitalism' (Boito and Berringer 2013: 32).

As is well known, the main principles of *the old developmentalism* (*desarrollismo*—in Spanish, *desenvolvimentismo*, in Portuguese) were based on ideas of Hans Singer and Raúl Prebisch. These prominent thinkers, pioneers in development studies, provided a conceptual foundation for the strategy of inward-looking development (*desarrollo hacia adentro*) and import substitution industrialisation aimed at the growth of domestic markets with strong state regulation of external trade, an active role for the state in the construction of infrastructure and heavy industry, social security for unionised labourers and some elements of the welfare-state for urban inhabitants. This strategy, with numerous variations, had been accepted by governments across the continent until the lost decade of the 1980s when it accomplished its 'historical mission' and declined.

The term 'new developmentalism' was introduced into scientific discourse for the first time by Luiz Carlos Bresser-Pereira, a Brazilian economist and minister of the Cardoso government in 1995–1999 (Bresser-Pereira 2019: 227–234) (see references to his other works in this chapter above). However, as a new current of economic thought with the following adjective 'liberal' and later 'social', it actually arose earlier, on the eve of the new century (the

(continued)

Box 6.2 (continued)

so-called Consensus of Buenos-Aires, as a reaction to both economic politics experienced in Latin America over the last four–five decades of the twentieth century—simultaneously to the 'hard neoliberalism' of the 1990s and the old developmentalism with all its shortcomings. In a concentrated form, the new developmentalism was performed as 'the Manifesto of São Paulo' entitled 'Ten Theses on New Developmentalism' (Fundação Getúlio Vargas... 2010) signed by many well-known economists apart from Bresser-Pereira: Alice Amsden, Werner Baer, Robert Boyer, Ha-Joon Chang, Aldo Ferrer, Kwame Sundaram Jomo, José Antonio Ocampo, Gabriel Palma, Adam Przeworski, Robert Wade and others.

Similar to the old developmentalism, the new developmentalism recognises a role for the state in the economy, particularly in achieving full employment, but also in the conditions of price and financial stability. It recognises a necessity to develop the internal market, too, but, at the same time, orients nationally based firms to expansion abroad because of the realities of globalisation. The new developmentalism underlines the significance of structural changes in the economy (in this respect it partly coincides with the old developmentalism) by increasing the weight of branches and enterprises with a high level of value added. It does not defend trade protectionism and accepts the idea of an open economy. According to the new developmentalism, industrial policy must be aimed at the elevation of national firms' competitiveness on a global scale by means of their technological upgrading and innovations. An important tool of the new industrial policy is the regulation of an exchange ratio for avoiding the excessive appreciation of the local currency ('Dutch disease') and simultaneous oppression of inflation as well.

Underlining the importance of the control of inflation, new developmentalism does not see the only way to this goal as the manipulation of interest rates. Rather, it treats inflation as a complicated, multi-factor process originating not solely in the monetary sphere. It accepts the necessity of capital flow control, preferring the growth of domestic savings for investment instead of the increase of foreign indebtedness.

The new developmentalism puts attention to a gradual elevation of the minimal wage, cash transfers to the poor and the improvement of human capital as a whole. Meanwhile, in contrast to the practice of the old developmentalism, it refuses the possibility of supporting effective demand by means of the fiscal deficit because the latter leads to financial instability and uncontrolled inflation. The new developmentalism requires progressive taxation of high incomes and redistributive policy for the eradication of poverty and other acute social problems. In this respect, it has often been associated with *social-developmentalism*, although some economists think that there are

(continued)

Box 6.2 (continued)
some conceptual differences between the latter and new developmentalism (Ban 2012; de Medeiros Carneiro 2012, esp. 767–776). In particular, social-developmentalism, not rejecting the pivotal principles of the new developmentalism as a whole, puts a resolution of the social problems, including, of course, the problems of poverty and excessive inequality, at the centre of development. Moreover, it interprets social development as a key to economic growth and technological innovation because poor quality of human capital and abnormal inequality are the main obstacles to the increase of demand and growth in such country as Brazil.

Considering the plans of industrial policy announced by the PT during its employment, we can conclude that there was discordance between the technocratic vision of economic and technological modernisation, on the one hand, and real social policy, on the other. Such discordance could hardly facilitate resolving the problem of premature deindustrialisation, transforming the latter into a 'mature' one upon a contemporary scientific-technological, innovative basis. In addition, the intention of the PT government, probably sincere in itself, to approach to this profound problem, economic and social at the same time, underwent the temptation to sacrifice the long-term, strategic solutions for the sake of obvious, rapidly achievable results. (Here I do not consider whether there was another choice or not.) So what then led Brazil astray? It wasn't the biblical temptation of the snake in the garden, nor was it the glittering 'Alliance for Progress'-style project as under the Kennedy administration, nor was it the misconceived FTAA/ALCA programme of George Bush Jr. No, ironically, it was the former 'friend' of the poor and 'wretched of the earth'—the 'Red Dragon' itself—the People's Republic of China.

6.3 The "Friendship" with China and the Interests of Agribusiness

The industrial growth of China and the rapid transformation of this previously poor but huge country into the 'world's workshop' coincided with profound structural changes in Chinese economy. The fascinating growth of industry, particularly its export-oriented sector, hugely augmented the demand for primary resources. At the same time, the growing industry and urbanisation required expanded territory for them at the expense of agricultural lands. It led to a relative shortage of agricultural products in relation to the expanding demand and to the respective increase of food importation. (China did not carry out 'a green revolution'—in contrast to India, Thailand and some other Asian countries where this technological revolution in agriculture started in the 1950s–1960s and enabled a notable improvement in food supply. Supposedly, the Chinese leaders, the 'builders of socialism with Chinese

Table 6.4 The volume of trade (FOB) between Brazil and China, millions US$ and as percentage of total Brazilian trade, 2005–2018

	Exports from Brazil		Imports to Brazil		Total (the sum of exports and imports)	
Years	US$	%%	US$	%%	US$	%%
2005	6827	5.76	5337	7.25	12,164	6.33
2010	30,748	15.23	25,591	14.08	56,339	14.68
2013[a]	44,305	18.26	37,326	15.58	81,631	16.93
2015	35,550	18.60	30,715	17.91	66,265	18.28
2018	64,206	26.76	34,730	19.16	98,936	23.49

[a]2013—the year when the volume of trade between two countries reached its maximum before a temporary decrease in 2014–2016
Sources and counted on: IPEA (2019)

specificity', did not deliberately stimulate such revolution, having a fear of the rocketing growth of rural unemployment with inevitable social-political destabilisation and threat to the 'Communist' party's power. Indeed, even 'ordinary' liberalisation of the agricultural economy in the early-1980s had succeeded in the increased economic overpopulation in rural areas.) Henceforth, a search for new sources of raw materials and agricultural products was an indispensable solution for the Chinese state and business. In this respect, Latin America, with a developed extractive industry and agriculture and much more productive than the least-developed African countries, looked a more attractive and preferable partner than Africa with its numerous risks. It is worth noting the rapid growth of Chinese importations from Latin America—from 5 billion US$ in 2000 to 103 billion in 2015 (da Rocha and Bielschowsky 2018: 10–14). Therefore Brazil, as the biggest and developed country of the continent, would play a key role in the Chinese economic expansion into Latin America (Bruno et al. 2011: 91–92).

The crisis of 2008–2009 had become a milestone in the reorientation of the old external economic ties of Brazil from the North American and EU markets to China. During this period, China outstripped the USA and EU as the main trade partner of Brazil. This situation did not arise suddenly; it had been growing since 2000–2001 when the trade between two countries began intensively developing. This trade, which in 2000 exceeded 2 billion US$ (1.085 billion—the export of goods from Brazil; 1.022, the import of goods to Brazil)—1.9 per cent of the total external trade of Brazil at the time—was followed by the volume of trade by goods (without services) between two countries growing strongly in the subsequent years (Table 6.4).

The extending economic ties with China helped Brazil and other Latin American countries to withstand the turbulence of 2008–2009 with small losses. They minimised the costs of the global crisis for the continent, and Latin America as a whole, in particular Brazil, looked—maybe, for the first time in history—better than many other regions of the world during the conditions of recession. The reserves accumulated in the preceding years, thanks to the trade with China (trade with a positive balance for Brazil), softened the negative effects of the crisis in the manufacturing industry and services. In this connection, some of my Russian colleagues devised a narrative of the transformation of Latin America as 'the crisis-proof region'. However, this story is an example of when, at first, short-term advantages hide long-term, strategic losses, and, secondly, when the label of views, in contrast to that of other articles, "cheats not only the buyer but often also the seller", as Marx noted once (Marx 1978: 360).

Certainly, the penetration of China into Latin America as a whole and, in particular, into Brazil would be almost inevitable independently on the political colour of the governments that ruled in the continent's countries during the first decade of the new century. Namely, it would be inevitable due to China's expansion, but the latter could hardly be possible at the recently observable scale, if the governments and some of the continent's business circles, including, of course, Brazilian ones, weren't interested, economically and politically, in development of the economic ties with the emerging Asian giant. What concerned the Left and Left-centrist governments in Latin America was that they conceived of the economic ties with China not only from an economic point of view (as a kind of *business and nothing more*) but also as an alternative to the North American and West European domination of the world economy and politics. They intensified these ties partly because of a sincere intention to diversify the external economic relations of their countries, partly because of their previous Leftist anti-hegemonism (implicitly—anti-Americanism). The latter had been fed, to a large degree, by nostalgic reminiscences rooted in the 'legendary 1960s', when the theories of dependency, revolutionary romanticism and dreams 'of repeating the Cuban experience' by means of the guerrilla inspired 'heads and hearts' of the young, 'reddening' generation in the continent. In the case of Brazil, the 'soft' anti-Americanism of Lula was for him and the PT also a mode to distinguish himself from the preceding administration of Cardoso in foreign policy, while the continuity of the financial-economic policy was obvious. In addition, Lula and his advisers, including the Minister of Foreign Affairs, Celso Amorim, proceeded with the conviction that global power was shifting from the relatively weakening 'old West' to the new emerging actors, primarily, of course, to China but also to India, Russia and neighbouring South American countries (Vieira and Ouriques 2016: 410–414). Consequently, the PT Southwards-looking policy appeared as the logically consistent 'correction' (but not full disruption) of the multi-vectored foreign policy of their predecessor in Planalto (Burges 2017: 40–42, 174–198, 224–226; Christensen 2013, 273–281; Suyama et al. 2016, 31–37). At the same time, it was notable that the first foreign country visited by Dilma Rousseff after her inauguration was China.

The traditional anti-Americanism of the Left in power, including the PT government in Brazil (whose anti-Americanism was, however, very moderate in comparison to that of Evo Morales in Bolivia or Hugo Chávez in Venezuela and did not exclude a broad collaboration with the USA in many respects), nevertheless, had rebounded on them. When the Left and Left-centrist governments in Latin America began developing their economic ties with China, they, at first, sought for ways of deliverance from the centurial dependency on their Northern neighbour and, secondly, saw the 'friendship' with 'the Red Dragon' as the efficient alternative to the discontentment with globalisation in its neoliberal forms. In inviting Chinese firms, and signing various trade agreements or contracts with China, they seemingly hoped that collaboration with China would contribute, at least, indirectly, to the socioeconomic development of their countries. They did not understand that their Chinese partners, in contrast, for example, to the former Soviet Union, were not going to introduce a model of development which would be an alternative to capitalism in Latin America, particularly in its neoliberal forms. The Left and Left-centrist 'friends' of China in Latin America, including the PT in Brazil, underestimated that the Chinese policy is adherent to only one ideological principle—the pragmatic principle of economic advantage for China. Thus the Latin American Left (of different shades of 'redness') with their deep-seated anti-Americanism did not comprehend that the Chinese fascinating success story has been the other side of neoliberalism in the USA and other developed countries. Possibly, they inattentively read the well-known book and concomitant papers by two authors, Fernando Henrique Cardoso and Enzo Faletto, about the associated-dependent development in Latin America (Cardoso and Faletto 1970, 1978; Cardoso 1972: 88–94, 1973: 144–149). Meanwhile, the rapid growth of China since 1979 has been a brilliant illustration of such development—the outward-looking development associated with the neoliberal economic practices and structural shifts in the core of the world system. These shifts, as was initially in the case of the first-tier 'tigers' (Hong Kong, Singapore, Taiwan and South Korea), opened niches for manufactured goods from East Asia (and later of course from China also), facilitating, thereby, economic development there. In fact, the process of apparent liberalisation in economies of the West, beginning from Thatcherism in the UK and Reaganomics in the USA, and the activity of *the developmental states* in East/Southeast Asia have actually been different, seemingly (and only seemingly) opposite aspects of the same process.

When the Latin American Left in power opened doors to Chinese firms, both private and state-owned, hoping to weaken the previous dependency on Uncle Sam, they changed one form of neoliberalism for another form, for its 'other being', as Hegel would say. In essence, the 'friendship' with China led the PT government (as well as the other Left governments in Latin America) to the same ends, against which they protested and which they intended to avoid. This 'friendship' gave nothing or, at best, only a small amount of genuine technological and economic modernisation of the continent and had, from the long-term strategic point of view, an even worse effect than the direct implementation of neoliberal reforms in the 1990s for Latin American countries. As we know, these reforms stabilised the financial systems, oppressed destructive inflation, strengthened competition, favoured a selective modernisation in some branches of economy (telecommunications, banking services, transport, retail trade) and improved, though not anywhere to the same degree, the institutional conditions for businesses (a defence of the property rights, etc.). Of course, the costs of transformations were often excessive, combined with the negative effects: the structural degradation of economies, precocious deindustrialisation, the growth of unemployment and deepening social differentiation in some cases, although those effects were different across different countries of the continent, and the balance of positive and negative results of neoliberalism in Latin America have been in dispute until today.

Meanwhile, it is difficult to say anything about the contribution of China to modernisation anywhere in the continent. Indeed, when did a Chinese firm ever invest in the development of an advanced manufacturing industry of Brazil or any other Latin American country—in contrast to greedy multinationals that built the new industrial enterprises in the years of 'miracle', albeit for the privileged, upper minority? Rather, on the contrary, the trade with China hindered the process of development, not curing the disease but softening its symptoms. The economic ties with the emerging Asian giant led Latin America back to the predicament, from which the continent tried to escape for over six decades, often through tears, pain and blood – that is the position of a supplier of raw materials with all the associated and inevitable vulnerabilities to the capricious world market of commodities. In fact, the economic ties with China pushed Brazil and other Latin American countries back to the world periphery again, whereas China began occupying the position of the industrially developed centre in bilateral relations with Latin America (Corsi et al. 2019: especially 177–189).

Thus, while intending to abolish economic dependency on the excessively obtrusive Northern neighbour, the Latin American Left governments, including the PT government, did not eliminate their dependency as a whole. Moreover, because of this dubious 'friendship' with China, Brazil together with many other Latin American countries returned to the old forms of dependency that corresponded to the nineteenth century. This return had not only direct economic effects, aggravating premature deindustrialisation and technological degradation (simplification) of industry. It also succeeded in serious changes in political life because it favoured the strengthening of social forces of the past. *Forces of the past* were, of course, the abovementioned financiers, the main beneficiaries of neoliberal reforms in the 1990s and inheritors of 'coronels' (*coroneis*) performing now as an export-oriented large agribusiness. The influence of the latter on the process of economic decision-making and politics was disproportionately bigger than its visible weight in economy performed by the formal indicators. Indeed, at a first glance, the primary sector, including agriculture, has apparently been insignificant for the national economy, being equal to small percentage of GDP—around 5 per cent for agriculture with forestry, fishery, etc. and 3–4 per cent for extractive industry. Nevertheless, these branches have been important sources of foreign currencies, and their successes or, on the contrary, failures determine, to a big degree, the exchange ratio of the real to other currencies and to overall financial stability. Respectively, the enlarged agribusiness together with extraction of iron ore and some rare-earth metals (e.g. niobium) began impacting on the conditions of accelerating deindustrialisation and on the financing of social programmes to an ever-increasing degree. A decrease of commodities' prices after 2012–2013 was immediately succeeded by budget shortfalls with negative effects for social policy (Pahnke 2018: 1662–1668).

Box 6.3 The Second Edition of 'The Open Veins of Latin America'?

Almost a half-century ago, in 1971, the Uruguayan journalist Eduardo Galeano published a book that has rapidly become a bestseller, not just in Latin America, but across the world, 'The Open Veins of Latin America' ('Las venas abiertas de América Latina'). This book, a brilliant example of journalism with historical excurses and a strongly expressed ideological inclination, although very far from respectable but tedious academism, ran numerous editions in many countries and remains popular and widely read among Latin American Leftists to this day. The author imposed a full responsibility for mass poverty, shocking inequality and sufferings of the continent's peoples on the economically developed countries that exploited Latin America for their own advantage and economic prosperity, plundering the people, nature and resources of the continent. Of course, they acted with co-participation of the local oligarchy and indigenous 'sons of bitches'. Galeano even explained the rise of industrial capitalism by such exploitation of overseas lands. In particular, he asserted that neither the steam engine of Watt nor the cannons of Washington could be invented without Caribbean and Brazilian plantation slavery because the capital accumulated from the sugarcane trade and plantation slavery in the New World was used for the initial start of industrial revolution (Galeano 1997: 78–81, 2004: 106–110). As many Leftists who accuse 'the imperialist powers' of the unhappiness and others discontents of Latin America, real either though up by ideologically inclined consciousness, Galeano did not put the simple, elementary questions: Were the plantation slavery and sugar trade more significant for the industrial development of the North than the internal contradictions of early capitalism with manufactory production? Did slavery in the Caribbean and Brazil hinder the industrial revolution, postponing it for some decades? Wouldn't the industrial revolution have started earlier if plantation slavery did not exist at all?

Certainly, the open veins of Latin America, that horrible pillage in the name of 'civilisation and Christianisation', indirectly contributed to the enrichment of North America and Western Europe but were not the causes of the rise of capitalism. Moreover, perhaps, without the exploitation of the world periphery, the core countries would have developed faster, and the British, Dutch, French and later American capitalist class would have begun thinking about innovations and the attribution of a 'human face' to capitalism in the nineteenth century and not 100 years later.

However, the problem emphasised in the book by Galeano concerns the 'friendship' with China, too. It is not accidental that the academic journal 'Latin American Perspectives' devoted two issues in 2018 and 2019 under the general title 'Open Veins Revisited' to the problem of extractivism and re-primarisation of Latin American economies. At first glance, the Left and Left-centrist governments used the extracted natural resources to solve acute

(continued)

Box 6.3 (continued)
social problems, not just redistributing incomes from exports of primary goods for the reduction of poverty but also financing healthcare and education. The main, though not only, actor in this process has been the state as the leading regulator and controller—in contrast to the past times when the extractive industries pertained mostly to foreign companies, often in alliance with local oligarchic groups. Probably, people like Galeano (he died in 2015) should be glad that, at last, the democratically elected, socially oriented governments began controlling the use of natural wealth for the vast majority of the continent's population. But state control for resources did not change the economic fundamental of Latin American societies. Strictly speaking, the socially oriented policy of the Left ('Pink-tide') governments appeared as the specifically coloured continuation of the Washington Consensus and neoliberalism in their 'softened' forms. In essence, the Latin American Left governments, including the PT government in Brazil, have been performing as social inheritors of the conservative forces of the past (Farthing and Fabricant 2018: 6–8; Svampa 2013: 35–37). For instance, an enlargement of sugarcane plantations for the production of bio-ethanol ('Movido á Bio-Diesel', you can read on boards of many urban buses in São Paulo) has been accompanied by the expulsion of peasants from their lands, a worsening environment and—this a culmination of the Left's policy—through the use of labour that does not principally differ from slavery labour (Mendonça 2010: 133–136; Teixeira Assis and Rocha Franco 2018: 42–43, 45–47).

Therefore, the 'Veins' of Latin America remain open, and the Right-turn observable now in many countries of the continent looks as the conservative 'correction' of a temporary 'deviation' from 'the approved path'.

A conservation of the status quo, with the ascendance of big agribusiness in a position of significant socioeconomic actor, presupposed a peculiar role of the North and North-East regions in the political life of the country. Thus the large rural areas, with mass poverty and patrimonial relationships, were the main 'fortress' of the internal periphery from where millions of under-proletarians migrated to the growing cities and industry. It was impossible to eradicate this periphery and its poverty without the radical bourgeois agrarian reform which could subvert the system of landlordism with the extreme socioeconomic polarisation of society.

However, as it was already said above, modernisers such as Vargas and Kubitschek did not approach profound agrarian reform. Goulart intended to do so but was overthrown before he had time to begin. The military-bureaucratic regime of 1964–1985 conceived an acuteness of rural backwardness and attempted to solve the agrarian problem, though in full accordance with the algorithm of conservative modernisation: not destroying the system of latifundia but enlarging technical opportunities for the few successful peasants (farmers) to develop their businesses on new soils like Stolypin did in Russia in 1906–1910 in a framework of Russian autocratic modernisation.

According to the Constitution of 1988, the necessity of agrarian reform was widely declared, but real attempts to implement it began under the Cardoso presidency. At the same time, the MST (*Movimento dos Trabalhodores Rurais Sem Terra*—the Movement of Rural Landless Labourers), the main radical proponent of agrarian reform, became one of the most important actors of Brazilian political life, propping the PT from the Left side of political spectrum.[10]

Considering the problem of agrarian reform and Brazilian agriculture as a whole, it is necessary to note that very important changes occurred in this sphere of the economy since the 1970s. Due to conservative modernisation, previous latifundia, *fazendas*, became big entities in modern agribusiness. Agriculture ceased to be a backward sector, the Cinderella of the national economy. Moreover, in the last two to three decades, it developed faster and much more successfully than industry. For instance, the share of value added in agriculture, including its peculiar sub-branches such as forestry, fishery, etc., almost did not change from 2000 up until today. It was 5.52 per cent in 2000 and had increased a little to 5.66 per cent in 2016, whereas the share of people occupied in this sector of economy fell from 21.24 per cent in 2000 to 13.06 per cent—in 2016 (or, in absolute terms, from 16.7 to 13.1 million people) (IBGE 2016b: tables 10.4, 13.4, 15.4 and author's calculations; see also Mattei 2015: 41–46). This data illustrates the good growth in productivity and the effectiveness of the given sector of economy—in contrast to the tendencies observable in the manufacturing industry. But this growth has been provided mostly by big agribusiness. The latter concentrates a lion's share of the natural, technical and financial resources of the branch. 1 per cent of the biggest establishments held about 45 per cent of land used in agriculture. At the same time, farms and other agricultural entities with squares of land below 10 hectares (about 50 per cent of all establishments in agriculture) held only about 2.5 per cent of the total agricultural land. The degree of concentration and inequality of land ownership did not significantly change since 1995 during the period of the Left-centrist rule in spite of all the programmes of aid to small land proprietors, family farms and self-employed peasants. Even a notable decrease in the number of landless agricultural labourers and peasants—by one third from 1995–1996 to 2006–2007, when many of those, who were obliged to rent land and/or to be hired, became proprietors—did not succeed in diminishing disparities and inequalities in the distribution of land ownership (Hoffmann and Gomes 2010: 45–46, 48–50; Sabourin 2014: 36–37, 43–44).

Indeed, the reform, formally aimed at the distribution of non-cultivated agricultural lands among landless peasants and rural workers, had been carrying out in a full relation to the algorithm of conservative modernisation. There were not (and could not be) instant confiscations of the landlords' properties, as in the case of South

[10]In interview to the author of these lines in September 2009, Cardoso said that he met with the representatives of the MST, and these meetings helped to correct the pace and path of reform in different states (Cardoso 2010: 33–34).

Korea and Taiwan, where the Japanese landlords were expelled by the US occupational administrations from these territories after defeat of Japan in 1945, and their lands were distributed among peasants with a subsequent positive effect for the internal market and restraint of corruption (Jong-Sung You 2014, 2017, esp. 539–540, 544–549). In Brazil the procedure of land transfer into new ownership was very long. It could last 3–4 years, and the previous proprietor might appeal against its results in a court of law. The lands expropriated spontaneously by activists of the MST, without legally established procedures, were not recognised as lawfully transferred with the respective registration of property rights. But in the case of legal property's transfer, the new owners often met various difficulties of an infrastructural and social character: poor transport communications, a shortage of necessary tools and equipment, a lack of medical assistance and schools for children, etc. The reforms did not principally diminish an outflow of the rural population. In particular, young people who did not see prospects for themselves in the rural areas left their native countryside, migrating into cities where they replenished the ranks of precariously employed labourers.

Even the moderates, surrounded by numerous formalities of reform, encountered serious resistance from the local 'coronels'—landlords and oligarchic groups. The latter did not hesitate to use military force and paramilitary groups, many of which were of criminal origin, to oppress the activists of MST who were required to implement the reforms as soon as possible and often occupied the non-used lands of proprietors. The amount of assassinated landless peasants and activists of the MST ran into hundreds (223 in total for 1995–2001), although it shrank under the Cardoso rule (Pessanha Neves 2003: 183), but did not principally decrease under the PT. In particular, on April 17, 1996, the police assassinated 21 people who blockaded a highway in the state of Pará, protesting against postponement of the reform in the state (the so-called 'massacre of Eldorado dos Carajás').[11] (Today, after the 2016 parliamentary coup, it began increasing again as the effect of aggravating social struggle in Brazilian countryside.)

The presidency of Cardoso accelerated the pace of reform after 1995 (Ondetti 2007: 12–19). In 1996, the national programme of support for familial agriculture was launched and began operating. (Supposedly, in this respect Cardoso-the-sociologist, understanding that the historical roots of Brazilian poverty lay in the specific character of agriculture with the relics of slavery, prevailed over Cardoso-the-president who was obliged to find compromises with conservative political forces, in particular, with the *coronels* from the North-East.) The number of families that officially got access to land in 1995–2001 was 584,655, much bigger than under the military regime in 1964–1984 (218,033 families) (Pessanha Neves 2003: 182). However, the pace of reform slowed down in the years of the second term of Cardoso

[11] Neither the then governor of Pará Almir Gabriel, who gave orders to unblock the highway, nor the state's secretary for public security Paulo Câmara, who authorised a use of police force, nor the coronel Mario Colares Pantoja with the mayor José Maria Pereira de Oliveira, were held accountable judicially.

and under the PT rule all previous promises of Lula to intensify it notwithstanding (Gaulard 2019: 80–81; Gómez Bruera 2015: 317–323). Thereby, PT leaders contested the requirements of the MST which supported the party but insisted on radicalisation of the reforms. But such slowdown was not accidental; it was the effect of inevitable compromises of the PT with the Right-centrist forces. Lula and Dilma Rousseff did not risk confronting big agribusiness because the latter increased income from commodities exports (to China) for financing the social programmes, primarily, *Bolsa Família*. Such attitudes of the party and its leaders corresponded to the larger context of conservative modernisation promoted under the slogans of strong social policy. It avoided aggravating socio-political conflicts, and it redistributed a part of incomes without elevating taxes for the rich and upper social groups when any attempt to revise taxes would be rejected by the National Congress. Therefore, in Brazil's conditions at the time, a further radicalisation of the agrarian reform might have succeeded in a decrease of agricultural output and exports with an inevitable shrinkage of the resources for social policy and corresponding erosion of the electoral base of the PT. Moreover, as Graziano da Silva, the principal counsellor to Lula on agrarian issues, said, agrarian reform is unnecessary from the point of view of the capitalist development of productive forces (Sabourin 2014: 41–42). From the point of view of the PT, the main reason for the reform's continuation consisted—in a framework of the general socioeconomic policy of the party—in the reduction of rural poverty but without the elimination of its profound structural sources. In fact, the agrarian reform did not essentially impact on trends that already existed in the economy and society despite its positive effect for the reduction of rural poverty. In particular, poverty in Brazil is mostly urban poverty, and the poor in their prevailing majority are urban inhabitants, so the agrarian reform could only affect poverty in the country as a whole indirectly. Meanwhile, the slow pace of agrarian reform and existence of numerous landless rural labourers favoured the conservation of archaic social relationships such as slave labour.

Box 6.4 The Capitalist Development and Reproduction of the Pre-capitalist Relationships

In many respects the contemporary situation is reminiscent of the practices of early capitalism when rapid capitalist development in the centre of the world system had been accompanied by the re-establishment or conservation of the archaic, pre-capitalist social order and relationships at the periphery. In particular, plantation slavery in Brazil, as well as in the South of the USA, was the satellite of the mercantilist and early-industrial capitalist development in Europe. The establishment of repressive archaic regimes in Central America, like the regime of Somoza family in Nicaragua, in the 1930s was indistinguishable from the Fordist-Keynesian revolution in the USA because those regimes provided, in institutional respect, a supply of coffee and fresh fruits for the growing mass consumption in North America. Later, their significance

(continued)

Box 6.4 (continued)
strengthened in the conditions of Cold War. Respectively, we can presuppose that the rise of post-industrial, knowledge-based economies in developed countries may accompany the return to some archaic forms of social relationships in semi-peripheral countries.

It is paradoxical, at first glance, that Brazil is among the world 'leaders' on the issue of 'enforced labour' (equivalent to 'slave labour' but without the market of slaves) and, at the same time, in the fight against such labour that has been marked by the International Labour Organization. The existence of slave labour as one of the serious social vices was officially recognised at the highest level of political authority in 1995 by Cardoso who initiated the institutional and legal measures for eradicating this intolerable phenomenon. Later, in 2003, Lula launched the national plan to abolish the latter. In 2005 he approved the National Pact for the Eradication of Slavery Labour (*O Pacto Nacional pela Eradicação do Trabalho Escravo*) (OIT/ILO 2011: 151–152).

However, before fighting against evil, it is necessary to know its size and scale, i.e. to estimate how many people and where they are involved in slavery. Evidently it is very difficult to count the exact number of people subject to enforced labour because of illegal character of such activity. For example, the office of the ILO in Brasília estimated their number as 9762 persons in the period from November 2002 to March 2007 (Ibid.: 56), but this amount reflected only the cases discovered by the police and NGOs' activists. How many cases have not been found and investigated in the far off places of Amazonas, Pará or Maranhão where the local *fazendeiros* personify an archaic unity of economic and administrative power? Answers to this question can be only estimations.

Despite undeniable successes in the struggle against slavery labour in 1995–2015, there were serious institutional obstacles to such a struggle. Often those activists and NGOs who exposed cases of slavery were met with bureaucratic procrastination and police indifference. The local police and authorities had informal, sometimes crony, ties with *fazendeiros* that used slavery labour, not to mention the cases of obvious corruption (Rezende Figueira and Antunes Prado 2014: 26–30).

Today, a practice of slave labour or enforced labour in conditions similar to slavery is, in essence, one of the forms of precarious employment, mainly, of course, in rural areas. It has been applied in cattle-breeding, harvesting of sugar cane, soya, coffee, etc., and precariousness is probably its main characteristic feature (Issa 2017: 95–97; Maranhão Costa 2010: 71–72). As a rule, people who fall into slavery are poor with very low levels of educational attainment or simply illiterate. They do not have a choice and agree with seemingly attractive offers from recruiters ('gatos'/ 'cats') who are intermediaries between them and *fazendeiro*. Sometimes, a fall into the slavery trap can be caused by debts: a rich *fazendeiro* promises to pay out debts of peasants, often landless or bankrupted, thus requiring to work for him. This practice, formally illegal, of course, spread throughout the years of authoritarian regime, which combated, rather in words than actuality, slave labour on the one hand—in a framework of its modernisation strategy—but simultaneously also created conditions, through impoverishment of peasantry, for 'debt slavery' on the other (Esterci 2008: 61–66).

In many cases, the products of slave labour have been supplied as intermediary goods to the advanced branches of the Brazilian economy. The increased production of bio-ethanol, this indisputable technological achievement of Brazil, lifted the respective demand for cane. Meanwhile it is disadvantageous to mechanise harvesting of cane because of abundance of cheap labour force, including, in particular, slave labour (Alves de Almeida 2014; Alves and Novaes 2014).

Today, after 'the turn to the Right' when the conservative Congress often supports the Rightist president's initiatives that revoke many laws and ordnances concerning the social and environmental programmes introduced under Cardoso, not to mention Lula and Rousseff, slave labour, particularly in the depths of the North, North-East and Centre-West regions (the states Amazonas, Acre, Maranhão, Mato Grosso, Mato Grosso do Sul, Pará, Tocantins), can become a steadily spreading practice in Brazilian socioeconomic life. It is difficult to presuppose that Jair Bolsonaro will launch any plan for combating such a practice.

* * *

Thus, the social policy of the PT had a flip side, namely, it involuntarily favoured the structural degradation of the economy, the rise of dependency on China (in the quality of commodities adjunct to the latter) and the conservation of several obsolete, archaic forms of social relationships. We can discuss, of course, whether it was 'a good price' for achievements in social policy or not. Nonetheless, it is relevant to put other questions: how truly significant were these achievements from the point of view of long-term trends? How profoundly did they change the social structure of Brazilian society?

References

ABDI (Agência Brasileira de Desenvolvimento Industrial). (2008). *Política de Desenvolvimento Produtivo: Inovar e investir para sustentar o crescimento*. Brasilia, DF: ABDI.

ABDI. (2014). *Plano Brasil Maior. Inovar para Competir, Competir para Crescer. Balanço Executivo 2011-2014*. Brasilia, DF: ABDI.

Alves de Almeida, A. (2014). Pastorais lutam por trabalho livre e digno. In R. Rezende Figueira, A. Antunes Prado, & H. Antunes de Sant'Ana Junior (Eds.), *Trabalho Escravo Contemporâneo: Um debate transdisciplinar* (pp. 32–53). Rio de Janeiro: Mauad X.

Alves, F., & Novaes, J. R. P. (2014). Precarização e pagamento por produção: A lógica do trabalho na agroindústria canavieira. In R. Rezende Figueira, A. Antunes Prado, & H. Antunes de Sant'Ana Junior (Eds.), *Trabalho Escravo*. (pp. 86–113).

Arend, M., & Dutra Fonseca, P. C. (2012). Brasil (1955-2005): 25 anos de catching up, 25 anos de falling behind. *Revista de Economia Política, 32*(1), 33–54.

Arendt, M. (2015). *A Industrialização do Brasil ante a Nova Divisão Internacional do Trabalho Texto para discussão*. Brasília: IPEA (Instituto de Pesquisa Econômica Aplicada).

Ban, C. (2012). Brazil's liberal neo-developmentalism: New paradigm or edited orthodoxy? *Review of International Political Economy, 1*, 1–34. https://doi.org/10.1080/09692290.2012.660183.
Bell, D. (1973). *The coming of post-insdustrial society: A venture in social forecasting*. New York: Basic Books.
Berthelot, J. (1991). Politique industrielle et politique économique au Brésil. *Caravelle*, 57. Numéro consacré au Brésil, pp. 5–51. Retrieved June 21, 2019, from https://doi.org/10.3406/carav.1991.2466., https://www.persee.fr/doc/carav_1147-6753_1991_num_57_1_2466
Bizberg, I. (2019). *Diversity of capitalisms in Latin America*. Cham: Palgrave Macmillan.
Boito, A., Jr., & Berringer, T. (2013). Brasil: Classes sociais, neodesenvolvimentismo e política externa nos governos Lula e Dilma. *Revista de Sociologia e Política, 21*(47), 31–38.
Bresser-Pereira, L. C. (2012). A taxa de câmbio no centro da teoria do desenvolvimento. *Estudos Avançados, São Paulo, 29*(75), 7–28.
Bresser-Pereira, L. C. (2013). The value of the exchange rate and the Dutch disease. *Brazilian Journal of Political Economy (Revista de Economia Política), 33*(132), 371–387.
Bresser-Pereira, L. C. (2016). Reflecting on new developmentalism and classical developmentalism. *Review of Keynesian Economics, 4*(3), 331–352.
Bresser-Pereira, L. C. (2019). Do desenvolvimentismo clássico e da macroeconomia pós-keynesiana ao novo desenvolvimentismo. *Revista de Economia Política, 39*(155), 211–235.
Bresser-Pereira, L. C., Nassif, A., & Feijó, C. (2016). A reconstrução da indústria brasileira: a conexão entre o regime macroeconômico e a política industrial. *Revista de Economia Política, 36*(144), 493–513.
Bruno, M., Halevi, J., & Marques-Pereira, J. (2011). Les défis de l'influence de la Chine sur le développement du Brésil: Avantages comparatifs et conflit distributif. *Revue Tiers Monde, 208*, 83–102.
Burges, S. W. (2017). *Brazil in the world: The international relations of a South American Giant*. Manchester: Manchester University Press.
Cano, W. (2012). A desindustrialização no Brasil. *Economia e Sociedade, 21*, 831–851.
Cardoso, F. H. (1972). Dependency and development in Latin America. *New Left Review, 74*, 83–95.
Cardoso, F. H. (1973). Associated-dependent development: Theoretical and practical implications. In A. Stepan (Ed.), *Authoritarian Brazil: Origins, policies, and future* (pp. 142–176). New Haven: Yale University Press.
Cardoso, F. H. (2010). To be stable, democracy needs to be effective in reducing mass poverty and social inequality (interview). *Svobodnaya Mysl (Free Thought), 1*, 29–38. in Russian.
Cardoso, F. H., & Faletto, E. (1970). *Dependencia y desarrollo en América Latina. Ensayo de interpretación sociológica*. México: Siglo XXI (1-ra edición – 1969).
Cardoso, F. H., & Faletto, E. (1978). *Dependency and development in Latin America* (Translated by Marjory Mattingly Urguidi). Berkeley, Los Angeles: University of California Press.
CEPAL/ECLAC. (2017). *Anuario estadístico de América Latina y el Caribe/Statistical Yearbook for Latin America and the Caribbean 2016*. Santiago de Chile: NU. La versión electrónica. Cuentas nacionales/National counts. Retrieved February 17, 2020, from http://interwp.cepal.org/anuario_estadistico/Anuario_2016/es/index.asp
Christensen, S. F. (2013). Brazil's foreign policy priorities. *Third World Quarterly, 34*(2), 271–286. https://doi.org/10.1080/01436597.2013.775785.
Clark, C. (1957). *The conditions of economic progress* (3rd ed.). Macmillan: St. Martin's Press (1st edition – 1940).
Coronel, D. A., Zago de Azevedo, A. F., & Carvalho Campos, A. (2014). Política industrial e desenvolvimento econômico: a reatualização de um debate histórico. *Revista de Economia Política, 34*(134), 103–119.
Corsi, F. L., dos Santos, A., & Camargo, J. M. (2019). A América Latina: Ciclo de Commodities e Crise do Capitalismo Global. *Austral: Revista Brasileira de Estratégia e Relações Internacionais, 8*(15), 168–194.

da Rocha, F. F., & Bielschowsky, R. (2018). La búsqueda de China de recursos naturales en América Latina. *Revista de la CEPAL, 126*, 9–29.

Dabène, O., & Louault, F. (2013). *Atlas du Brésil: Promesses et défis d'une puissance émergente. Cartographie: Aurélie Boissière*. Paris: Autrement.

Dasgupta, S., & Singh, A. (2006). *Manufacturing, services and premature industrialization in developing countries: A Kaldorian Analysis*. WIDER Research Paper N 2006/49. Helsinki: WIDER.

Dávila-Fernández, M. J. (2015). Desindutrialização e o investimento na infraestutura como instrumento conciliador de uma política industrial base no Brasil. *Revista de Economia Política, 35*(140), 576–600.

de Medeiros Carneiro, R. (2012). Velhos e novos desenvolvimentismos. *Economia e Sociedade, 21*, 749–778.

Denison, E. (assisted by J.-P. Poullier). (1967). *Why growth rates differ: Postwar experience in nine western countries*. Washington, DC: The Brookings Institution.

Esterci, N. (2008). *Escravos da Desigualdade. Un estudo sobre o uso repressivo da forэa do trabalho hoje*. Rio de Janeiro: Centro Edelstein de Pesquisas Sociais.

Farthing, L., & Fabricant, N. (2018). Introduction. Open veins revisited: Charting the social, economic, and political contours of the New Extractivism in Latin America. *Latin American Perspectives, 22*(222), 4–17. https://doi.org/10.1177/0094582X18785882.

Feijó, et al. (2005). *Ocorreu uma desindustrialização no Brasil?* IEDI.

Fourastié, J. (1949). *Le Grand Espoir du XXe Siècle. Progrès technique, progrès économique, progrès social*. Paris: Presses Universiataires de France.

Fourastié, J. (1953). *La civilisation de 1975*. Paris: Presses Universitaires de France.

Fundação Getúlio Vargas. Escola de Economia de São Paulo da Fundação Getúlio Vargas. (2010). *Ten theses on new developmentalism (available online in English and Portuguese)*. Retrieved January 27, 2020, from https://cnd.fgv.br/en/node/404

Galeano, E. (1997). *The open veins of Latin America. Five centuries of the pillage of a continent* (Translated by Cedric Belfrage. 25th Anniversary Edition. Foreword by Isabel Allende). New York: Monthly Review Press.

Galeano, E. (2004). *Las venas abiertas de América Latina. 76-a edición, revisada y corregida*. México, Buenos Aires, Siglo XXI editores (1-a edición – 1971).

Gaulard, M. (2016). Les responsabilités de la désindustrialisation précoce dans la crise brésilienne actuelle. *Outre-Terre, 47*, 66–81.

Gaulard, M. (2019). *L'économie du Brésil* (2-e ed.). Paris: Bréal.

GGDC (Groningen Growth and Development Centre). (2013). *Maddison Historical Statistics. Maddison Project Database 2013*. Last modified – 11.01.2018. Retrieved June 19, 2019, from https://www.rug.nl/ggdc/historicaldevelopment/maddison/data/mpd_2013-01.xlsx

Gómez Bruera, H. F. (2015). *Lula, el Partido de los Trabajadores y el dilema de gobernalidad en Brasil. Traducción de Ana Inés Fernández*. México: Fondo de Cultura Económica, Centro de Investigación y Docencia Económica.

Gonçalves, S. M., Nunes, W., & Perissinotto, R. (2019). Ideias, instituições e coalizões: as razões do fracasso da política industrial lulista. *Revista de Economia Política, 39*(157), 736–754.

Hallward-Driemeier, M., & Nayyar, G. (2018). *Trouble in the making? The future of manufacturing-led development*. Washington, DC: World Bank.

Hoffmann, R., & Gomes, N. M. (2010). Evolução Recente da Estrutura Fundária e Propriedade Rural no Brasil. In J. Garcia Gasques, J. E. Ribeiro Vieira Filho, & Z. Navarro (Eds.), *A Agricultura Brasileira: Desempenho, desafios e perspectivas* (pp. 45–64). Brasilia: IPEA.

IBGE. (2016a). *Indústria e Construção. Pesquisa Industrial Mensal de Emprego e Salário – PIMES. Dezembro 2015. Pessoal ocupado assalariado por seção da indústria (índice de base fixa mensal com ajuste sazonal), dezembro 2000 - dezembro 2015*. Atualizado em 18.02.2016. Retrieved June 20, 2019, from https://www.ibge.gov.br/estatisticas/economicas/industria/9298-pesquisa-industrial-mensal-de-emprego-e-salario.html?=&t=resultados

IBGE. (2016b). *2016 Sistema de Contas Nacionais: Brasil. Tabelas sinóticas – 2010-2016*. Retrieved June 20, 2019, from ftp://ftp.ibge.gov.br/Contas_Nacionais/Sistema_de_Contas_Nacionais/2016/tabelas_xls/

IPEA. (2019). *IPEAdata. Comércio Exterior. Exportações (FOB), 1974-2018, Exportações (FOB) – destino: China, Importações (FOB), 1974-2018, Importações (FOB) – origem: China*. Atualizado em 27.03.2019, 03.05.2019. Retrieved June 06, 2019, from http://www.ipeadata.gov.br/Default.aspx

Issa, D. (2017). Reification and the human commodity: Theorizing modern slavery in Brazil. *Latin American Perspectives, 44*(6), 90–106.

Jenkins, R. (2015). Is Chinese competition causing deindustrialization in Brazil? *Latin American Perspectives, 42*(6), 42–63.

Laplante, M., & Laplante, A. (2017). Planes industriales y los desafíos del desarrollo sostenible en Brasil. In M. Cimoli, M. Castillo, G. Porcile, & G. Stumpo (Eds.), *Políticas industriales y tecnológicas en América Latina* (pp. 133–174). Santiago de Chile: NU (CEPAL).

Maddison, A. (1987). Growth and slowdown in advanced capitalist economies: Techniques of quantitative assessment. *Journal of Economic Literature, 25*(2), 649–698.

Maranhão Costa, P. T. (2010). *Combatendo o Trabalho Escravo Contemporâneo: O exemplo do Brasil*. Brasília: OIT.

Marconi, N., & Rocha, M. (2012). Taxa de câmbio, comércio exterior e desindustrialização precoce – o caso brasileiro. *Economia e Sociedade, 21*, 853–888.

Marx, K. (1978). Capital. A critique of political economy. In F. Engels (Ed.), *The process of circulation of capital* (Vol. II). Moscow: Progress Publishers.

Marx, K. (1987). Economic manuscripts of 1857-1858 (First version of capital). In K. Marx & F. Engels (Eds.), *Collected works* (Vol. 29). Moscow: Progress Publishers.

Massi, E., & Nem Singh, J. (2018). Industrial policy and state-making: Brazil's attempt at oil-based industrial development. *Third World Quarterly, 39*(6), 1133–1150. https://doi.org/10.1080/01436597.2018.1455144.

Mattei, L. (2015). Emprego agrícola: Cenários e tendências. *Estudos Avançados, 29*(85), 35–52.

Mendonça, M. L. (2010). Le myth brésilien d'un éthanol socialement et environnement propre. *Alternatives Sud, 17*, 123–137.

MoF (Ministry of Finance of Malaysia). (1998). *Economic Report 1998/1999*. Kuala Lumpur: MoF.

Nassif, A. (2015). As armadilhas do tripé da política macroeconômica brasileira. *Revista de Economia Política, 35*(140), 426–443.

Nassif, A., Feijó, C., & Araújo, E. (2017). A structuralist-Keynesian model for determining the optimum real exchange rate for Brazil's economic development process: 1999-2015. In *CEPAL Review* (Vol. 123, pp. 188–208).

OECD/OCDE. (1979). *National Accounts of OECD countries/Comptes Nationaux des pays de l'OCDE, 1960-1977* (Vol. II). Paris: OECD.

OIT/ILO (Organização Internacional do Trabalho/International Labour Organisation). (2011). *Perfil dos Principais Atores Envolvidos no Trabalho Escravo Rural no Brasil*. Brasília: OIT.

Ondetti, G. (2007). An ambivalent legacy: Cardoso and land reform. *Latin American Perspectives, 34*(5), 9–25.

Oreiro, J. L., & Feijó, C. A. (2010). Desindustrialização: conceituação, causas, efeitos e o caso brasileiro. *Revista de Economia Política, 30*(118), 219–232.

Pahnke, A. (2018). The contradictions of neo-extractivism and social policy: the role of raw material exports in the Brazilian political crisis. *Third World Quarterly, 39*(8), 1656–1674. https://doi.org/10.1080/01436597.2018.1428088.

Palma, J. G. (2005). Four sources of "de-industrialization" and a new concept of the "Dutch disease". In J. A. Ocampo (Ed.), *Beyond reforms: Structural dynamics and macroeconomic vulnerability* (pp. 71–116). Washington, DC: World Bank.

Pessanha Neve, D. (2003). La réforme agraire au Brèsil: Une conquête sinueuse. In J. Picard (dir.), *Le Brèsil de Lula: Les défis d'un socialisme démocratique à la périphérie du capitalisme* (pp. 177–186). Paris: Karthala.

Rezende Figueira, R., & Antunes Prado, A. (2014). Trabalhadores Denunciam o Trabalho Escravo. *Hendu, 4*(1), 22–40.

Rodrik, D. (2015). *Premature deindustrialization*. National Bureau of Economic Research. Working Paper 20935. Cambridge, MA: NBER. The electronic version. Retrieved June 20, 2019, from http://www.nber.org/papers/ w20935

Rodrik, D. (2016). Premature deindustrialization. *Journal of Economic Growth, 21*(1), 1–33. https://doi.org/10.1007/s10887-015-9122-3.

Rowthorn, R., & Ramaswamy, R. (1998). *Growth, trade, and deindustrialization. IMF Working Paper 98/60* (p. IMF). Washington, DC.

Sabourin, É. (2014). L'agriculture brèsilienne en débat: Évolutions récentes, contraverses et politiques publiques. *Problèmes d'Amérique latine, 95*, 33–55.

Salama, P. (2012a). China – Brasil: Industrialización y "desindustrialización temprana". *Cuadernos de Economía, 31*(56), 223–252.

Salama, P. (2012b). *Les économies émergentes latino-américaines: Entre cigales et fourmis*. Paris: Armand Colin.

Salama, P. (2014a). Chine – Brésil: Une comparaison instructive. *Problèmes d'Amérique latine, 95*, 11–31.

Salama, P. (2014b). *Des pays toujours émergents*. Paris: La Documentation Française.

Salama, P. (2019). Amérique latine: goodbye industrie, hello stagnation. *Alternatives Sud, 26*(2), 65–86.

Santarcángelo, J. E., Schteingart, D., & Porta, F. (2018). Industrial policy in Argentina, Brazil, Chile and Mexico: A comparative approach. *Revue Interventions économiques,* n 59, mis en ligne le 01 janvier 2018. Retrieved June 27, 2019, from http://journals.openedition.org/interventionseconomiques/3852, https://doi.org/10.4000/interventionseconomiques.3852

Solow, R. M. (1957). Technical change and the aggregate production function. *The Review of Economics and Statistics, 39*(3), 312–320. https://doi.org/10.2307/1926047.

Suyama, B., Trajber, W. L., & Costa, L. I. (2016). Brazil as a development partner under Lula and Rousseff: Shifts and continuities. In J. Gu, A. Shankland, & A. Chenoy (Eds.), *The BRICS in international development*. London: Palgrave Macmillan. https://doi.org/10.1057/978-1-137-55646-2.

Svampa, M. (2013). "Consenso de los Commodities" y lenguajes de valoración en América Latina. *Nueva Sociedad, 244*, 30–46.

Teixeira Assis, W. F., & Rocha Franco, S. H. (2018). Coloniality in the appropriation of nature: Agrofuel production, dependency, and constant primitive accumulation in the periphery of capitalism. *Latin American Perspectives,* 22(5), 35–51. https://doi.org/10.1177/0094582X17707924.

Thatcher, A. R. (1979). Labour supply and employment trends. In F. Blackaby (Ed.), *De-industrialisation* (pp. 26–55). London: Heinemann Educational Books.

UK Central Statistical Office. (1961). *Annual abstract of statistics, 1961*. London: Her Majesty's Stationary Office.

UK Central Statistical Office. (1965). *Annual abstract of statistics, 1965*. London: Her Majesty's Stationary Office.

UK Central Statistical Office. (1970). *Annual abstract of statistics, 1970*. London: Her Majesty's Stationary Office.

UNCTAD (United Nations Conference on Trade and Development). (2020). *UNCTADstat. Gross domestic product: GDP by type of expenditure, VA by kind of economic activity, total and shares, annual*. Retrieved February 07, 2020, from http://unctadstat.unctad.org/wds/TableViewer/tableView.aspx

US Bureau of the Census. (1956). *Statistical abstract of the United States: 1956*. Washington, DC: US Bureau of the Census.

US Bureau of the Census. (1959). *Statistical abstract of the United States: 1959*. Washington, DC: US Bureau of the Census.

US Bureau of the Census. (1961). *Statistical abstract of the United States: 1961*. Washington, DC: US Bureau of the Census.

US Bureau of the Census. (1965). *Statistical abstract of the United States: 1965*. Washington, DC: US Bureau of the Census.

Vieira, P. A., & Ouriques, H. R. (2016). Brazil and the BRICS: The trap of short time. *Journal of World-System Research, 22*(2), 404–429. https://doi.org/10.5195/JWSR.2016.628.

You, J.-S. (2014). Land reform, inequality, and corruption: A comparative historical study of Korea, Taiwan, and the Philippines. *The Korean Journal of International Studies, 12*(1), 191–224. https://doi.org/10.14731/kjis.2014.06.12.1.191.

You, J.-S. (2017). Demystifying the Park Chung-Hee Myth: Land reform in the evolution of Korea's Developmental State. *Journal of Contemporary Asia, 47*(4), 535–556. https://doi.org/10.1080/00472336.2017.1334221.

Chapter 7
How Did the Incomes of Brazilians Change Under the Left Government?

Starting from the questions posed at the end of preceding chapter, we could presuppose that the growth in consumption among Brazil's poor, as well as partial improvements in education under the PT rule, might increase the proportion of the labour force that had skills that could contribute to the strategic task of transitioning to a new type of development, with a strong innovative component. The national statistics of household income and expenditure helps to clarify these complicated issues.

7.1 Incomes of Brazilians: Are They Big or Small?

Firstly, we can scrutinise the income levels of different groups of the country's population, in particular the shares of persons of 10 and more years of age[1] according to categories of monthly income, measured by quanta of minimal salaries/wages (Tables 7.1 and 7.2).

The presented data look somewhat paradoxical in light of the apparent achievements in social policy in Brazil since 1995 and particularly after 2003. Despite the obvious social orientation of the PT economic policy, the number of people aged 10 and over whose per capita monthly income did not exceed half of minimal salary was much less in the period of the Plano Real (with its stronger neoliberal component!) than under the PT rule. The number of people who either received no income, subsisted only on social benefits, or were occupied in informal sector with low wages and without whatever social insurance/security over 16 years, from 1995 to 2011, remained approximately the same. Its decrease in 2014 (although with subsequent

[1] 10 years are the age at which many children from poor families begin working to help to their parents to provide for families. Since 2013 the low level of such age was lifted to 15 years.

V. Krasilshchikov, *Brazil - Emerging Forever?*, Societies and Political Orders in Transition, https://doi.org/10.1007/978-3-030-50208-9_7

Table 7.1 Number of people (in thousands) of 10 and more years old (from 1985 to 2011) and 15 and more years old (in 2014 and 2015) receiving monthly income, measured in nominal minimal salaries (wages)

Groups by Monthly income	1985	1990	1995	1998	2001	2004	2007	2009	2011	2014	2015
Up to 1/2 minimal salary	9775	7150	4360	3894	6858	11,365	11,314	13,105	11,588	11,975	12,047
From 1/2 to 2 min. salaries	25,664	27,273	32,724	34,342	42,208	51,893	59,867	63,560	65,330	71,365	74,362
From 2 to 5 min. salaries	13,266	18,329	19,384	21,332	21,701	22,315	23,095	23,433	25,032	28,731	25,903
More 5 minimal salaries	8213	14,456	14,349	14,770	12,571	11,446	10,888	9719	9929	10,240	10,072
Without incomes[a]	41,092	45,906	49,163	52,093	53,058	51,170	52,261	50,620	50,850	33,857	37,472
Non-declared	243	516	956	1302	1291	1571	1936	2371	4257	3076	1937
Total	98,253	113,629	120,936	127,733	137,687	149,760	159,361	162,808	166,986	159,243	161,792

[a]Including persons who received only benefits

Sources and the author's calculations on: IBGE 1986: 8; IBGE 1990: 50 (table 3.3); IBGE 1997; 15 (table 4.1); IBGE 1999: 14 (table 4.1); IBGE 2002: 45 (table 4.1); IBGE 2005: 51 (table 4.1); IBGE 2008b: 57 (table 4.1); IBGE 2009: 59 (table 4.1); IBGE 2012: 58 (table 4.1); IBGE 2015a: table 4.1, IBGE 2016: table 4.1

Table 7.2 The share (as percentage) of persons of 10 and more years old (from 1985 to 2011) and 15 and more years old (from 2012 to 2015) receiving monthly income measured in nominal minimal salaries (wages)

Groups by monthly income	1985	1990	1995	1998	2001	2004	2007	2009	2011	2014	2015
Up to 1/2 minimal salary	9.95	6.29	3.61	3.05	4.98	7.59	7.10	8.05	6.94	7.52	7.45
From 1/2 to 2 min. salaries	26.12	24.00	27.06	26.89	30.65	34.65	37.57	39.04	39.12	44.81	45.96
From 2 to 5 min. salaries	13.50	16.13	16.03	16.70	15.76	14.90	14.49	14.39	14.99	18.04	16.01
More 5 minimal salaries	8.36	12.72	11.86	11.56	9.13	7.64	6.83	5.97	5.95	6.43	6.23
Without incomes[a]	41.82	40.40	40.65	40.78	38.54	34.17	32.79	31.09	30.45	21.26	23.16
Non-declared	0.25	0.45	0.79	1.02	0.94	1.05	1.21	1.46	2.55	1.93	1.20
Total	100.00	100.00	100.00	100.00	100.00	100.00	100.00	100.00	100.00	100.00	100.00

Calculated on the sources of the preceding table

[a]Including persons who received only benefits

elevation by 3.6 million people in 2015) can be explained as the result of accounting changes: since 2012 the total number of observable people fell by 17 million because the age threshold was lifted from 10 to 15 years.[2]

In addition, over the 30 years from 1985 to 2015, we see the steady growth of the number of people receiving monthly income per capita between 0.5 and 2.0 minimal salaries, i.e. the vast majority of them and/or their parents, senior brothers, etc., which were poorly paid labourers. The number of such people with low and 'almost low' incomes had increased approximately 2.5 times from 1985 to 2011 and continued increasing up to 2015, although the total number of observable people decreased because of changes in the methodology of counting. The share of such people had grown, too, from 27.06 per cent in the beginning of the Cardoso presidency to 39.12 per cent in 2001 and to 46.0 per cent in 2015, whereas the total number of observable people diminished after 2011. Moreover, it is notable that the number of people whose incomes were between 2 and 5 minimal salaries, i.e. people with low-middle and 'medium-middle' per capita incomes, increased from 1995 to 2014 only by approximately 50 per cent and from 1995 to 2011 (the years of comparable data!) only by 30 per cent, whereas *the share* of such people did not change or changed insignificantly either since 1990 or 1995. It remained almost the same with small fluctuations over 20–25 years.

Finally, even in 2013, at the end of the 'golden' period, just before decline of the PT's rule, 77.6 per cent of Brazilians[3] had incomes per capita up to 2 minimal salaries, including 54.7 per cent with incomes within the limit of one minimal salary (then 672 RS$ per month). In the poorest region, the North-East, the shares of people with such per capita incomes were 87.1 and 73.1 per cent, respectively [counted on: (IBGE 2014: 158, table 5.2)]. When the economic situation worsened and the country entered the recession, these indicators worsened. In 2016 the share of people, residents in particular households, with incomes per capita up to 2 minimal wages, increased to 81.7 per cent and the share of those whose incomes did not exceed one minimal wage (880 RS$) to 57.2 per cent. In the states of the North-East, these indicators were worse: 91.0 and 76.1 per cent, respectively [counted on: (IBGE 2017: table 2.2)].

Since 2016 the IBGE began counting people who live beneath the international poverty lines: US$ 1.9 per day on PPP (parity of purchasing power), the line of absolute poverty; US$ 3.2 per day on PPP, the line of 'ordinary' poverty; and US$ 5.5 on PPP, the line of poverty for upper-middle income countries. In 2018 the shares of people who lived beneath the called lines of poverty in Brazil were 6.5, 12.4 and 25.3 per cent, respectively. (In 2014, the last 'good year' of the PT rule—4.9, 9.9 and 22.8 per cent, respectively.) (IBGE 2019b: table 2.14 UF).

---

[2]See the country's population data in the same surveys of households (PNAD).

[3]Strictly speaking, these were not all Brazilians but those who were 'residents in particular households' (*pessoas residentes em domicílios particulares*), then their total number was 200,976 thousand people, only a little less than the total population, 201,033 thousand, at the mid-year.

These data allow us to presuppose that the reduction of poverty attained in Brazil under the Left-centrist governments consisted mostly in transformation of many extremely poor people into the 'moderately poor'.

Indeed, since the presented data are based upon the quotas of nominal minimal wages, whereas the latter raised from year to year, it is also worth considering how the incomes of lower income groups correlate with the minimal salaries and average incomes. In addition, it is necessary to take into account the concrete aggregate value and real amount of minimal salaries that have been used as a measure of incomes in this case.

Considering the ratio of the average income per capita of each income group to minimal salary, we can see that the incomes of the poor (those people[4] who had per capita monthly income below 2 minimal salaries) in their ratio to minimal salary were lower in 2011–2015 than in 1995 or 1998. This suggests that the increase in incomes for the poor groups that took place due to the PT's social policy was insufficient for substantial improvement of their living conditions. The same ratio for middle- and upper-income groups fell to an even bigger degree than for the lower income groups, and this relative fall meant a loss of rents from those with higher levels of education, an additional reason for their discontent to the end of the PT's rule (Table 7.3).

Now let us consider how the average income per capita in each income group changed over the long term, 30 years, in the ratio to the total average income per capita (Table 7.4).

Box 7.1 Comments to Tables 7.1, 7.2, 7.3, and 7.4

The sources of data presented in Tables 7.1, 7.2, 7.3, and 7.4 are yearbooks of the *National Household Sample Survey* (*Pesquisa Nacional por Amostra de Domicílios* – PNAD) that were published by the Brazilian Institute of Geography and Statistics (Instituto Brasileiro de Geografia e Estatística—IBGE) from 1967 to 2015. Since 2016 it has become a brief quarterly publication, mainly in the electronic version, deprived of many details and data which were available in previous editions. The first year performed in Tables 7.1 and 7.2 is 1985 when the military-bureaucratic authoritarianism conceded state power to civil politicians. The next reference marks are the years 1990, when the then President Fernando Collor de Mello attempted 'to kill a tiger of inflation by one shot' but transformed it into hyper-inflation, and 1995, the first year of the Fernando Henrique Cardoso presidency when the *Plano Real* was fully implemented. The year 1998 was the last year when this plan operated before

(continued)

[4]At the age of 10 or more years up to 2011 and 15 or more years, in 2014–2015. Obviously, if including observations of children beneath 10 and 15 years, the situation will be very similar as the incomes per capita in each income group, particularly among the poorest families where, as a rule, there are many children, will be lower.

Table 7.3 Ratio of the average income of each income group to the minimal salary (upon the base of current amount of each income in respective currency), 1985–2015

Groups by monthly income	1985	1990	1995	1998	2001	2004	2007	2009	2011	2014	2015
Up to 1/2 minimal salary	0.331	0.448	0.340	0.315	0.289	0.262	0.258	0.267	0.264	0.269	0.253
From 1/2 to 1 min. salary	0.831	1.063	0.930	0.915	0.894	0.904	0.897	0.910	0.917	0.923	0.911
From 1 to 2 min. salaries	1.477	1.864	1.600	1.554	1.494	1.508	1.445	1.458	1.461	1.461	1.462
From 1/2 to 2 min. salaries	1.183	1.490	1.283	1.228	1.222	1.238	1.200	1.217	1.229	1.230	1.227
From 2 to 3 min. salaries	2.497	3.145	2.630	2.477	2.472	2.450	2.413	2.404	2.446	2.432	2.440
From 3 to 5 min. salaries	3.941	4.993	4.100	3.838	3.917	3.823	3.787	3.802	3.855	3.873	3.744
From 2 to 5 min. salaries	3.240	4.194	3.363	3.206	3.155	3.158	3.010	3.055	3.004	3.000	2.984
From 5 to 10 min. salaries	7.184	9.074	7.340	7.077	6.956	7.058	6.711	6.845	6.807	6.851	6.551
From 10 to 20 min. salaries	14.282	17.868	14.660	14.092	13.778	14.027	13.495	13.366	13.615	13.461	13.298
More 20 minimal salaries	35.715	50.492	38.640	36.731	35.450	34.269	32.724	32.905	32.152	30.874	31.062
More 5 minimal salaries	12.493	17.972	13.846	13.111	12.325	11.579	10.665	10.761	10.473	10.405	9.886
Total (average)	1.824	3.310	2.540	2.415	2.028	1.823	1.653	1.602	1.613	1.816	1.697

Calculated on the sources of Table 7.1

Table 7.4 Ratio of the average income of each income group to the average income (upon the base of current amount of each income in respective currency), 1985–2015

Groups by monthly income	1985	1990	1995	1998	2001	2004	2007	2009	2011	2014	2015
Up to 1/2 minimal salary	0.182	0.135	0.134	0.131	0.142	0.143	0.156	0.166	0.164	0.148	0.149
From 1/2 to 1 min. salary	0.456	0.321	0.366	0.379	0.441	0.496	0.543	0.568	0.569	0.508	0.537
From 1 to 2 min. salaries	0.810	0.563	0.630	0.643	0.737	0.827	0.874	0.910	0.906	0.805	0.862
From 1/2 to 2 min. salaries	0.648	0.450	0.505	0.509	0.603	0.679	0.726	0.760	0.762	0.677	0.723
From 2 to 3 min. salaries	1.369	0.950	1.035	1.025	1.219	1.344	1.460	1.501	1.516	1.339	1.438
From 3 to 5 min. salaries	2.161	1.509	1.614	1.589	1.932	2.097	2.291	2.373	2.390	2.132	2.206
From 2 to 5 min. salaries	1.776	1.267	1.324	1.327	1.556	1.732	1.821	1.907	1.863	1.652	1.758
From 5 to 10 min. salaries	3.939	2.741	2.890	2.930	3.430	3.871	4.061	4.272	4.221	3.772	3.861
From 10 to 20 min. salaries	7.831	5.398	5.772	5.834	6.795	7.694	8.166	8.342	8.441	7.411	7.838
More 20 minimal salaries	19.583	15.254	15.213	15.207	17.482	18.797	19.801	20.538	19.935	16.998	18.307
More 5 minimal salaries	6.850	5.429	5.451	5.428	6.078	6.351	6.453	6.717	6.493	5.729	5.827
Minimal monthly salary	0.548	0.302	0.394	0.414	0.493	0.549	0.605	0.624	0.620	0.551	0.589

Calculated on the sources of Table 7.1

Box 7.1 (continued)
the start of 'free floating' and devaluation of real. Beginning from 1998, the presented data are taken over each 3 years except 2010 when the IBGE did not publish the annual household survey, so the years 2009 (the crisis) and 2011 are chosen for consideration. The last years included in the tables are: (a) 2014, when Dilma Rousseff was re-elected for the second presidential term and, simultaneously, the PT's development model was factually exhausted; (b) 2015, the first year of recession in Brazilian economy, the last full year of Dilma Rousseff's presidency before her impeachment and the last year when the annual survey under our scrutiny was published. Since 2016 the IBGE publishes the monthly and quarterly surveys that contain less data about the structure of income distribution. In particular, it has ceased to measure the personal incomes by quantum of minimal wage. The last issue of the 'Synthesis of Social Indicators' (*Síntese de Indicadores Sociais*) presents only the data about the poorest persons whose monthly incomes do not exceed a half of the minimal wage (the latter was equal to 937 R$ in 2017): 29.4 per cent of the total population in 2018, whereas this indicator accounted for 28.0 per cent in 2014 (IBGE 2019b: table 2.14a UF). It can be presupposed that the changes in methodology of statistics non-occasionally coincided with the dismissal of Dilma Rousseff from Planalto and have been conditioned by intention of the conservative political forces which have come to power in 2016 to hide an unpleasant situation in social sphere. It reminds us of the original name of statistics attributed to this branch of knowledge by its father-founder William Petty in the seventeenth century: the *political arithmetic*.

The original data concerning the amount of minimal salary in Brazil in the years 1985 and 1990 for Tables 7.3 and 7.4 have been recalculated taking into account the galloping increasing inflation. In particular, the minimal salary was raised three times over the year 1985 and ten times over the year 1990. In 1985, it was equal to 166,560 cruzeiros (CRs$) over the first 4 months, then it was raised to 332,120 CRs$ and was held at this level over 6 months, finally reaching 600,000 CRs$ in November–December. In January 1990, the minimal salary was equal to 1283.95 New cruzados (NCz$). On the first of February that year, it raised to 2004.37 NCz$ and on the first of March to 3674.06 NCz$. This level of the minimal salary persisted over the next 3 months but began increasing from the first of June onwards, each first day of every month. In December 1990 the minimal salary was 8836.82 NCz$. In the tables, the minimal salaries in 1985 and 1990 are calculated as the weighted averages over 12 months of each observed year.

As the tables show, the poorest groups, whose incomes per capita did not exceed the level of 2 minimal wages, augmented their relative incomes in the ratio to the total average income per capita very moderately since 1985 or since 1995. Their relative incomes reached the maximum over the observable period in 2007–2009, during the second term of the Lula's presidency, but decreased a little after this ended. In fact, the incomes of the lower income groups lagged from the average income to the end of the PT's rule only a little less than in the mid-1980s. As such, even the poorest groups, to which the governments of Lula and Dilma Rousseff paid particular attention, did not benefit very much from the proclaimed PT's social policy.

Every ratio, i.e. the *relative* indicator, has real content that can be expressed in absolute terms. Indeed, what is hidden behind the ratios of incomes to the average income and minimal salary? How did the real incomes of each income group change over the time period of interest? To answer to these questions, it is necessary to recalculate the income of each group in constant 1995 prices (when the Plano Real was completely implemented) and in 2010 prices (when the PT's policy blossomed to a full degree). The recalculations are presented in the respective Tables 7.5 and 7.6.

Both tables prove firstly that the year 2014 was the last year of the PT's achievements in social policy. The real incomes of all income groups fell after 2014, instigating the rise of broad disappointment in the Left government, even independently on the *Lava Jato* ('Car Wash') scandal, which began moving ahead with police investigation at that year. (This story played a key role in the evolution of the post-PT's rule crisis.) Secondly (and this is much more important for assessment of the PT's policy than temporary fluctuations of conjuncture and incomes), the tables prove that incomes of the poorest income groups only grew a very small amount between 1995 and 2014.

Finally, we can compare the real minimal salaries in the period of the PT rule to those in the past. Certainly, such a comparison is very relative because of the concrete structure of labourers' consumption changes in the course of time, so it is difficult to compare wages in the 1960s–1970s and, for instance, in 2010–2015 to each other. Nevertheless, even a relative comparison can be a useful tool for assessing the real dynamics of wages. Recalculation of these amounts accounting for consumer prices indices, according to the IPEA[5] data, allows us to conclude that the real minimal wage under the PT rule in 2015–2016 and up to today has been lower than in 1959–1962 under the Kubitschek and Goulart presidency. Indeed, it began exceeding the real minimal wage that existed under the military dictatorship only in 2007–2009 after a long fall in the 1980s–1990s (IPEA 2019; see also Bojikian Calixtre 2019: 46). Hence the PT policy in regard to wages cannot be seen as an outstanding achievement. Rather, it returned the workers' consumption to a level that had been reached in the past.

This modesty of the PT achievements is clearly demonstrated when considering all incomes from labour, whether they are salaries (wages) in the formal and informal sectors, or incomes of self-employed people (petty sellers, artisans, etc.).[6] In

[5]IPEA—Instituto de Pesquisa Econômica Aplicada (Institute for Applied Economic Research)

[6]The incomes of entrepreneurs from their labour on management, organisation and supervising are counted in the calculation of the average incomes from labour.

Table 7.5 Income of persons of 10 and more years old (from 1995 to 2011) and 15 and more years old (in 2014 and 2015) according to the categories of received monthly income measured in minimal salaries (wages), constant 1995 RS$

										Increment 1995–2014	
Groups by monthly income	1995	1998	2001	2004	2007	2009	2011	2014	2015	Absolute	%
Up to 1/2 minimal salary	34	35	36	35	45	51	53	60	55	26	76
From 1/2 to 1 min. salary	93	101	110	122	155	174	183	205	199	112	120
From 1 to 2 min. salaries	160	172	184	203	250	279	291	324	319	164	103
From 1/2 to 2 min. salaries	128	136	151	167	207	233	245	273	268	145	113
From 2 to 3 min. salaries	263	275	305	330	417	461	487	540	533	277	105
From 3 to 5 min. salaries	410	425	484	515	655	729	760	860	817	430	110
From 2 to 5 min. salaries	336	355	390	426	521	586	598	666	651	329	98
From 5 to 10 min. salaries	734	784	859	951	1161	1312	1356	1521	1430	787	107
From 10 to 20 min. salaries	1466	1562	1701	1891	2334	2562	2712	2988	2902	1522	104
More 20 minimal salaries	3864	4071	4377	4619	5660	6307	6405	6853	6778	2989	77
More 5 minimal salaries	1385	1453	1522	1561	1845	2063	2086	2309	2157	925	67
Total (average)	254	268	250	246	286	307	321	403	370	149	59
Minimal monthly salary	100	111	123	135	173	192	199	222	218	122	122

Sources and counted on: CEPAL 2005, cuadro A-23; CEPAL 2012, cuadro A-26; CEPAL 2018, cuadro A-26; IBGE 1997: 15 (table 4.1); IBGE 1999: 14 (table 4.1); IBGE 2002: 44 (table 4.1); IBGE 2005: 50 (table 4.1); IBGE 2008b: 56 (table 4.1); IBGE 2009: 60 (table 4.1); IBGE 2012: table 4.1; IBGE 2015a: table 4.1; IBGE 2016: table 4.1; Salário Mínimo Brasileiro

Table 7.6 Income of persons of 10 and more years old (from 1995 to 2011) and 15 and more years old (in 2014 and 2015) according to the categories of received monthly income measured in minimal salaries (wages), constant 2010 RS$

										Increment 1995–2014	
Groups by monthly income	1995	1998	2001	2004	2007	2009	2011	2014	2015	Absolute	%
Up to 1/2 minimal salary	87	90	92	91	115	131	135	154	142	66	76
From 1/2 to 1 min. salary	239	261	284	313	399	448	469	526	511	287	120
From 1 to 2 min. salaries	411	443	474	522	642	718	747	833	819	422	103
From 1/2 to 2 min. salaries	330	350	388	429	533	600	629	701	688	372	113
From 2 to 3 min. salaries	676	706	784	848	1073	1184	1252	1387	1368	711	105
From 3 to 5 min. salaries	1053	1093	1242	1324	1683	1873	1973	2208	2098	1155	110
From 2 to 5 min. salaries	864	913	1001	1094	1338	1505	1537	1710	1672	846	98
From 5 to 10 min. salaries	1886	2016	2206	2444	2982	3372	3484	3906	3671	2020	107
From 10 to 20 min. salaries	3766	4014	4370	4858	5998	6584	6967	7674	7453	3908	104
More 20 minimal salaries	9927	10,462	11,243	11,868	14,544	16,209	16,454	17,601	17,409	7674	77
More 5 minimal salaries	3557	3734	3909	4010	4740	5301	5359	5932	5541	2375	67
Total (average)	653	688	643	631	735	789	825	1035	951	383	59
Minimal monthly salary	257	285	317	346	444	493	512	570	560	313	122

Sources: see note to Table 7.5

Table 7.7 Ratio of average incomes from labour to the level of minimal salary in Brazil and by grand regions, 2001–2018

	2001	2004	2007	2012	2014	2016	2018
Brazil	3.48	2.95	2.51	2.36	2.38	2.30	2.27
	3.03	2.44	2.06	1.87	1.92	1.70	1.75
North-East	2.07	1.82	1.59	1.62	1.56	1.53	1.51
	4.19	3.42	2.39	2.68	2.74	2.69	2.61
South	3.63	3.30	2.30	2.57	2.62	2.47	2.48
Centre-West[a]	3.82	3.46	3.00	2.84	2.80	2.54	2.53

[a]Including the Federal District Brasília where incomes from labour (salaries) always exceed the salaries in other regions of Brazil. For example, in 2018 the ratio of incomes from labour to the minimal salary (954 R$) was 3.93, and in 2012 it was 6.35 (622 R$)
Counted on: IBGE 2003: 127 (table 4.16); IBGE 2006: table 3.13; IBGE 2008a: 225 (table 4.40); IBGE 2013: table 4.5; IBGE 2015b: table 4.10; IBGE 2019c: table 1.6 rend UF

particular, we can compare how the ratio of average salary to minimal salary changed from 2001 (on the eve of the PT's rise to presidency) to 2018, in the country as a whole and by grand regions (Table 7.7).

As the table demonstrates, there has been the steady tendency to convergence of the average incomes from labour with the level of minimal salaries in Brazil as a whole and in each region. Certainly, this convergence is mostly the direct effect of the rising minimal salary, but, at the same time, it testifies a slow increase in all wages which exceeded the established minimum. Hence, salaries and wages of a vast majority of Brazilian labourers did not notably differ from the fixed minimum, exceeding the minimal level of salaries/wages only a little. Moreover, a big proportion of the employed Brazilians earned remuneration for their labour at a level comparable to the minimal salary or even beneath it. For example, in 2014, when Dilma Rousseff was narrowly re-elected for a second presidential term, the average salary in the informal sector was 1165 Rs$ in the country as a whole and 750 Rs$ in the North-East region (for women it was lower, 887 and 603 Rs$, respectively). Meanwhile, the informal sector embraced 42.3 per cent of all occupied people in the country, 59.8 per cent in the North-East region, or 41,501 and 15,001 thousands of people, respectively [IBGE 2015b: 72, 70 (tables 4.10, 4.8)]. Therefore, it is necessary to recognise that most Brazilians had relatively low incomes, although it could not be said that Brazil is a poor country.

Comparing the presented data with those from other emerging economies, it could be said that the countries with successful modernisation stories (Japan after 1945, the East Asian 'tigers' of the both tiers, later Vietnam and China) began their rapid lifting on the ladder of development due to very low salaries of most workers. The low level of labour remuneration operated as a stimulus, instigating people to work harder for the sake of deliverance from poverty. However, the situation in contemporary Brazil, beginning from the 1980s up today, is another matter. Certainly most wages in Brazil are low, but they are, on the one hand, already insufficiently low for stimulation of hard work, and on the other hand they are too low for the large-scale stimulation of innovations and transition towards a knowledge-based economy. Brazil passed the stage at which low wages could be one of the factors of fast modernisation many years ago, and the country (which stagnated at the upper-middle level of development and incomes over a long time) could not use the same methods and tools that were very efficient at the lower levels of development for further modernisation. One of the main strategic tasks of Brazil consists in overcoming of its past heritage, i.e. moving on from *an economy of cheap labourers* ('cheap' from the point of view of the innovative, 'brain-intensity' development). However, as it has become clear, the solution of this problem is not easy.

7.2 The Structure of Private Expenditures: Consumption of Material and Immaterial Goods

The difficulty of deliverance from *an economy of cheap labourer* can be seen from analysing the structure of household consumption from the beginning of the 2000s to 2017/2018. Indeed, how many resources do Brazilians, particularly poor and 'semi-poor', expend for subsistence and for personal development, which determines a quality of labour force? Table 7.8 helps to answer to this question.

Perhaps, it is also worth measuring these expenditures in constant prices for better and clearer comparisons of the expenditures' dynamics on different kinds of expenses among different income groups. However, we must remember that a recalculation of the presented data at constant prices does not reflect the dynamics of expenditures of different income groups for different goals: the index of consumer prices is the *average* magnitude, whereas the real rate of inflation is not the same for all social groups on different kinds of expenditures. For instance, inflation of food products for the lower income groups is often higher than the average pace of consumer price growth. Therefore it is relevant to consider *the structure* of expenditures of different income groups for different needs and goals in its dynamics over a specified time. The changes of distribution (structure) of those expenditures are presented in Table 7.9.

Box 7.2 Comments to the Tables 7.8 and 7.9

Only the main types of households' expenditures are presented in the given tables. As a rule, they unite 'sub-types' of small importance and embrace them as a sum of such 'sub-types' of expenditures according to methodological explanations of the IBGE. The tables perform expenditures in monetary and non-monetary forms together. The expenditures in non-monetary form account for 17–18 per cent of all expenditures. Such expenditures include, for example, food planted by peasants for themselves and subsequently consumed by themselves, various objects appropriated by exchange for other

(continued)

Table 7.8 Brazilian households' monthly expenditures in monetary and non-monetary forms measured in current prices (in rounded off R$) according to income group, measured as quanta of minimal salary in 2002–2003 (I), 2008–2009 (II) and 2017.2018 (III)[a]

Types of expenditures	Groups of households by incomes (quanta of minimal salary)														
	Up to 2 min. salary			From 2 to 3			From 3 to 6[b]			From 10 to 15			Average[c]		
	I	II	III	I	II	III	I	II	III	I	II	III	I	II	III
Food	149	207	330	196	279	449	234	379	634	398	655	1144	304	422	658
Housing and concomitant services	188	304	616	264	447	908	357	659	1275	790	1522	2847	581	868	1500
Clothes	24	40	63	38	59	92	53	97	150	122	202	296	83	118	160
Transport	37	72	142	57	124	266	101	248	527	419	836	1493	270	419	680
Hygiene, healthcare, personal beauty	29	61	164	46	98	266	67	157	383	176	357	882	127	205	439
Education, recreation, culture	7	15	55	14	28	97	25	57	188	141	232	620	95	108	272
Other expenditures	8	23	79	24	49	167	48	124	351	248	495	1452	198	280	601
All current expenditures	442	722	1449	639	1084	2245	885	1721	3508	2294	4299	8734	1658	2420	4310
Non-consumption and other expenditures	13	23	52	19	41	106	36	90	197	156	479	668	120	206	339
Total	455	745	1501	658	1125	2351	921	1811	3705	2450	4778	9402	1778	2626	4649

[a]Minimal salaries used in the table have been 200, 415 and 954 R$, respectively
[b]2002–2003, from 3 to 5 minimal salaries
[c]Counting expenditures of the upper groups whose incomes are between 5 and 10 and/or exceed 15 minimal salaries per month
Sources: IBGE 2004: table 1.1.1; IBGE 2010a: table 1.1.1; IBGE 2019a: table 1.1.1.

Table 7.9 Structure of Brazilian households' expenditures in monetary and non-monetary forms (as percentage) according to income groups measured as quanta of minimal salary in 2002–2003 (I), 2008–2009 (II) and 2017–2018 (III)

Types of expenditures	Groups of households by incomes (quanta of minimal salary)														
	Up to 2 min. salary			From 2 to 3			From 3 to 6[a]			From 10 to 15			Average[b]		
	I	II	III	I	II	III	I	II	III	I	II	III	I	II	III
Food	32.7	27.8	22.0	29.8	24.8	19.1	25.4	20.9	17.1	16.2	13.7	12.2	17.1	16.1	14.2
Housing and concomitant services	41.3	40.7	41.0	40.0	39.7	38.6	38.8	36.4	34.4	32.2	31.9	30.3	32.7	33.1	32.2
Clothes	5.3	5.4	4.2	5.7	5.2	3.9	5.8	5.3	4.1	5.0	4.2	3.2	4.7	4.5	3.4
Transport	8.2	9.7	9.5	8.6	11.1	11.3	10.9	13.7	14.2	17.1	17.5	15.9	15.2	16.0	14.6
Hygiene, healthcare, personal beauty	6.5	8.3	10.9	7.0	8.7	11.3	7.3	8.7	10.3	7.2	7.5	9.4	7.1	7.8	9.4
Education, recreation, culture	1.6	2.0	3.6	2.1	2.5	4.1	2.7	3.1	5.0	5.7	4.8	6.6	5.3	4.1	5.9
Other expenditures	1.8	3.1	5.3	3.9	4.4	7.1	5.2	6.8	9.5	10.2	10.4	15.4	11.1	10.7	12.9
All current expenditures[c]	97.2	96.9	96.5	97.1	96.4	95.5	96.2	95.0	94.7	93.6	90.0	92.9	93.3	92.1	92.7
Non-consumption and other expenditures	2.8	3.1	3.5	2.9	3.6	4.5	3.8	5.0	5.3	6.4	10.0	7.1	6.7	7.9	7.3
Total	100.00	100.00	100.00	100.00	100.00	100.00	100.00	100.00	100.00	100.00	100.00	100.00	100.00	100.00	100.00

[a]2002–2003, from 3 to 5 minimal salaries
[b]Counting expenditures of the upper groups whose incomes are between 5 and 10 and/or exceed 15 minimal salaries per month
[c]The sum of data in each column from the line 'Food' to one 'other expenditures' may differ a little from the amount in the line 'all other expenditures' because the original data (see Table 7.8) are rounded off, whereas the data in the respective IBGE table are performed in reals (R$) and centavos
Sources: IBGE 2004: table 1.1.2; IBGE 2010a: table 1.1.2; IBGE 2019a: table 1.1.2

Box 7.2 (continued)

objects and consumed, too, gifts, various donations (e.g. gifts presented by employer to her/his employees on occasion of holidays), medicines consumed by diseased in hospitals, and so on.

Food (Alimentação) includes expenditures for food consumed at home either out of home (in restaurants, cafés, canteens, etc.).

Housing (Habitação) includes all expenditures for services, such as gas, electricity and water supply, garbage disposal, TV, the Internet, etc., stationary and mobile phones and maintenance of residence (current repair, purchase and maintenance of necessary domestic equipment, payment for rented housing).

Clothes (Vestúario) includes all expenditures for properly cloth, shoes, belts, bijouterie, tissues and jewellery.

Transport means expenditures for the public transport of all kinds (bus, tram, underground, taxi, trains) for urban, intercity, urban-rural (and vice versa) and foreign travels, expenditures for gasoline and/or ethanol for proper car, maintenance of the latter and purchase of accessories for it, payment for parking and obligatory insurance.

Hygiene and healthcare include expenditures for articles of hygiene and beauty (perfumes, goods for hairdressing, shaving, creams, toothpaste, soap, etc.), medicines, dentist treatment, expenditures for ambulatory treatment and stay in hospitals.

Education, recreation and culture embrace expenditures for education at all levels, from pre-school to post-graduation, including vocational education, various courses for improvement of professional skills, purchase of manual books, didactic books and journals, folders, bags for books, pens, school uniform, games, software, belletristic literature in printed either electronic form, expenditures for sports, theatres, cinema, visitation of museums, excursions and other similar expenses.

Other services and expenditures include hairdressing, key-makers services, mail services, payment of estate and vehicles' property taxes, income taxes, payments for life and health insurance certificates, property estate, vehicles and other belongings insurance, services of banks, services of attorneys (advocates), etc.

Since the column 'Average' presents expenditures of all income groups, including the upper and upper-middle ones with incomes from 6 to 8, from 8 to 10, from 15 to 20 and more minimal salaries, the data in this column are not apparently correlating with the data in other columns of the given table. What is important here is the demonstration of the consumption structure of most Brazilians, i.e. the people and households whose monthly incomes do not exceed three minimal salaries.

As Tables 7.8 and 7.9 demonstrate, the expenditures of poor and 'semi-poor' households for education, recreation, culture (entertainments) and healthcare grew much more rapidly than their expenditures for food, clothing and housing, overtaking the pace of consumer price index (the latter accounted for the period 2002–2017 about 3.5). Moreover, the share of household expenditures for food purchasing, particularly among the lower income groups (up to 3 minimal salaries per household), decreased faster than the same share in average and among all other income groups. Simultaneously we see growth in the shares of expenditure for education, recreation and culture among households with incomes beneath the specified quanta of minimal salaries, which covers the vast majority of Brazilian families. Figure 7.1a–c, where the level of expenditures in 2002–2003 is equal to 1.00, illustrate this very clearly.

These changes in household expenditure structure, namely, the notably diminished shares of expenses for basic needs, food and clothes on the one hand and the increased expenses for healthcare (in a broad sense), education and culture on the other, can be seen as one of the most significant achievements of the Left-centrist social policy. Seemingly, the increased share of such expenditures corresponds to the importance of education on the spending choices of Brazilians. Indeed, as already noted above in the discussion of Cardoso's election for presidency (Box 5.1), the prestige of knowledge and education has always been very high in all strata of Brazilian society, including those groups that could not access education at all. The wide-scale poll carried out in a framework of the United Nations Development Programme in 2009–2010 also gives evidence for this societal preference for knowledge and education. The questionnaire surveyed people in all states of the country and contained the following question: 'What is necessary to change in Brazil for a genuine improvement of your life?' The results of the poll are presented in Fig. 7.2, which shows education being highlighted by the greatest number of respondents as the most important change needed.

At the same time, we must not over-evaluate the growth of poor and 'semi-poor' households' expenditures for education and healthcare or, in other words, for human development. They are actually modest in absolute terms. As the both Tables 7.8 and 7.9 show, Brazilian society as a whole and its groups with low and low-middle incomes have mainly been oriented to the growth of material goods' and services' consumption, namely, to the improvement of living conditions such as housing and concomitant services. The biggest part of the *increment* of incomes of Brazilians over the period of relative well-being was used for the latter, and it is understandable, taking into account the concrete situation in this sphere. In this regard, we have to recognise that the Left-centrist social policy in Brazil has definitely been significant for reduction of poverty, but this policy did not (and could not) succeed in the emergence of numerous labourers capable of moving Brazil ahead to the new frontiers of development according to the contemporary challenges.

The insufficiency of the social policies and changes in the structure of the population's consumption are also seen when evaluating the achievements of this policy in the sphere of education. The evident improvement of various educational indicators does not necessarily relate to a radical elevation of educational quality. Indeed, deficiencies and poor quality of Brazil's educational system are evident in two respects.

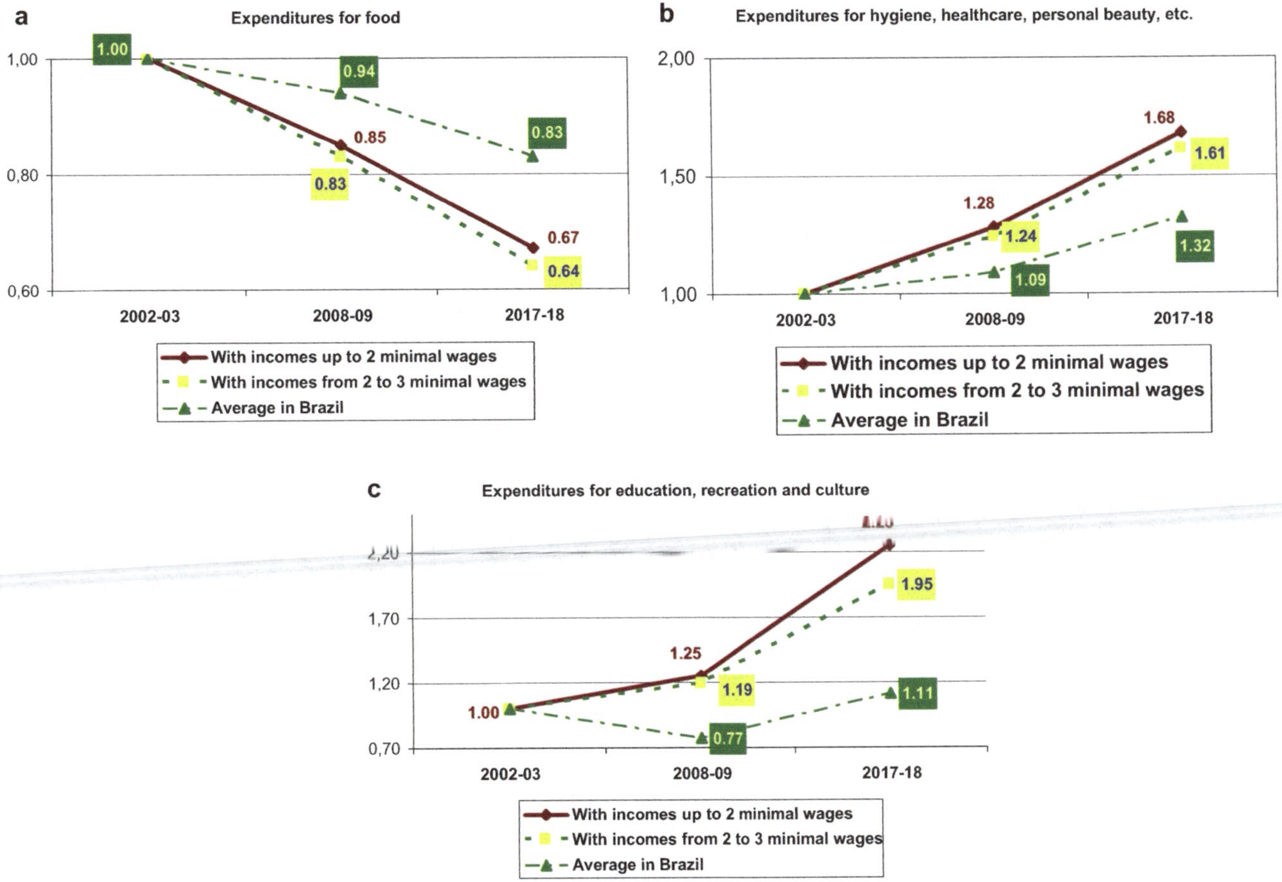

Fig. 7.1 (**a–c**) Dynamics of expenditures of the households with low (up to 2 minimal salaries) and low-middle (from 2 to 3 minimal salaries) for food (**a**), hygiene and healthcare (**b**), education and culture (**c**) in comparison to the average level of the same expenditures in Brazil upon the base of percentage of total expenditures, 2002–2018, the level of 2002 = 1.00. Sources: the data in Table 7.9

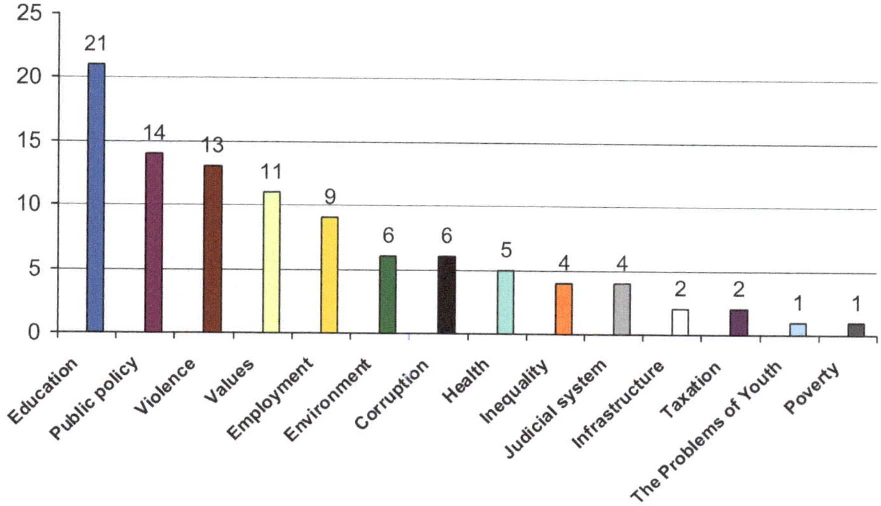

Fig. 7.2 Answers of Brazilians to the question 'What is necessary to change in Brazil for a genuine improvement of your life', as percentage of all answers. Source: PNUD Brasil 2009: 38–39. One of the most interesting and paradoxical at a first glance results of the pool concerned education. The biggest significance of education for improvement of social and personal life, 38.8 per cent, was fixed in Pernambuco, one of the poorest states in North-East with low level of education of the population, whereas the smallest one, 17.1 per cent, was in São Paulo, the state with the biggest and developed economy among all other states of Brazil (PNUD Brasil 2009: 40)

Table 7.10 Rate of functional illiteracy among people aged 15 and over, Brazil and Grand Regions, as percentage, 1992–2009

	1992	1999	2001	2004	2007	2009
Brazil	36.9	29.4	27.3	24.4	21.7	20.3
	33.2[a]	28.7[a]	26.3[a]	29.1	25.0	23.1
Nord-East	55.2	46.2	42.8	37.6	33.5	30.8
	29.4	22.3	20.4	18.1	15.9	15.2
South	28.9	21.8	21.2	18.6	16.7	15.5
Centre-West	33.8	27.1	25.9	22.0	20.3	18.5

[a]Only urban areas

Sources: IBGE 2001, table 3-2; IBGE 2003, table 3-2; IBGE 2006, table 2-2; IBGE 2008c, table 2-3; IBGE 2010b, table 2-3

Firstly, a large proportion of adult Brazilians are functionally illiterate. They are not illiterate from the formal point of view; but these people cannot understand a sense of the text they read, they cannot make simple calculations in a framework of four arithmetical operations and are unable to comprehend a schedule of buses or flights. Up to 2009, the IBGE published statistical data about functional illiteracy of the country's population (Table 7.10) but ceased doing it from this year, seemingly because the results cast a shadow on the pro-government propaganda.

Secondly it is necessary to recognise that Brazilian students fare poorly compared to international students on results of international control tests. For example, in

2007 the knowledge and skills of most Brazilian schoolchildren did not correspond to contemporary requirements. Only 27.9 per cent of fourth form pupils had acquirements in Portuguese corresponding to their age, and only 23.4 per cent in mathematics. Among students of the eighth form, the situation was even worse, with only 20.5 per cent attaining the required level of knowledge and skills in Portuguese, and 14.3 per cent in math (Fagnani 2013: 76). Eight years later, in 2015, serious shortcomings in the educational system of Brazil continued existing. According to the OECD tests of PISA (Programme for International Student Assessment) on mathematics and natural sciences, 15-year-old students from Brazil occupied the 63rd position out of 70 countries in natural science test (situated between Indonesia and Perú), and the 65th position in mathematics (near Jordan and Northern Macedonia). Moreover, Mexico and the neighbours of Brazil on the Southern cone of Latin America, Argentina, Chile and Uruguay, demonstrated better results than Brazil. Only the Dominican Republic occupied the lowest 70th position in both kinds of the tests. (In total, ten countries from Latin America and the Caribbean took part in the tests; these were also Colombia, Costa Rica and Trinidad and Tobago.) (OECD 2016: 67, 177). Obviously, the situation could not principally change in the next 3 years, and the PISA-2018 tests demonstrated intolerably poor results of the Brazilian students at the age of 15 years in maths and natural sciences again (OECD 2019b: 103–109, 112–117).

Undoubtedly, these results look very bad for the country that has the seventh or eighth economy in the world, manufactures civil aircrafts for international markets and is the continental leader in life sciences and biotechnologies. Such results testify to the ongoing elitist character of education in Brazil, in spite of all efforts of the social-democratic governments and the PT to enlarge access for talented youngsters from poor families to good education. This elitist character has been supported by the structure of expenditures for education in Brazil in the absolute terms and, in addition, as the ratio of such expenditures for the secondary and tertiary education to those for the primary one. At the same time, it is worth comparing the structure of expenditures for education in Brazil to that in the OECD countries. All these data and comparisons are presented in Tables 7.11 and 7.12.

As the presented data demonstrate, the expenditures for higher education (including research and development in universities in Brazil per student do not principally differ from the respective expenditures in developed countries such as Finland or Germany. The difference between Brazil and the average OECD data in this respect is even less significant than between Brazil and these countries. However, the expenditures for tertiary education per student in Brazil exceed those for the primary and secondary education to a much greater degree than in the OECD countries, including Chile. The gap between financing of the tertiary and elementary (primary and secondary together) education has somewhat shortened under the PT rule but remains excessive. Such a focus on higher education means a relative shortage of resources for the improvement of primary and secondary education quality. Also this preference for higher education at the cost of elementary education is a kind of social discrimination that advantages the middle and upper social groups (Mendes 2014: 186–190) because a poor quality of primary and secondary education restrains

Table 7.11 Annual expenditures per student by the level of education in Brazil and some OECD countries (in US dollars on parity of purchasing power for GDP), 2007–2012–2016

	Levels of education, years								
	Primary education			Secondary education			Tertiary education[a]		
Countries	2007	2012	2016	2007	2012	2016	2007	2012	2016
Brazil[b]	1862	3095	3762	1750	3020	3872	10,950	10,455	14,261
Chile[c]	2268	4476	5371	2222	3909	5278	6626	7960	9769
Finland	6234	8316	9447	7829	9985	10,427	13,566	17,863	17,541
Germany	5548	7749	8960	7841	10,650	12,268	13,823	17,157	17,429
Korea	5437	7395	11,029	7860	8355	12,370	8920	9866	10,486
USA	10,229	11,030	12,184	11,301	12,442	13,845	27,010	26,652	30,165
OECD average	6741	8247	8470	8267	9518	9968	12,907	15,028	15,566

[a]Includes expenditures for R&D in universities
[b]In 2007, the public institutions only; data for 2015 instead of 2016 (data for 2016—are not available)
[c]Data for 2006 instead of 2007; for 2013, instead of 2012; for 2017, instead of 2016
Sources: OECD 2010: 202 (Table B1.1a); OECD 2015: 219 (Table B1.1a); OECD 2018: 254 (Table C1.1); OECD 2019a: 274 (Table C1.1).

Table 7.12 Ratio of annual expenditures per student at the levels of the secondary and tertiary education in Brazil and some OECD countries to the level of expenditures for the primary education (the level of expenditures for the primary education = 1.00), 2007–2012—2016[a]

	Levels of education, years					
	Secondary education			Tertiary education		
Countries	2007	2012	2016	2007	2012	2016
Brazil[b]	0.94	0.98	1.03	5.88	3.37	3.79
Chile[c]	0.98	0.87	0.98	2.92	1.78	1.82
Finland	1.26	1.20	1.10	2.18	2.15	1.86
Germany	1.41	1.37	1.37	2.49	2.21	1.95
Korea	1.45	1.13	1.12	1.64	1.33	0.95
USA	1.10	1.13	1.14	2.64	2.42	2.48
OECD in average	1.23	1.15	1.18	1.91	1.82	1.84

[a]With the same notes as to Table 7.11
[b]In 2007, the public institutions only; data for 2015 instead of 2016 (data for 2016—are not available)
[c]Data for 2006 instead of 2007; for 2013, instead of 2012; for 2017, instead of 2016
Sources: the author's calculations on Table 7.11

opportunities for the poor to pass university entrance exams. The racial quotas introduced under the rule of Dilma Rousseff for equalising chances of young Afro-Brazilians and mulattos to access higher education have been ineffective, as well as the abovementioned (Chap. 5) 'ProUni'. Of course, this measure cannot be assessed as completely useless, but, in essence, it has alleviated, rather than eradicated, the causes of inequality in education. (Today, under the right-wing government, even the already limited access of higher education for the poor families' youth is under question. Moreover, we cannot be sure that Brazil will be able to save the qualitative elitist education attained in the years of authoritarian modernisation.)

What has to be done (and what could be done) to resolve this problem? Would it be sufficient to increase expenditures for education, as the PT's governments did up to 2016? Were there more serious and profound obstacles to continuation of the previous social policy than administrative mistakes and a shortage of resources?

In my opinion, answers to these questions have to be found, firstly, in the context of opportunities and limitations of social policy in the contemporary world, and not only in the concrete case of Brazil. Secondly, answers to these questions lie in the social-professional structure of contemporary society in Brazil. Anticipating further considerations of this complicated issue, it is worth noting that this structure has been indistinguishable from the social policy of Brazilian governments since 1995. And the PT, ruling from 2003 to 2016, has been not only hostage to the concrete global conditions that existed independently from the will of its leaders but also victim of the proper policy.

References

Bojikian, C. A. (2019). Sociedade salarial e resiliência: reflexões sobre a economia política da mudança estrutural. In M. V. Chiliatto Leite (organizador), *Alternativas para o desenvolvimento brasileiro: Novos horizontes para mudança estrutural com igualdade* (pp. 35–49). Santiago de Chile: Comissão Econômica para a América Latina e o Caribe (CEPAL).

CEPAL. (2005). *Balance preliminar de las economías de América Latina y el Caribe 2005*. Santiago de Chile: NU (Naciones Unidas).

CEPAL. (2012). *Balance preliminar de las economías de América Latina y el Caribe 2012*. Santiago de Chile: NU (Naciones Unidas).

CEPAL. (2018). *Balance preliminar de las economías de América Latina y el Caribe 2018*. Santiago de Chile: NU (Naciones Unidas).

Fagnani, E. (2013). Desafios e oportunidades para o desenvolvimento brasileiro—aspectos sociais. In CGEE (Centro de Gestão e Estudos Estratégicos). *Desafios ao desenvolvimento brasileiro: uma abordagem social-desenvolvimentista* (pp. 67–104). Brasilia, DF: CGEE.

IBGE (Instituto Brasileiro de Geografia e Estatística). (1986). *PNAD (Pesquisa Nacional por Amostra de Domicílios) 1985. Volume 9, t. 1 (Brasil e Grandes Regiões)*. Rio de Janeiro: IBGE.

IBGE. (1990). *PNAD 1990. Volume 14, n 1. Brasil e Grandes Regiões*. Rio de Janeiro: IBGE.

IBGE. (1997). *PNAD 1995. Volume 17, n 1. Brasil*. Rio de Janeiro: IBGE.

IBGE. (1999). *PNAD 1998. Volume 20. Brasil*. Rio de Janeiro: IBGE.

IBGE. (2001). *Síntese de indicadores sociais: Uma análise das condições de vida da população brasileira 2000*. Rio de Janeiro: IBGE.

IBGE. (2002). *PNAD 2001. Volume 22. Brasil*. Rio de Janeiro: IBGE.

IBGE. (2003). *Síntese de indicadores sociais: Uma análise das condições de vida da população brasileira 2002*. Rio de Janeiro: IBGE.

IBGE. (2004). *Pesquisa de Orçamentos Familiares 2002–2003. Primeiros resultados. Brasil e Grandes Regiões. 2-a edição*. Rio de Janeiro: IBGE.

IBGE. (2005). *PNAD 2004. Volume 25. Brasil*. Rio de Janeiro: IBGE.

IBGE. (2006). *Síntese de indicadores sociais: Uma análise das condições de vida da população brasileira 2005*. Rio de Janeiro: IBGE.

IBGE. (2008a). *PNAD. Síntese de indicadores 2007*. Rio de Janeiro: IBGE.

IBGE. (2008b). *PNAD 2007. Volume 28. Brasil*. Rio de Janeiro: IBGE.

IBGE. (2008c). *Síntese de indicadores sociais: Uma análise das condições de vida da população brasileira 2008*. Rio de Janeiro: IBGE.

IBGE. (2009). *PNAD 2009. Volume 30. Brasil*. Rio de Janeiro: IBGE.

IBGE. (2010a). *Pesquisa de Orçamentos Familiares 2008-2009. Despesas, Rendimentos e Condições de Vida. Rio de Janeiro: IBGE. Tabelas em Excel, versão eletrônica*. Retrieved July 06, 2019 and February 07, 2020, from https://www.ibge.gov.br/ estatisticas/sociais/ rendimento-despesa-e-consumo/9050-pesquisa-de-orcamentos-familiares.html?=&t=downloads

IBGE. (2010b). *Síntese de indicadores sociais: Uma análise das condições de vida da população brasileira 2010*. Rio de Janeiro: IBGE.

IBGE. (2012). *PNAD 2011. Volume 31. Brasil*. Rio de Janeiro: IBGE.

IBGE. (2013). *Síntese de indicadores sociais: Uma análise das condições de vida da população brasileira 2013*. Rio de Janeiro: IBGE.

IBGE. (2014). *Síntese de indicadores sociais: Uma análise das condições de vida da população brasileira 2014*. Rio de Janeiro: IBGE.

IBGE. (2015a). *PNAD 2014. Volume 34. Brasil. Rio de Janeiro: IBGE. Tabelas em Excel, versão eletrônica*. Retrieved July 02, 2019, from ftp://ftp.ibge.gov.br/Trabalho_e_Rendimento/Pesquisa_Nacional_por_Amostra_de_Domicilios_anual/2014/Volume_Brasil/Brasil/brasil_tc_brasil_trabalho_xls.zip

IBGE. (2015b). *Síntese de indicadores sociais: Uma análise das condições de vida da população brasileira 2015*. Rio de Janeiro: IBGE. Tabelas en Excel, versão eletrônica: Trabalho. Retrieved

July 03, 2019, from ftp://ftp.ibge.gov.br/Indicadores_Sociais/Sintese_de_Indicadores_Sociais/Sintese_de_Indicadores_Sociais_2015/xls/trabalho_xls.zip

IBGE. (2016). *PNAD 2015. Volume 35 (Volume Brasil).* Rio de Janeiro: IBGE. Tabelas em Excel, versão eletrônica. Retrieved June 14, 2019, from ftp://ftp.ibge.gov.br/Trabalho_e_Rendimento/Pesquisa_Nacional_por_Amostra_de_Domicilios_anual/2015/Volume_Brasil/Brasil/Brasil_xls.zip

IBGE. (2017). *Síntese de indicadores sociais: Uma análise das condições de vida da população brasileira 2017.* Rio de Janeiro: IBGE. Tabelas em Excel, versão eletrônica: Rendimento. Retrieved July 02, 2019, from ftp://ftp.ibge.gov.br/Indicadores_Sociais/Sintese_de_Indicadores_Sociais/Sintese_de_Indicadores_Sociais_ 2017/xls/rendimento_xls.zip

IBGE. (2019a). *Pesquisa de Orçamentos Familiares 2017-2018. Despesas, Rendementos e Condições de Vida.* Rio de Janeiro: IBGE. Tabelas de despesas em Excel, versão eletrônica. Retrieved February 6, 2020, from ftp://ftp.ibge.gov.br/Orcamentos_Familiares/Pesquisa_de_Orcamentos_Familiares_2017_2018/Primeiros_resultados/tabelas_despesas/tabelas_despesas_xls_20191108.zip

IBGE. (2019b). *Síntese de indicadores sociais: Uma análise das condições de vida da população brasileira 2019.* Rio de Janeiro: IBGE. Tabelas em Excel, versão eletrônica: Rendimento. Retrieved July 3, 2019 and February 07, 2020, from ftp://ftp.ibge.gov.br/Indicadores_Sociais/Sintese_de_Indicadores_Sociais/Sintese_de_Indicadores_Sociais_ 2019/xls/2_Rendimento_xls.zip

IBGE. (2019c). *Síntese de indicadores sociais: Uma análise das condições de vida da população brasileira 2018.* Rio de Janeiro: IBGE. Tabelas em Excel, versão eletrônica: Trabalho. Retrieved February 04, 2020, from ftp://ftp.ibge.gov.br/Indicadores_Sociais/Sintese_de_Indicadores_Sociais/Sintese_de_Indicadores_Sociais_ 2018/xls/1_Trabalho_xls.zip

IPEA. (2019). *IPEAdata. Salário mínumo real.* Atualizado em 08.05.2019. Retrieved May 31, 2019, from http://www.ipeadata.gov.br/Default.aspx

Mendes, M. (2014). *Inequality, democracy and growth in Brazil: A country at the crossroads of economic development.* Amsterdam: Elsevier.

OECD. (2010). *Education at a glance 2010: OECD indicators.* Paris: OECD.

OECD. (2015). *Education at a glance 2015: OECD indicators.* Paris: OECD.

OECD. (2016). *PISA 2015 Results (Volume I). Excellence and equity in education.* Paris: OECD.

OECD. (2018). *Education at a glance 2018: OECD indicators.* Paris: OECD.

OECD. (2019a). *Education at a glance 2019: OECD indicators.* Paris: OECD.

OECD. (2019b). *PISA 2018 results (volume I): What students know and can do.* Paris: OECD.

PNUD Brasil (Programa das Nações Unidas para o Desenvolvimento). (2009). *Relatório de Desenvolvimento Humano 2009/2010. Brasil Ponto a Ponto: consulta pública.* Brasilia: PNUD.

Salário Mínimo Brasileiro. *The constantly renovable resource.* Retrieved February 11, 2020, from http://portalbrasil.net/salariominimo.htm

Chapter 8
Brazilian Society as the Obstacle to Self-Modification

Each government, whether it is authoritarian or democratically elected, intends to exaggerate its achievements and to hide or, at least, to deflect from its shortcomings, not to mention failures. This is one of each government's jobs. The governments of the PT in Brazil, particularly under Dilma Rousseff, when the first signs of forthcoming economic difficulties appeared on the horizon, were not exclusions from this rule. In the course of the 2010 electoral campaign and later, during the first presidential term of Dilma, the Brazilian government thought up and propagated the idea to transform Brazil into a country with a prevalent middle class. What motivated this approach by the PT leaders? To what degree did it correspond to the real state of society? Did the social structure of Brazilian society substantially change in the last 20–30 years?

8.1 The 'conto de fada' About the New Middle Class in Brazil

Before considering the assertion about the growth of the middle class in Brazil, it is relevant to note that the PT government was not prone to wishful thinking on this issue. Such an attitude corresponded to the worldwide trend of the 2000s, when various authors and international institutions began discovering the shift towards the middle-class domination in social structures of developing countries' societies.

These 'discoveries' have been the conceptual 'co-brothers' in belief about the global shift of the world-system core towards East Asia. They are, so to speak, the co-products of the prognoses considered above in Chap. 2. For instance, Homi Kharas argued that:

V. Krasilshchikov, *Brazil - Emerging Forever?*, Societies and Political Orders in Transition, https://doi.org/10.1007/978-3-030-50208-9_8

> there is good reason to be optimistic about a new Asian consumerism emerging at a scale and timing sufficient to replace the forecast shortfalls in US consumer demand growth . . . several Asian countries, in particular, China and India, have reached a tipping point where large numbers of people will enter the middle class and drive consumption. (Kharas 2010: 8; see also Kharas 2017: 11–16)

The analysts of Goldman Sachs linked 'the shift in spending power towards middle income people' to the rise of middle-income countries, too (Wilson and Dragusanu 2008: 3–6). Thus, the global emergence of the 'non-West' has been driven by and coincides with the rise of new middle classes out of the North/West where the middle class, on the contrary, is contracting (Damon 2019: 40–44; OECD 2019). In particular, according to World Bank analysts, the process of middle-class growth embraces not only the East and South Asia (the region-champions in the growth of the middle class) but Latin America as well. As these experts argued, being evidently enchanted by impression of the 'golden decade' (2002–2011), the number of middle-class people in Latin America had augmented from 103 million in 2003 to 152 in 2009 (just 6 years!), and the continent was on the way to becoming the region of the middle class (Ferreira et al. 2013a: 1–4, 137, b: 1–4, 147). But 'to be on the way' does not yet mean that it 'has already become', so the same authors remind us that:

> despite positive trends, the region is not yet a 'middle-class society' where most people earn a sufficiently high income to consume, live, and behave like middle-class citizens. (Ferreira et al. 2013a: 136, b: 146–147)

However, it is relevant to ask: what are criteria of the middle class? What groups of population can be considered middle class?

It is necessary to underline that there is no broad agreement on this issue. For example, the criteria for middle class proposed by the World Bank have been constructed primarily upon a quantitative indicator: the level of daily income on parity of purchasing power (PPP) of a country's currency. The lower boundary of this definition is typically based on the poverty line in the USA and was set at 11US$ on PPP in 2011. The upper boundary is 50 or 100 US$ on PPP in 2005 (110 US$ on PPP in 2011), according to different authors (Berrou et al. 2019: 16–17; Birdsall 2010: 161–164; Castellani et al. 2015: 103–108; Dayton-Johnson 2015: 8–14; Kharas 2010: 8–12, 2017: 3–4; Ravallion 2009: 3–5). In regard to such criteria, obviously very uncertain and amorphous, Martin Ravallion remarked:

> The developing world's middle class is defined as those who are not deemed 'poor' by the standards of developing countries but are still poor by the standards of rich countries. (Ravallion 2009: 4)

The PT governments in Brazil, particularly in the years of the Dilma Rousseff presidency, defined the Brazilian middle class broadly using the World Bank indicator. In 2012, on the eve of the long recession, the government defined the low and upper boundaries of middle class monthly and daily income per capita in Brazil as 291 and 1019 R$ or, respectively, between 9.7 and 34.0 R$. For households the respective levels of monthly incomes were 1115 and 4807 R$ in 2008. It was therefore not difficult to proclaim that the middle class population increased by

30 million and, henceforth, 53 per cent of Brazilians, 104 million people, pertained to the country's middle class (Clément et al. 2018: 20–21; Neri et al. 2009: 6–7, 17, 2010: 12–14; SAE 2012: 7, 10, 12–14).[1] According to such an approach, the number of the middle class had increased from 2003 to 2014 (on the eve of the PT policy's decline!) by 52 million and reached 118 million people (Neri 2015: 79–80). This notable change in the income pyramid occurred hand in hand with the growth of mass consumption society in Brazil. Perhaps for the first time in history, the obvious signs of such a society began to appear in the country (Cary 2010: 82–90), in contrast to the past situation under the authoritarian regime when mass consumption grew only for the upper 25–30 per cent of the population. It is notable that customers within class C (who have middle-class incomes, according to the Brazilian classification) purchased in supermarkets approximately the same 40 types of goods as customers of the upper classes A and B in 2012–2013, towards the end of the 'happy period' of PT rule. In 2002, before the PT came to power, people of this category mostly purchased only 28 kinds of goods (Gaulard 2019: 133).

Certainly, taking this income-based indicator of the middle class, it is easy to paint a rosy picture of socioeconomic prosperity achieved under the PT governments. However this indicator, being incomplete by itself, is not strictly clear; it allows a choice of various lower and upper boundaries of middle-class incomes, which can be narrowed or broadened. The French scholars who studied the middle class and social policies in Brazil underlined the arbitrariness of such an indicator (Clément et al. 2018: 19–23). The same can be said about the income criteria of the global middle class because:

> [However,] as indicators of demand for various types of nonessential consumer goods, income-based measures of the middle class not only suffer from arbitrariness and major inconsistency but are also subject to a number of serious measurement problems. (Dadush and Ali 2012: 5)

Meanwhile, even from the point of view of incomes, whether they are calculated per capita or per household, it is difficult to classify a big part of the called middle class, 50–55 per cent of the Brazilian population in total, as people who really make up the country's middle class. As we saw in the preceding chapter, the majority of people aged 15 years and over received monthly incomes that did not exceed two minimal salaries. If we take into account the whole population, including children up to 15 years, then the share of persons with monthly incomes within reach of two minimal salaries notably increases. Thus, assertions about transformation of Brazil into a middle-class society did not correspond to reality, being, at best, a kind of wishful thinking. Such assertions deluded primarily the PT government, leading them away from an unpleasant truth.

In addition, using an income-based criterion of middle class ignores or, at best, underestimates important parameters relating to the means of production, accumulated households' assets (wealth), the attained level of education and the types of

---

[1] As Marcelo Neri noted in this connection, 'the limits (low and upper, respectively—V.Kr.) of class C would be as boundaries for the Indian and Belgian sides of our Belindia' (Neri et al. 2010: 29).

occupation. Meanwhile, the significance of non-income indicators is increasing today, while scientific knowledge, skills, intellectual and creative capabilities (in other words, human and cultural capital) become specific 'means of production' in the post-industrial era. A consideration of the social-professional structure of the so-called new middle class arisen in Brazil in the years of the PT rule induces doubt in the credibility of the official data about the growth of the middle class. And if it was possible to relate a part of manual skilled workers to the middle class in industrially developed countries in the 1950s–1970s, today, in the conditions of precocious deindustrialisation of Brazil, it is hardly relevant to include labourers with 2–3 minimal salaries into the middle class.

Now, when various non-economic factors become more and more important in the process of social groups' and inequality formation, and when the heterogeneity of societies (not only in Latin America but across the world) increases,[2] new social-cultural aspects become more significant in determining class boundaries. In this regard we must not forget that human capital and its most important part, cultural capital, have been formed and accumulated primarily in families, from childhood, while parents inculcate habits and skills, including a habit to acquire knowledge, to their children, and some Left-oriented Brazilian sociologists especially underline this rarely recognisable fact (Souza 2015: 240–241, 2017: 9–10, 173; see also Milanovic 2016: 214–217; Rivas 2019). Relatedly, however, we can disappoint the contemporary Left critics of liberal and vulgar Marxist approaches on the issue of class formation: when it comes to recognising a family's significance for children's nurture and education and the consequent effects on their well-being/poverty, these critics have predecessors in the neoconservative ideologists of the 1970s–1980s. For example, George Gilder, the author of *Wealth and Poverty* (a favourite book of Reagan), underlined a key role for family in the reduction of poverty and, therefore, for social mobility. The French neoconservative Jean-Louis Michau wrote that family plays 'the primordial role in education of children' (Gilder 1981: 69; Michau 1987: 49). Thus, we can see some coincidence of the seemingly opposite views on the significance of family for children's education and, in the end, for the formation of social classes. Such a coincidence reflects real patterns in social development, though different actors may draw different conclusions from the same facts.

By the way, it is also worth drawing attention to the role that has been attributed to family by the Brazilian social consciousness. As the polls carried out in a framework of the programme 'Brasil Ponto a Ponto' demonstrated, recognition of this role in nurture and education of children is broadly accepted among Brazilians. For instance, 43.1 per cent of the interviewed people marked the primary significance of family in this process, whereas only 24.8 per cent gave the same responsibility to school (as a social institution) (PNUD Brasil 2010: 100).

---

[2]Here I do not consider the cases of social-political archaisation that simplifies a socioeconomic structure of society. These are the cases of some African and Central Asian countries (e.g. Turkmenistan or Kyrgyzstan) as well as the dominating trend in Russia.

Considering not only incomes but also the attained level of education, character of occupation, material and non-material (intangible) assets and familial origin (the entire complex of socioeconomic and social-cultural factors that determine the formation of classes), we come to a clear conclusion: all assertions about the transition of Brazil to the state of a middle-class society have been 'fairy tales' ['contos de fada' (Souza 2015: 244–245)]. The role of fairy was performed by Dilma Rousseff when the socioeconomic policy of the PT had reached its objective limits in the changing situation and had to be modified.

The increase of labourers' incomes and enlargement of formal employment (which allowed the PT leaders and their economists to proclaim the fast growth of new middle class), took place mostly thanks to widespread computerisation in Brazil. A big part of new jobs, about 90 per cent, was created in the service sector with low productivity (while productivity in manufacturing industry, except a few branches, declined) (Aldright and Colistete 2015: 184–191). Jobs in the manufacturing industry do not require many special skills except, perhaps, a capability of pressing buttons on a keyboard. In particular teleoperators, including operators of call centres, made up the most numerous group of new comers at the labour market, so the so-called new middle class has mostly been *the new working class* (Antunes 2018: 78–80, 156–164 et ff.; Braga 2012: 143–158; 175–177, 2017: 106–107, 114–117, 165–176; Mansor de Mattos 2015: 77–79; Sicsú 2013: 41; Singer 2018: 88–98; Souza et al. 2012: 61–84). The average labour income of these people is about 1.5 or, at best, 2.0 minimal salaries. They work at centres and offices that function 24 h/day, 7 days/week. The length of their working day is often 9–10 h and positions can be short term and temporary, existing only for accomplishment of one or another project. Many of them are occupied for between 2 and 6 months and are obliged to change their place of work without alteration of job's character. It is hardly an exaggeration to say that a big part of the so-called new middle class has actually been not only a large new group of working class but, prima facie, the new *precariat*, though with formal employment, *carteiras de trabalho* and banking cards.[3] One of its character features consists in having higher levels of education and potential skills than is necessary for the work (Salama 2019: 52; Standing 2014: 970, 972). It succeeds in feeding dissatisfaction and alienation within the labourers, which becomes a source of social tension and motivates protests.

In Brazil this large stratum of labourers has mostly been the socioeconomic 'inheritor' of the under-proletariat created during the period of accelerated industrialisation. In contrast, the industrial working class, the social co-product of industrial boom in the past, has declined due to deindustrialisation. Hence, from the point of view of employment and its structure, the changes that could have been viewed as the growth of the middle class in Brazil in the years of the PT rule were

[3]Seemingly, there is formally a logical contradiction between assertions about the enlargement of the formal employment and the growth of precarious jobs. Really, both are sides of the same coin: what actually took place could be called as *the process of formalisation of precarious employment* (with signed contracts, transfer of salaries to the banking accounts, etc.).

insignificant (Scalon and Salata 2012: 395–398) or perhaps even negative. The World Bank experts quoted above estimated the share of middle class in Brazil more moderately than the former PT governments: about one third of the total population (although this amount is very debatable, too – V. Kr.), underlining its vulnerability to fluctuations in economic conditions (Ferreira et al. 2013a: 140–141 (Box 5.1), 144, 2013b: 150–151 (recuadro 5.1), 155).[4] Even those scholars who glorify the social achievements of the PT recognise that the *new* middle class does not exist in Brazil (Sicsú 2013: 60–72). In my opinion, it would be more correct to say that the new middle class did not *considerably grow* in the years of the PT rule; groups such as engineers, scientists, university professors, high school teachers, officials/technocrats, etc. continue to exist since the times of industrialisation but did not numerically increase to a notable degree.

Therefore, all talks of a fantastic rise of a Brazilian middle class camouflage an important fact: the Brazilian economy remains an economy of cheap labourers with deep socioeconomic and social-cultural discrimination of the majority by a privileged few.[5] This situation has not principally changed (or has changed very slowly) in decades: the internal periphery exists as always, supplying a lot of cheap labour to the economy, and, moreover, it has been reproducing (as we saw in Chap. 6, briefly scrutinising the practice of new slavery).[6] Since 2016, when Dilma Rousseff was impeached, this process has intensified.

In the light of these tendencies, including the use of enforced labour in rural areas, we have to ask ourselves: can these negative trends be overcome through the development of education?

Box 8.1 Study of Mathematics as a Threat to Authoritarianism (Implications of the Soviet Experience for Brazil Today)

Considering the tightly interconnected problems of education, on the one hand, and the reduction of poverty and precariousness, on the other, it is worth remembering the Soviet experience, which could have far-reaching implications for social policy in Brazil. The well-known achievements of the former USSR in mass education and several strands of scientific-technological progress created large groups of labourers who did not believe blindly in the official ideological dogmas. They had a critical consciousness and did not think that the so-called really existing socialism was 'the apotheosis of social progress'. These people gravitated towards autonomous jobs and were creative

(continued)

[4]'. . .as the poor move upward, in most cases, they do not jump all the way into the middle class' (Ferreira et al. 2013a: 135, 2013b: 145).

[5]Here, I do not consider the gender and race differences even *within* the total precarious employment. Although these differences decreased over the PT rule, they are still significant, showing the gender and race discrimination at the Brazilian labour market (Proni and Gomes 2015: 141–148).

[6]Certainly, today this internal periphery is mostly not rural but urban.

Box 8.1 (continued)
and negatively viewed any incompetence of the party *nomenklatura*. Their attitude to the Soviet system, sometimes semi-loyal, sometimes deeply critical, played a big role in the decline of that 'socialism'. It would not be an exaggeration to say that the Soviet achievements in sciences and education played a significant part, together with many other factors, of course, in the social-political death of the USSR. Unfortunately, however, ultimately it was not the most educated social groups who picked up the yields of 'perestroika' and subsequently transformed the old Soviet system into a bureaucratic-oligarchic capitalistic model with features of a criminal kleptocratic state.

Thus, the diffusion of scientific knowledge, particularly in mathematics and physics, as the Soviet experience showed, approved the aphorism of Mikhail Lomonosov, the founder of Moscow University in the eighteenth century: it is worth studying mathematics because this science establishes good order in the brain. By the way, it was not accidental that the Argentine junta in 1976–1983, one of the most detestable and obscurantist repressive regimes in the entire history of Latin America, expelled some subdivisions of mathematics from the school curricula because this discipline elaborates critical thinking which threatens authoritarian rule.

With regard to Brazil, the old elites ('elites do atraso') may sleep quietly whilst the quality of mass education, particularly in mathematics and physics, leaves much to be desired. How long will this state of affairs continue?

As said above, the governments of Brazil since 1995 applied considerable efforts to improvement of the education system, but those efforts were not very effective because they only created a small change in the social-occupational structure of Brazilian society. The profound problem of education in Brazil consists both in scant funding and poor teaching at the primary and secondary levels, as was already noted. Adequate funding is a necessary but still insufficient measure to radically elevate the quality of education in Brazil to a desirable level. Basic growth of expenditures for education alone is unlikely to help schoolchildren from poor families to learn because, as a rule, they are not accustomed to concentrate their attention in lessons. Indeed, if parents have not been able to help their children to evolve their intellectual capabilities, being occupied at hard and poorly paid work, it is difficult for such children to master the curriculum compared to children from the middle- and upper-class families. Even those poor families who do not overuse alcohol, work in good faith, are not involved into criminal 'business' and try to steer their children towards the acquisition of knowledge cannot give them all the habits and skills necessary for an adequate comprehension of curricula subjects (Souza et al. 2009: 213–214, 251–255, 286–288; Souza 2017: 88–89, 96–99).

Thus it became evident that to disrupt the vicious circle of 'poverty-illiteracy-poverty' (this circle began gradually disrupting under the Cardoso administration) was actually much more difficult than it seemed initially. In fact, this circle expanded into another with the inclusion of an 'additional' link: 'poverty-poor education-precarious employment-'improved' poverty'. This 'modification' is not only seen in Brazil; it has universal implications for many other emerging countries that are searching for an exit from the middle-development trap. Maybe this phenomenon has occurred in Brazil in sharper forms because of wider its pre-existing socioeconomic disparities, but this does not revoke its universality across the developing world. Brazil demonstrates how difficult it is to graduate from the status of mid-level development country when society is not ready for deep structural changes.

8.2 Conservatism of the Poor

The social policy of the PT, pulling out tens of millions of Brazilians from poverty and enlarging the channels of vertical mobility for them, could not transform these people, mostly under-proletarians by their origin, into contemporary labourers capable of operating with technologically complicated equipment and ready to permanently extending innovations. According to assessments of some Brazilian sociologists, about one third of the economically active population of Brazil (approximately 30 million people to the end of the 'golden' period, 2010–2012) were unfit for advanced labour activity (Singer 2012: 43; Souza et al. 2009: 21–22, 122, 479–480). Work in the service sector including work of teleoperators ['info-proletarians' (Antunes et al. 2009)], has been the most complicated job they can do, often being live 'supplements' to computer networks.

The new labourers (the *formalised precariat* of the informatisation/globalisation era) together with a big part of the 'old' unionised workers (the people whose wages have mostly been within the corridor between 1 and 2 minimal salaries) became the new additional social and electoral base of the PT. And this base significantly impacted the choice of socioeconomic policy of the PT government; the policy that finally favoured to the Right turn in 2016–2018.

As is well known, the PT was politically born in 1980 as the new party-movement under conditions of weakening dictatorship when the military-bureaucratic authoritarianism was transforming into *dictablanda*, the 'soft' dictatorship. It would not be an exaggeration to say that the regime, carrying out accelerated industrialisation, bred the proper social-political gravedigger. The PT was rooted in syndicalism of the industrial working class, and its geographical motherland was the industrially developed South and South-East, mainly the ABC triangle: Santo André, São Bernardo do Campo and São Caetano plus Diadema, the industrial belt around São Paulo. In the North-East, the region with the poorest states, the newly born party was not popular. Moreover, up to the beginning of the 1990s, some part of the urban middle class arisen as the social effect of fast industrialisation, too, supported the PT which had then been perceived as 'unlike all other parties'. Meanwhile, the process of *de*industrialisation, on the one hand, and the political struggle for power, on the other hand, changed the social and electoral base as well as the character of the PT. Already by the end of the first term of Lula da Silva (2005–2006), the PT began losing its initial base in the South/South-East and became the party of the North-East. In other words, it ceased being the party of unionised industrial labourers and began transforming into the party of the precariat and poor, the former and recent under-proletariat. The successful capture of parliamentary seats, governors' and mayors' offices and, at last, the electoral 'capture' of Planalto in 2002 allowed it access to solid resources. Many former trade-union activists occupied positions in various endowments and financial institutions, including pension funds, whereas the previous ties with the mass grassroots movements began weakening. As a result, the process of professionalization and bureaucratisation of the party evolved to an extending degree, together with its political-ideological de-radicalisation. The PT did not require 'radical disruption' to capitalism, as it was in the 1980s and the first half of the 1990s. Instead it began resembling the traditional social democratic parties with bureaucrats and professionals. Beginning as the party-movement, symbolising the deep transformation of society as the concomitant effect of authoritarian modernisation, the PT, transforming from the party of the South-East into the party of the North-East, became simultaneously 'the party of Order'[7] (Antunes 2018: 193–204, 221–225, 227–228, 275–276; Braga 2017: 101–105, 110–111; D'Araujo 2009, esp. 21–32, 57–79; Goirand 2019: 90–100, 177–183, 223–243, 252–263, 274–283; Samuels 2004, esp. pp. 1002–1017).

It would be very easy to explain the evolution of the PT by the necessity to seek political compromises in Congress, by the pressure of the international financial institutions or by the gradual bureaucratisation of the party machine. Certainly all these and other factors played a role in the transformation of the formerly almost 'anti-systemic' party-movement into a respectable political organisation 'like all others'. However, it would be excessive over-simplification to suggest that the PT defended the interests of the global financial capital and, respectively, to paint Lula da Silva – as a 'manager' for the advantages of 'big money', as Francisco de Oliveira and his colleagues do (de Oliveira 2010: 373–376; Paulani 2010: 123–130).[8] This visible defence of the financial capital corresponded to the current, momentary interests of those people who made up the electoral base of the PT in the 2000s.

The people who supported Lula and Dilma Rousseff made up, to a large degree, their new "disorganised and passive" electoral base (Boito and Berringer 2013: 34), who consciously voted for the PT in 2006, 2010 and 2014, because they were the main beneficiaries of the party's social policy. They were simultaneously interested in the conservative financial-economic policy aimed at low inflation with the respective rate of banking interest and strong real. This policy enabled them to enlarge access to relatively cheap consumer credits and to purchase goods importable from other less developed countries of Latin America and from China, even at the cost of deindustrialisation within Brazil. The growth of private consumption,

[7]Calling the PT as 'the party of Order', Ricardo Antunes refers to 'The Eighteenth Brumaire of Louis Bonaparte' by Karl Marx.

[8]Francisco de Oliveira wrote: "Lulism is a political regress, the vanguard of backwardness and the backwardness of vanguard." (de Oliveira 2010: 376).

including consumption of durable goods not only improved the everyday life of formerly poor and 'semi-poor' people but also softened some of the hardship and inconveniences of monotonous labour, when, in addition to undertaking unpleasant jobs, they had to spend 3 or 4 h in transport travelling from home to their place of work and back. (This is a widespread feature of everyday life for many labourers in São Paulo or Recife.) The growth of consumption raised the people who just now escaped from poverty in their own eyes; it was a mode of self-fulfilment for them, narrowing, often only in a psychological respect, the social gap between them and the genuine middle class, whereas all other ways of self-realisation and social ascension were unknown for them (Klein et al. 2018: 89–91; Souza et al. 2009: 138–142). Thus, the old principle of Brazilian conservative modernisation (modernisation for the sake of permanently extending consumption) spilled over the social boundaries of the privileged, upper and middle classes, and spread to the former poor.

Involvement of the large masses of poor into the race for consumption did not touch the existing system of financial capital dominance in alliance with the exporters of commodities. It did not principally modify that system even within the capitalist framework, in direction to the leadership of more advanced industrial sectors. It did not erode the profound socioeconomic fundaments of poverty, so some scholars who study the PT policy aimed at reduction of poverty call it *social liberalism* (Antunes 2018: 223–225, 228–230; Goirand 2019: 284–287). In this respect the current interests of the mass of ordinary people, new labourers and new consumers, coincided with the interests of the conservative circles of financiers and exporters of commodities, including big agribusiness, the social strata that were not worried about such things as, for example, industrial development, the rate of investment in new machinery, technological breakthroughs and other 'relics' of the twentieth-century capitalism. In fact, conservatism of the lower classes, the phenomenon brilliantly described by Karl Marx in *The Eighteenth Brumaire of Louis Bonaparte*, coincided with the 'old merry' conservatism of the upper social groups. This coincidence, temporary and unstable by its social nature, predetermined the strange political alliances of the Left-centrist PT with the Right and Right-centrist parties, the LP (the Liberal Party) and the PMDB (Party of the Brazilian Democratic Movement), the party that existed since the times of dictatorship. Such an alliance was conditioned by inevitable 'political flexibility', because otherwise it would be impossible to promote one or another bill through a labyrinth of various groups of interests in the National Congress. Also, it was propped up thanks to 'the common points' of conservatisms of the upper and lower social groups, which might exist until the economic situation allowed the redistribution of incomes in order to implement various social programmes, not touching the incomes of the upper strata.

However, this situation, depending to a large extent on the demand of China for commodities, could not last permanently. When China, this new 'friend' of Brazil and other Latin American countries, began approaching her 'perestroika' with the strategic goal to stimulate internal demand on the base of technological advances, the prices of commodities began falling. This fall was sufficient to subvert the growth in Brazil and to create fiscal difficulties. Simultaneously, the premature deindustrialisation undergone by Brazil restrained the opportunities for maintenance of economic growth at its previous pace, as in 2003–2012. Then the economic policy should have been changed in line with more consistent implementation of the plans PAC and *Brasil Maior* (see above Chap. 6). However it was not done. On the contrary, the government of Dilma Rousseff, not without 'friendly advice' of *companheiro Lula*, turned to more conservative financial-economic policy with emphasis on inflation targeting (as if Brazilian inflation would be merely the monetary phenomenon!), high interest rates and shrinkage of social expenditures. Yes, of course, this looked like a concession to the interests of financiers (known as *rentistas*) in a framework of the approved PT policy of compromises. Actually it was a choice for pro-recessive policy which led to further slowdown of the economic growth, to increased unemployment and other concomitant discontents (Sawaya 2015: 107–108; Singer 2015: 54–70, 2018: 53–76).

Could the government of Dilma Rousseff prevent the coup, radically changing the financial-economic policy? Was the political relevance of compromises with 'unfriendly' political forces the only reason to continue the conservative financial-economic policy when the global situation changed?

Unfortunately, the problem did not consist only in the political compromises with financiers and commodities exporters interested to maintain their financial stability. Additionally the problem was enclosed in the social and electoral base of the Left government. Any attempt to stimulate economic growth with partial re-industrialisation in the conditions of Brazil would lead to an acceleration of inflation and therefore could depreciate incomes of the poorest groups. It could also raise the prices of imported goods for everyday consumption because even restricted devaluation of the real would make the Chinese, Paraguayan or Peruvian shoes, clothes, cosmetics, etc. more expensive and hard to access for those Brazilians who sincerely believed in 'good mother' Dilma and her economic wisdom. Moreover, the necessity to fund social programmes (by the way, Dilma Rousseff was obliged to cut some of them, such as subsidies to some medicines and even expenditures for education) required an increase in the exportation of commodities despite the prices for primary goods beginning to decline. Involuntarily this succeeded in further economic and political strengthening of agribusiness whose representatives became irreconcilable opponents to the PT and conquered, step by step, one for one position on the political scene.

In addition, we have to take into account that many former trade unionists, 'people of comrade Lula', held important posts in various financial institutions, such as pension and social insurance endowments. They would hardly agree with whatever losses of incomes from financial instruments, whereas such losses would become inevitable in the case of redistribution of resources from financial to industrial sectors of the economy.

Finally, the fractions of industrialists who initially supported the government's intentions to intensify pro-industrial policy in 2011–2012 began distancing from the government when the situation worsened and the strikes in industry occurred with alarming frequency during 2013–2014.

As a result of unfavourable conditions, the PT government met a contradiction that could not be resolved by the framework of its policy. An attempt to restrain inflation through the manipulation of interest rates (although the *real* was then depreciating) meant a respective necessity to restrict the increased bargaining power of labourers. These measures could obviously cause discontent within PT voters. Meanwhile, the Brazilian inflation has rather been the cost-push inflation, being fuelled by monopolisation of the local, regional and national-wide markets (imperfect competition, in other words), so it was difficult to target inflation when using only monetary tools. [About contradictions and inflation targeting policy of the PT, see (Summa and Serrano 2018, esp. pp. 350–354, 358, 365–366)]. The government lost support of all social forces: the financial circles did not trust to the PT; industrialists were disappointed; agribusiness saw itself as an autonomous player; the middle class protested against corruption (see below) and decrease of its incomes; and the labourers (the main voters of the PT) suffered from deterioration of the economic situation (Costa Pinto et al. 2016: 21–31).

Box 8.2 The Alliance of Conservatisms of the Poor and Rich: Is the Case of Brazil Unique?

Since Brazil is one of the so-called emerging countries, it is worth asking the following question: Is the alliance of the two seemingly antagonistic social groups, the financial rentiers and exporters of commodities, on the one hand, and the new labourers, mostly employed precariously, on the other, rich and poor, respectively, inherent to the concrete Brazilian situation, unique in its social nature? Does Brazil principally differ in this respect from other emerging countries?

Not considering the group of all emerging countries, very diverse by their sizes, population, levels of development, social structure, culture, etc., it is relevant to mention two other countries belonging to the BRICS block: South Africa and Russia, whose prospects are, at least, unclear.

In South Africa the rule of the ANC (African National Congress) since the end of apartheid has resembled, in many respects, the rule of the PT in Brazil. The party, which is close to social democracy by its slogans and proclaimed goals, built its practical policy upon compromise with big financial and extractive capital for funding social programmes and assistance to poor people of African origin. Thus the poorest social groups gained from the ANC policy, whereas the richest, privileged strata strengthened their economic and social domination. Evidently, Ruy Braga had solid foundations to devote some parts of his book about the rise of the precariat in South Africa (Braga 2017: 67–93, 139–162, 201–219), where the changes had a formal character consisting in the juridical eradication of apartheid but did not erode the socioeconomic and cultural base of the former race and class inequality.

(continued)

Box 8.2 (continued)

In Russia ('Brasil é uma Russia tropical') the authoritarian rule of Putin and the party 'United Russia' ('the party of swindlers and thieves', as one oppositionist eloquently called it) had been based upon the coincidence of two conservatisms, too. One was of the lower social groups with their nostalgic reminiscences about the imperial 'greatness' of 'mother Russia' and the former USSR. Their real incomes increased in the first 12 years of the Putin presidency, 2000–2012, although this growth took place primarily due to the enormous inflow of petrodollars, not because of 'wise' economic policy. Moreover, it is necessary to recognise that even people with low incomes lived better in that period than any other time in Russian/Soviet history, the growth of tremendous socioeconomic inequality notwithstanding. Meanwhile, these people were not interested in serious modernisation, partly because they lost their skills and professional experience over the years of 'reforms' and partly because modernisation would inevitably require a change in the character of activity (to intensify labour efforts (mostly in qualitative respect) and to agree with losses of status and incomes in the case of structural transformation that would be necessary for the country but unsuitable for them).

Another conservatism was of the upper, privileged oligarchic-bureaucratic clans whose consumption of luxury, 'prestigious' goods elevated them to unseen heights and became comparable to one of the leading world billionaires. These groups were content with the reached state and understood very well that even moderate modernisation would be dangerous to their privileges and status. The conservative financial-economic policy carried out by the governments and the Central Bank corresponded to their main goal: to maintain the status quo.

Like in the case of Brazil, such policy faced inevitable difficulties and discontents in the conditions of the changed world conjuncture. The informal consensus between the lower and upper conservatisms began disintegrating, and even the appropriation of Crimea in 2014 could prolong its social life only for the short term.

While the economic growth slowed down, the retreat of the government from pro-growth policy became less and less effective. The conservative forces prepared the counter-offensive, and it became almost impossible to maintain the previous alliances of the Left and Right-centrist political forces in Brazil. The compromise between them for the sake of the new version of conservative modernisation, now with the Leftist bias, began destroying itself.

8.3 The Rise of New Requirements, the End of Compromises and the Blind Alleys of Conservative Modernisation

The first visible signs of the PT decline arose not in 2012, when the economy slowed to 1.9 per cent and employment ceased to grow, but in June 2013 when the authorities elevated the fares of buses and underground travel in big cities to compensate for the increased (suddenly?) expenditures for the forthcoming World Cup 2014 and the Olympic Games 2016. At first glance the elevation was insignificant: only 6 per cent in São Paulo. Was it much or not? When I stayed in São Paulo for the first time in September 2009, the price of a single one-way ticket for the metro was 3 R$. In January 2019 the fare had become 4.30 R$.[9] In the both cases, the prices of single tickets were approximately equal to one euro (1 €) and did not significantly differ from the fares in Paris or Madrid, whereas wages in France and Spain were considerably higher than in São Paulo. Therefore, even a moderate increase of fares was tangible for the large masses of the 'new middle class' whose incomes fluctuated between 1.5 and 2.0 minimal wages, then 1017 and 1356 R$, which was equivalent to 342 and 456 euros, respectively.[10]

The decision to raise the public transport fares in São Paulo and other big cities of Brazil provoked mass protests. Initially they were directed against this decision but soon embraced a broad spectrum of requirements that concerned issues beyond urban transport. Among them was enlargement of access to the systems of healthcare and education together with radical improvement of their quality; stopping further privatisation of transport and other public goods; and a refusal for 'big projects', seemingly prestigious but useless for everyday life of ordinary people ('Stadiums like in the First World, hospitals like in the Third World!?' was one of the slogans-questions of demonstrators.[11]). In fact, the requirements of protesters expressed material as well as post-material needs of a big part of the urban, metropolitan population. They were, to some degree, the effects of steep aspirations of the young generation, students who were simultaneously obliged to work and labourers who had to combine work with studying, precariously (although formally) employed with a 'flexible' schedule of work. These youngsters experienced neither the dictatorship's repressions of the 1970s, nor the galloping inflation of the 1980s, nor the physical impoverishment of day-to-day life in the early 1990s. Their expectations for permanent improvements of life had risen in the conditions of improving well-being

[9]Data from the website of São Paulo metropolitan transport (http://www.metro.sp.gov.br/noticias/11-01-2019-a-partir-deste-domingo-13-a-tarifa-de-metro-e-trens-passa-para-r-430.fss. Viewed on 24.09.2019).

[10]According to the exchange rate on June 21, 2013 data of the European Central Bank for the periods from 01.IX.2009 to 25.IX.2009 and from 01.I.2013 to 01.VII.2013, respectively).

[11]Also, there was such one as 'Professor costs bigger than a soccer player', which reflected a disappointment of some part of the so-called new middle class (the class of new labourers) in insufficiency of the government's efforts in the sphere of education.

during 1995–1997 and 2004–2011, but there were no real opportunities for further improvements at the same pace and on the previous path.

One of the main aspirations of urban youngsters who came to the streets in June 2013 concerned the prospects of professional career development and social mobility. They felt discordance between the attainable level of education and the hard realities of the labour market. Certainly, such a discordance between the youth's level of education and career aspirations, on the one hand, and the actually existing structure of employment, including the newly risen job vacancies at the labour market, on the other hand, is not novel for contemporary capitalism, whether we consider the highly developed countries or the countries of middle level of development like Brazil. This discordance has been a consistent satellite of development, at least since the mid-twentieth century when capitalism began to need mass secondary and tertiary education, often under pressure of the workers' movement. But this discordance may be either a source ('moving force') for further technological and social development or create conditions for extending discontent and conflict. The latter is evidently inherent more to developing than developed countries. In particular, as the ILO and OECD studies show, many 15–29-year-old youngsters, students at the time of pool in 32 developing countries, would like to work in a high-skilled occupation, although the local labour markets cannot satisfy their aspirations. And this discordance between aspirations and reality has been dangerously widening, while the attained level of youth's education is elevating, though the mismatch with the reality of the labour market is less plain in more developed countries (OECD 2017: 23, 66–69). This can potentially lead to serious social-political consequences, such as the rise of protests movements, riots, etc. The main protagonist in these movements may be the new middle class, namely, its lowest and most numerous parts whose incomes exceed the level of poverty only by an insignificant amount. [As Frank-Borge Wietzke and Andy Sumner noted, criticising social scholars and politicians for neglecting the low-middle class' role, 'political scientists have only paid limited attention to recent lower middle class growth', although this growth may have very significant effects for political and social reforms (Wietzke and Sumner 2014: 3, 19–22)].

In the case of Brazil, even the very moderate achievements of the Left-centrist governments in education succeeded in an excessive rise in youth aspirations for adequate employment, whereas the actual labour market could offer almost nothing attractive apart from precarious jobs, though with all the formalities of labour contract, in the computerised service sector (Fauré 2014: 70–71). In addition, against the increased incomes of the poorest strata, the rent from education (this permanent feature of Brazilian modernisation under the military or civil regimes) began disappearing.

Thus there were serious reasons for the young generation of Brazilians to be discontented with the socioeconomic situation in 2013. The rise of urban transport fares was the catalyst rather than the underlying cause of the spreading dissatisfaction with the authorities' policy which was voiced through these protests. In essence, the mass protests against the new tariffs signified the rejection of neoliberalism and its financial-economic strategy even in its 'soft', social democratic version ('social liberalism') according to the principle 'to assist to poor for advantage of rich'. Henceforth it became clear that the PT policy of compromises and 'social liberalism' accomplished its 'historical mission' of farewell to 'era of Vargas' and came to social finish, exhausting itself (Antunes 2018: 232–235, 245–252; Braga 2017: 222–234; Singer 2018: 99–126).

The protests of June 2013 began seemingly as the movement of the Left-oriented youth required the government to pay attention to *the problems of sociality* in a broad sense. They expressed a disappointment of some part of the social, electoral base of the PT and other Left parties in their policy, which removed the mass social movements from political life. A transformation of the PT into the party 'like all other' and its bureaucratisation weakened the previous ties, both formal and informal, with grassroots organisations. The PT lost its 'sense of reality', not conceiving what was happening to its voters, how the mass needs and requirements changed and what the new trends in urban society were.

At the same time, a big part of the middle class (actual middle class but not thought up by the PT propagandists) and various old privileged groups expressed discontent, too, while the economic situation gradually became worse. This stratum, not very numerous but influential,[12] was dissatisfied with the relative diminution of its incomes against the incomes of the poorest groups (Singer 2018: 100–101) (see Tables 7.2, 7.3, and 7.4). Certainly, the gap between incomes of the actual middle class (but not one existing in the heads of the PT apologists) and the lower strata remained hugely wide. It was much wider than the respective gap in highly developed countries and even in many countries of Latin America. Nevertheless, even a small decrease of the income differences between the middle class and 'the low rest' beat on self-consciousness of the former and demolished its superiority to the 'common people' in proper eyes. To some degree, it was approximately the same

---

[12] Jessé Souza attempted to distinguish four large groups of the middle class in Brazil by their value and political orientation, not by the level of incomes. In his opinion, the first group (it can be subdivided into ultra-conservative and liberal-conservative subgroups – V.Kr.) is fully and voluntarily subjugated to the dominating class of financiers (*a elite de dinheiro*) and defends its interests, though often performs itself as 'critically thinking' and 'morally perfect' stratum. This group perceives 'ordinary people' with suspicion and sense of superiority, supposing that there is nothing good to expect from them.

The second group is liberal, supporting liberal values ('liberty for all'). It has partly the same character features as the first group has, including a blind belief in proper 'moral superiority', and sometimes criticises the upper class but intuitively supports it if it feels a social threat 'from below' to its privileges.

The third group ('expressivists') has been characterised by its adherence to the cosmopolitan post-materialist values, such as opportunities for self-fulfilment or defence of environment, and can be called as 'the middle class of Oslo'.

At last, the fourth group (with 'critical consciousness') refuses the really existing social order and intends to change it (Souza 2017: 166–179). It is possible to add to what Souza had written that this group is biased to see the roots of many social problems in capitalism and is largely presented by the Left intellectuals. Some of them participate in social-political struggle on the side of labourers and poor have tight contacts with the Leftist movements like the MST and sometimes critically assess the experience of the Left rule in Brazil.

situation that had risen in the second half of the 1970s when the economic conditions began worsening and the middle class, the socioeconomic child of the 'miracle' of 1967–1974, had been dissatisfied with the authoritarian regime. History repeated itself but in the new conditions and with new arrangements.

The dissatisfaction of the real middle class with the PT policy, being motivated at first glance economically, had one more, namely, socio-psychological aspect. The middle class of Brazil, not speaking about the richest and highest class of bourgeoisie, financial and industrial as well, reacted strongly to the narrowing gap between itself and the poorest groups of society, though this process proceeded at a snail's pace. The elite groups observed with anxiety how the PT governments opened the channels of vertical mobility, how youngsters of the lowest social groups entered prestigious universities and how the people who could formerly travel between cities and states only by buses became passengers of aircrafts (Sicsú 2013: 42–43). (Once flying from São Paulo to Recife, I saw how some passengers, apparently representatives of the old, traditional middle class, looked on a family couple of seniors, which, probably, flew for the first time in their life, with undisguised scorn for them.) This irritation of the middle and upper classes at the social effects of the PT policy expressed the old 'demophobia' deeply rooted in the era of slavery (Anderson 2011a, b: 37).

It was not surprising that the people who held Right wing views joined the demonstrators with their own slogans and requirements. They proclaimed a fight against corruption and incompetence of the PT government, building on the momentum from the initial protests of the Left-oriented youth. Activation of the forces that tolerated the PT rule but never were friendly to the Left policy symbolised the start of a counter-offensive of the conservative part of Brazilian society, henceforth not only in media but in real political life as well. The alliance and compromises between the opposite forces came to their logical end.

Yes, of course, the collaboration of the PT with the PMDB formally continued: Dilma Rousseff was re-elected in 2014 for a second term together with her Vice President Michel Temer. However, a split in this alliance was only a question of time.

If the events of June–July 2013 were the first significant frontier beyond which the decline of the PT rule became evident, the second frontier, or decisive turning point, was the corruption scandal, *Lava Jato* (Car Wash). In March 2014 the Federal police searched the office of currency exchange that operated under a roof of the car wash and refuelling station *Posto da Torre* in Brasília.[13] As it became clear, this was not only a station for washing cars but also a point for money laundering in huge amounts. The investigation revealed a colossal network of corruption in which ministers, deputies of both houses of the Congress, parties' functionaries, states governors and businessmen of top rank were involved. The state-controlled

[13]Strictly speaking, the sources of this story have been rooted in 2008 when businessman Hermes Magnus reported an attempt to launder money of suspicious origin through his company, *Dunel Indústria e Comércio*, that manufactured electronic components for other industries.

company Petrobras was one of the main actors involved in this story. Its top managers distributed orders, particularly in the construction industry, among definite firms and took bribes for these 'services'.[14]

The scandal Lava Jato (more exactly, Lava Jato – Petrobras) succeeded in genuine creating a political earthquake which reconfigured the political scene as a result. The scandal helped the Right and Right-centrist forces (for instance, the PSDB created in 1988 as the moderate Left-centrist party moved to the Right flange, and its leading figures, e.g. José Serra, became the radical opponents of the PT) to displace the PT from its positions in the Congress, at the level of states' governors and mayors of big cities, states' legislatures and below, including many municipal authority bodies. As a result of the deep crisis of the PT rule, Brazil, together with the narrow re-election of Dilma for the second term, had gotten the most conservative National Congress since 1985 when the general João Batistsa Figueiredo handed over the presidency to José Sarney, the first civil politician in Planalto after the coup of 1964.

Under these conditions, Dilma Rousseff started to retreat in the face of two factors: the rising economic difficulties and the political attacks of the Right. She attempted to follow the previous path of compromises with big banks, financiers, agribusiness, industrialists of São Paulo, etc., often consulting with Lula, but this line of policy aggravated her difficulties and further weakened her positions.

The Lava Jato story was the accidental motivation, though very significant, but not the real reason for the operation of impeachment in August 2016. The actual cause of impeachment was the counter-offensive of conservative forces against very moderate attempts of the Left-centrist government to change the centurial paradigm of Brazilian development within the capitalist system. Thus, there are real foundations to evaluate the impeachment as a parliamentary coup d'état carried out not by the generals in military uniform, as in 1964, but by civil politicians with assistance of the conservative mass media (*O Globo* played the leading role in this process). And this parliamentary coup corresponded to the interests of the same dominating social groups (perhaps with some modifications of small importance) which were the main beneficiaries of the events of 1964: the financial circles; agrarian oligarchs; upper groups of the middle class, including the state technobureaucracy; and, partly, industrialists (Antunes 2018: 259–263; Reis and Soares 2017: 53–54, 59–64; Vieira Santana 2018: esp. 85–101; Souza 2017: 154–156).

The impeachment of Dilma Rousseff and inauguration of Michel Temer opened the way to a large-scale counter-offensive of conservative forces. The policy of 'social liberalism' was rejected by the authorities. The conservative Congress and conservative president began competing with each other in reconsideration of the

[14] It is hardly worth describing here this case in details. It had such big resonance that its main episodes are vouchsafed in Wikipedia and Encyclopaedia Britannica. It is sufficient to mention that such political figures as Lula, his and Rousseff's former minister of finances Antonio Palocci, the former speaker of the Chamber of Deputies Eduardo Cunha who were sentenced to many years of prison. On March 21, 2019, Michel Temer, successor of Dilma Rousseff in the presidency, was arrested, too, being accused in a framework of Lava Jato story.

previous socially and environmentally oriented laws adopted not only under the PT rule but also under Cardoso. The expenditures for education and healthcare were frozen for the next 20 years. The rights of Amazonian Indians were hugely restrained and the spaces of jungles and savannah were cleared for enlargement of the cultivated lands in order to advantage agribusiness and augment production of food and cane (for ethanol). This aimed to increase agricultural exports to China, where the apparently 'pro-modernisation' authorities, as it was noted above (Chap. 5), were not hurrying to carry out the 'green revolution', preferring to import food products.

In the last years, the ruling circles of Brazil preferred to return back, not just to the period of authoritarian modernisation of the 1970s but further still to the pre-Vargas era. They persisted in enclosing the country in a prison of the past ('a prisão do passado') (Bojikian Calixtre 2019: 45), ignoring the mounting problems – social, economic, technological and ones at the level of everyday life, primarily, such as violence and security. Certainly, Brazil today differs in many respects from the Brazil that existed in 1964 when the preceding coup took place. The competitive elections have been carried out, neither political parties are prohibited nor can the president dissolve the National Congress. All democratic political and juridical institutions formally function as previously, and it is worth underlining, not worse but better than in many other countries of Latin America. However, this circumstance does not mean that the recent 'conservative experiment' will last 3–4 years until the next elections. *Today* some external and internal conditions are less favourable for development than 50 or 60 years ago. In particular, *then* the transnational capital was interested in relocating part of its industrial capacities to Brazil, thereby accelerating industrialisation of the country and supposedly constructing (in the context of Cold War) the tropical variant of the mass consumption society as an alternative to the Soviet and Cuban models. *Today*, the global capital, prima facie financial, creates few productive capacities and does not counteract the premature deindustrialisation of Brazil. *Then* some conservative circles were interested in fast development of the advanced manufacturing industries, even at a decreased technological level compared to those in the USA, France or Germany. *Today*, the industrialists of São Paulo may find themselves in the role of 'poor nephews' in relation to the 'rich Uncles' (financiers and agribusiness). The latter dominating groups in Brazil are hardly intending to re-industrialise the national economy with a new technological base. Certainly, manufacturing industry and its new technologies will be developing but at a much slower pace than is desirable for changing the general trajectory of Brazil. In addition, *today* there are many external restraints on the active industrial policy. In particular they are conditioned by the country's membership in WTO and Mercosul: any measure aimed at supporting one or another branch of industry can be seen by trade partners as a form of protectionism. *Then* the General-President Médici and Geisel were freer in this respect of the economic policy.

Apart from the abovementioned conservatism of the lower social groups, there are also other obstacles of social and social-psychological character in the way of profound changes to the Brazilian development path. Namely, there is an astonishing tolerance of both poles of society in regard to deep socioeconomic inequality. The large masses of ordinary labourers and poor (*a ralé brasileira*) tend to agree with this inequality, which seems intolerable and insupportable by the standards of any European country. (When they disagree, their disagreement with the extreme, unthinkable inequality often takes on anti-social forms, such as violence and criminality. Brazil is one of the most criminalised and violent middle-income countries in the world, exceeding even Mexico in this respect.) (Vidal 2016: 8, 2017: 86–88). At the same time, the upper social groups in their majority perceive the negative effects of shocking inequality as some 'inevitable evil' and prefer to build their settlements with tall hedges equipped by barbed wires and complicated alarm systems. In essence, a tolerance of inequality, which exceeds all reasonable and socially secure sizes, is one of the most obvious forms of Brazil's slavery heritage, whether it is viewed from the upper or lower strata of society.

This heavy heritage appears, by the way, to be preferred by many businessmen, particularly in the north-eastern states of Brazil, who hire workers with only primary, basic education. The low education level has been treated as important condition of weak aspirations of workers according to the old, 'pre-industrial' principle of management: poorly educated workers will agree with low wages and poor conditions of labour (de Ferranti et al. 2004: 186).

At the same time, many representatives of the Brazilian elite groups, whether they are businessmen, high-rank officials or professionals, recognise that the most acute problems of Brazil are those of poverty, extreme inequality, poor healthcare, housing and education. The latter is considered the main key to resolving the other social and economic problems. Meanwhile, as surveys at the beginning of the 1990s showed, the elite groups in Brazil do not feel responsible for changing the recent situation. They prefer to burden someone else (the state, local authorities, NGO and so on) but not themselves with expenditures for social policy. Then it remains unclear where the state can get money and other resources for these purposes (Reis 1999: 131–134, 2000: 182–188, 2012: 184–186, 188–193), while, as events in the last years demonstrated, the upper and middle strata have no desire to redistribute their incomes and privileges to fund the expenditures for social needs. A similar situation has been observed in Russia where entrepreneurs complain of the inadequate nature of youngsters' education ('they know nothing, they can do nothing', etc.) but do not invest in training graduation of specialists according to the needs of their businesses and economy as a whole.

Seemingly, there is the illogical contradiction in the views of the Brazilian elite. Indeed, how is it possible to insist on the necessity of resolving the social problems but not wanting to pay for the respective policy? Really, this contradiction reflects, on the one hand, being accustomed to an existence of the omnipresent and omnipotent state. This is a custom inherited from the periods of Vargas and generals-modernisers when the state played the leading role in development and was the main actor of modernisation policy. On the other hand, this contradiction is the effect of the old social-cultural gap and split between the top and bottom poles of society, the gap rooted in the epoch of slavery. A glance from the top strata to 'the common people' is, in essence, a view of masters on their slaves. The latter are bad, dirty, lazy, illiterate, etc., but their existence is inevitable: unfortunately, life is built that way, and it just cannot be helped.

One of the most significant obstacles of institutional character to Brazilian development is the system of taxation, which is regressive in its essence. This system contradicts the Brazilian Constitution of 1988 which proclaims the orientation of the state to social issues (Fandiño and Kerstenetzky 2019: 308–310, 320–323). As a whole, it is advantageous for those groups which have been called 'rentists' in Brazil, i.e. they earn their incomes mostly in the form of rent, whether the latter is financial (banking or from bond market) or ground rent (from agricultural activity, extraction of minerals or leasing of immobile property). Meanwhile, the maximal rate of taxes is 27.5 per cent of incomes; much less than in the USA, Canada or Japan, not to mention countries of the European Union. The rate of tax for heritable assets and property is from 2.0 to 4.0 per cent of the latter's value, unthinkably low by measure of developed countries. In addition, dividends earned by individuals are not subject to taxation: this practice actually justifies a legal tax evasion that is eminently suitable for holders of various bonds (Carneiro and Lima 2017). At the same time, the main charge of taxation is levied on labour and consumption; it includes the indirect taxes which have been paid by most people for whom salary is the only income (Fauré 2014: 72–73; IPEA 2011: 3–6, 12–13). The indirect taxes that are often included into various tariffs (e.g. for electricity or water supply) are very high in Brazil. Thereby, the poor groups partly finance the social expenditures, which ought supposedly to improve their conditions. In other words, one of the features of the Brazilian taxation system is the self-financing of the social programmes by those people who receive a part of their incomes and benefits due to such programmes.

Obviously, a reform of the country's taxation system appears an indispensable task. Meanwhile, it is insufficient only to reform the taxation system in direction to its more progressive and equitable character. It is also necessary to change the system of expenditures of collected taxes with a focus on improving human capital. Indeed, this is a general recommendation for taxation proposed by the OECD (O'Reilly 2018). As it was said above, the experience of Brazil demonstrated in the last 15–20 years that an augmentation of the expenditures for education is relatively ineffective because the children from poor families are unprepared to master school curricula at the required level. Therefore, it is necessary to revise the social policy aiming it at equalising, as far as possible, the chances of all children for successful studying independent of their social origin. In this regard, it is worth noting the analytical reports launched by the World Bank and Inter-American Development Bank some years ago about the principal importance of investment in early childhood (Berlinski and Shady 2015; Sayre et al. 2015). And let us not be surprised at such peculiar humanism of the Bretton-Woods institutions, though some Leftists have always been ready to expose 'a hypocrisy' of the global financial capital, etc., instead of comprehending why these institutions began worrying about the development of preschool-age children. The proposals of the mentioned reports reflect the necessity of modifying the principal approaches to social policy and aiming them at the elimination of the causes and sources of poverty, rather than only its quantitative reduction. Is Brazilian society ready for such radical change?

Today, we see these new contradictions rising in Brazil; between an insistent necessity of large-scale reforms (the new modernisation, in essence) and lack of motivation within society to modify itself. Unfortunately, this contradiction arises not only in Brazil but in many other emerging and developed countries across the world.

References

Aldright, M. D., & Colistete, P. R. (2015). Industrial growth and structural change: Brazil in a long-run perspective. In W. Naudé, A. Szirmai, & N. Haraguchi (Eds.), *Structural change and industrial development in the BRICS* (pp. 162–193). Oxford: Oxford University Press.

Anderson, P. (2011a, March 31). Lula's Brazil. *London Review of Books*, *33*(7), 3–12 (The electronic version. Retrieved September 27, 2019, from https://www.lrb.co.uk/v33/n07/perry-anderson/lulas-brazil; archive of the author).

Anderson, P. (2011b). O Brasil de Lula. *Novos Estudos, 91*, 23–52.

Antunes, R. (2018). *O Privilégio da Servidão: O novo proletariado de serviços na era digital.* São Paulo: Boitempo.

Antunes, R., Braga, R., et al. (2009). *Infoproletários. Degradação real do trabalho virtual.* São Paulo: Boitempo.

Berlinski, S., & Shady, N. (Eds.). (2015). *The early years: Child well-being and the role of public policy*. New York: Palgrave Macmillan – Inter-American Development Bank.

Berrou, J.-P., Clément, M., Combarnous, F., Darbon, D., Fauré, Y.-A., & Rougier, E. (2019). *L'essor des classes moyennes dans les pays en développement et émergents : une étude comparative des enjeux d'identification, de caractérisation et de politiques publiques. Brésil, Côte d'Ivoire, Turquie, Vietnam (Papiers de recherche AFD, n° 2019-89)*. Paris: AFD.

Birdsall, N. (2010). The (indispensable) middle class in developing countries. In R. Kanbur & M. Spence (Eds.), *Equity and growth in a globalizing world* (pp. 157–187). Washington, DC: The World Bank.

Boito Junior, A., & Berringer, T. (2013). Brasil: Classes sociais, neodesenvolvimentismo e politica externa nos governos Lula e Dilma. *Revista de Sociologia e Politica, 21*(47), 31–38.

Bojikian Calixtre, A. (2019). Sociedade salarial e resiliência: reflexões sobre a economia política da mudança estrutural. In Chiliatto Leite M.V. *(organizador).* Alternativas para o desenvolvimento brasileiro: Novos horizontes para mudança estrutural com igualdade. Santiago de Chile: Comissão Econômica para a América Latina e o Caribe (CEPAL), pp. 35-49

Braga, R. (2012). *A Política do Precariado: Do populismo á hegemonia lulista.* São Paulo: Boitempo (versão eletrônica).

Braga, R. (2017). *A Rebeldia do Precariado: trabalho e neoliberalismo no Sul global.* São Paulo: Boitempo.

Carneiro, M., & Lima, F. (2017, September 24). 'Desigualdade no Brasil é escolha política', diz economista. *Folha de São Paulo*. Retrieved October 02, 2017, from http://www1.folha.uol.com.br/mercado/2017/09/1921236-desigualdade-no-brasil-e-escolha-politica-diz-economista.shtml (archive of the author).

Cary, P. (2010). Réflexions sur la «société de consommation» brèsilienne. *Problèmes d'Amérique latine, 78*, 75–90.

Castellani, F., Parent, G., & Zenteno, G. J. (2015). Who is the Latin American middle class? Relative-income and multidimensional approaches. In J. Dayton-Johnson (Ed.), *Latin America's emerging middle classes. Economic perspectives* (pp. 101–129). Houndmills, Basingstoke: Palgrave Macmillan.

Clément, M., Fauré, Y.-A., Berrou, J.-P., Combarnous, F., Darbon, D., & Rougier, E. (2018). *Anatomie de la classe moyenne brésilienne : identification, caractérisation et implications pour les politiques publiques (Papiers de recherche AFD, n° 2018-67)*. Paris: AFD.

Costa Pinto, E., et al. (2016). *A economia política dos governos Dilma: acumulação, bloco no poder e crise. Texto para Discussão 004 – 2016*. Rio de Janeiro: UFRJ (Universidade Federal de Rio de Janeiro), Instituto de Economia.

D'Araujo M.C. (com participação de C. Lameirão). (2009). *A elite dirigente do governo Lula*. Rio de Janeiro: FGV (Fundação Getúlio Vargas).

Dadush, U., & Ali, S. (2012). *In search of the global middle class. A new index. The Carnegie papers. International economics*. Washington, DC: Carnegie Endowment for International Peace.

Damon, J. (2019). La dynamique des classes moyennes: Déclin au Nord, essor au Sud. *Futuribles, 432*, 33–47.

Dayton-Johnson, J. (2015). Making sense of Latin America's middle classes. In J. Dayton-Johnson (Ed.), *Latin America's emerging middle classes* (pp. 1–31). London: Palgrave Macmillan.

de Ferranti, D., Perry, G., Ferreira, F. H. G., & Walton, M. (2004). *Inequality in Latin America: Breaking with history?* Washington, DC: World Bank.

de Oliveira, F. (2010). O avesso do avesso. In F. Oliveira, R. de Braga, & C. Rizek (Eds.), *Hegemonia às Avessas: Economia, política e cultura na era da servidão financeira*. (pp. 369–376). São Paulo: Boitempo.

Fandiño, P., & Kerstenetzky, C. L. (2019). O paradoxo constitucional brasileiro: direitos sociais sob tributação regressiva. *Revista de Economia Política, 39*(2), 306–327.

Fauré, Y.-A. (2014). Bonheur privé, carences publiques. Retour sur la fronde sociale de mars-juin 2013 au Brésil. *Problèmes d'Amérique latine, 93*, 55–74.

Ferreira, F., Messina, J., Rigolini, J., López-Calva, L.-F., Lugo, M. A., & Vakis, R. (2013a). *Economic mobility and the rise of the Latin American middle class*. Washington, DC: World Bank. https://doi.org/10.1596/978-0-8213-9634-6.

Ferreira, F., Messina, J., Rigolini, J., López-Calva, L.-F., Lugo, M. A., & Vakis, R. (2013b). *La movilidad económica y el crecimiento de la clase media en América Latina*. Washington, DC: Banco Mundial. https://doi.org/10.1596/978-0-8213-9752-7.

Gaulard, M. (2019). L'économie du Brésil, 2e édition, Levallois-Perret, Éditions Bréal, coll. « Thèmes & débats ».

Gilder, G. (1981). *Wealth and poverty*. New York: Basic Books.

Goirand, C. (2019). *Le parti des travailleurs au Brésil: Des luttes sociales aux épreuves du pouvoir*. Paris: Karthala.

IPEA. (2011). *Equidade Fiscal no Brasil: Impactos Distributivos da Tributação e do Gasto Social*, Comunicados de IPEA, n 92.

Kharas, H. (2010). *The emerging middle class in developing countries* (OECD Development Centre Working Paper N 285). Paris: OECD.

Kharas, H. (2017). *The unprecedented expansion of the global middle class. An update* (Brookings institution global economy and development working paper N 100). Washington, DC: Brookings Institution. The online version. Retrieved July 29, 2019, from https://www.brookings.edu/wp-content/uploads/2017/02/global_20170228_global-middle-class.pdf

Klein, C. H., Mitchell, S. T., & Junge, B. (2018). Naming Brazil's previously poor: "New middle class" as an economic, political, and experiential category. *Economic Anthropology, 5*(1), 83–95.

Mansor de Mattos, F. A. (2015). Avanços e dificultades para o mercado de trabalho. *Estudos Avançados, 29*(85), 69–85.

Michau, J.-L. (1987). *Libérer le temps: Une nouvelle dimension de notre civilisation. Préface de François Guiraud. Avant-propos de Philippe Daublain*. Paris: Masson.

Milanovic, B. (2016). *Global inequality: A new approach for the age of globalization*. Cambridge, MA: Harvard University Press.

Neri, M. (2015). Brazil's new middle classes: The bright side of the poor. In J. Dayton-Johnson (Ed.), *Latin America's Emerging Middle Classes* (pp. 70–100). Houndsmills, Basingstoke: Palgrave.

Neri, M., et al. (2009). *Consumidores, Produtores e a Nova Classe Média: Miséria, Desigualdade e Determinantes das Classes*. Rio de Janeiro: FGV/IBRE, CPS.

Neri, M., et al. (2010). *A Nova Classe Média: O Lado Brilhante dos Pobres (The bright side of the poor)*. Rio de Janeiro: FGV/CPS.

O'Reilly, P. (2018). Tax policies for inclusive growth in a changing world. *OECD Taxation Working Papers*, no. 40. Paris: OECD.

OECD. (2017). *Youth aspirations and the reality of jobs in developing countries: Mind the gap*. Paris: OECD.

OECD. (2019). *Under pressure: The squeezed middle class*. Paris: OECD.

Paulani, L. M. (2010). Capitalismo financeiro, estado de emergкncia econфmico e hegemonia às avessas no Brasil. In F. Oliveira, R. de Braga, & C. Rizek (Eds.), *Hegemonia às avessas: economia, política e cultura na era da servidão financeira* (pp. 109–134). São Paulo: Boitempo.

PNUD Brasil (Programa das Nações Unidas para o Desenvolvimento). (2010). *Relatório de Desenvolvimento Humano Brasileiro 2009/2010. Valores e Desenvolvimento Humano*. Brasília: PNUD.

Proni, M. W., & Gomes, D. C. (2015). Precaridade ocupacional: Uma questão de gênero e raça. *Estudos Avançados, 29*(85), 137–151.

Ravallion, M. (2009). *The developing world's bulging (but vulnerable) "middle class"*. World Bank policy research working paper 4816. Washington, DC: World Bank.

Reis, E. P. (1999). Elite perceptions of poverty: Brazil. *IDS (Institute of Development Studies) Bulletin, 30*(2), 127–136.

Reis, E. P. (2000). Modernization, citizenship, and stratification: Historical processes and recent changes in Brazil. *Daedalus, 129*(2), 171–194.

Reis, E. P. (2012). Poverty in the eyes of Brazilian Elites. In A. Amsden, A. Di Caprio, & J. A. Robinson (Eds.), *The role of elites in economic development* (pp. 179–199). Oxford: Oxford University Press.

Reis, G. S., & Soares, G. (2017). O Fascismo no Brasil: O Ovo da Serpiente Chocou. *Desenvolvimento em Debate, 5*(1), 51–71.

Rivas, R. (2019). Factores hereditarios y sociales que explican la desigualdad en las habilidades tempranas: el caso de los niños chilenos. *Revista de la CEPAL, 128*, 207–223.

SAE (Secretaria de Assuntos Estratégicos). (2012). *Vozes da Classe Média. É ouvindo a população que se constroem políticas públicas adequadas*. Marco Zero: Brasília.

Salama, P. (2019). Le Brésil à reculons? *Les Possibles, 20*, 49–64.

Samuels, D. (2004). From socialism to social-democracy: Party organization and the transformation of the Workers' Party in Brazil. *Comparative Political Studies, 37*(9), 999–1024.

Sawaya, R. R. (2015). Poder, emprego e política econômica. *Estudos Avançados, 85*, 105–119.

Sayre, R. K., Devercelli, A. E., Neuman, M. J., & Wodon, Q. (2015). *Investing in early childhood development: Review of the World Bank's recent experience*. Washington, DC: World Bank. https://doi.org/10.1596/978-1-4648-0403-8.

Scalon, C., & Salata, A. (2012). Uma Nova Classe Média no Brasil da Última Década? O debate a partir da perspectiva sociológica. *Sociedade e Estado, 27*(2), 387–407.

Sicsú, J. (2013). *Dez Anos que Aabalaram o Brasil e o Futuro?* São Paulo: Geração Editorial.

Singer, A. (2012). *Os Sentidos do Lulismo. Reforma Gradual e Pacto Conservador*. São Paulo: Companhia das Letras.

Singer, A. (2015). Cutucando onças com varas curtas. O ensaio desenvolvimentista no primeiro mandato de Dilma Rousseff (2011-2014). *Novos Estudos, 102*, 43–71.

Singer, A. (2018). *O lulismo em crise: Um quebra-cabeça do periodo Dilma (2011-2016)*. São Paulo: Companhia das Letras.

Souza, J. (2015). *A tolice da inteligência brasileira, ou como o país se deixa manipular pela elite*. Rio de Janeiro: LeYa.
Souza, J. (2017). *A Elite do Atraso: Da Escravidão à Lava Jato*. Rio de Janeiro: LeYa.
Souza, J., et al. (2009). *Ralé Brasileira: Quem É e Como Vive*. Belo Horizonte: UFMG (Universidade Federal de Minas Gerais).
Souza, J., et al. (2012). *Os Batalhadores Brasileiros: Nova Classe Média ou Classe Trabalhadora?* Belo Horizonte: UFMG.
Standing, G. (2014). Understanding the Precariat through labour and work. *Development and Change, 45*(5), 963–980. https://doi.org/10.1111/dech.12120.
Summa, R., & Serrano, F. (2018). Distribution and conflict inflation in Brazil under inflation targeting, 1999-2014. *Review of Radical Political Economics, 50*(2), 349–369.
Vidal, D. (2016). Le Brésil, va-t-il aussi mal qu'on le dit? *Cahiers des Amériques latines, 81*, 7–15.
Vidal, D. (2017). *Le Brésil: Terre de possibles*. Nouvelle édition (électronique). Rennes: Presses Universitaires de Rennes (édition imprimée – 2016).
Vieira Santana, C. H. (2018). The geopolitics of the Brazilian coup d'état and its consequences. *Transcience, 9*(1), 75–110.
Wietzke, F.-B., & Sumner, A. (2014). *What are the political and social implications of the 'new middle classes' in developing countries?* King's International Development Institute. Working Paper 2014-3. London: King's IDI.
Wilson, D., & Dragusanu, R. (2008). *The expanding middle: The exploding middle class and falling global inequality (Goldman Sachs Global Economics Paper 170)*. S. l.

Chapter 9
Concluding Remarks: Some Prospects for Brazil and Other Emerging Countries or the Myth of Emergence?

The way up is littered with multiple obstacles, the way down may seem a pleasant stroll. Nonetheless, I know only too well, being an experienced mountain climber, that 75–80 per cent of all serious accidents in alpinism and mountain hiking occur while a team or hiker descends. The likelihood of facing and undergoing troubles and difficulties is much greater for those countries that stagnate and commit themselves to waves of spontaneity, probably while enjoying already attained well-being, than for those that apply serious efforts to chart the correct course in the rough ocean of historical time.

Today, Brazil, as well as other emerging countries, including China, encounters a series of threats which, maybe, are not yet seen in a full measure. One such threat consists of the intention of the ruling circle to resolve new problems by old methods; the latter, perhaps, were efficient in the past but today do not correspond to the changed reality and new conditions. Moreover, all attempts to return back—to the 'old merry principles' in politics—may aggravate the rising difficulties with the prospect of systemic crisis. These were the case of the former Soviet Union from the mid-1950s until the collapse of 1991 and the Argentine stories, whether under the obscurantist junta in 1976–1983 or under the presidency of señora Cristina Fernández de Kirchner that tried to recuperate the socioeconomic practice and rhetoric of Peronism. It could also be the case of China, where some attempts to strengthen the authoritarian power in the light of new strategic tasks may lead to an all-embracing crisis against the sincere endeavours of the rulers.

Over many decades Brazil followed the way of conservative modernisation, sometimes even in contrast to the intentions of the actors which initiated the movement. They were constantly obliged to search for compromises with the forces of the past that attempted to save their privileges and wealth at price of holding back the country. Consequently conservative modernisation cannot be even slightly effective. The period of 1995–2016 marks the historical limit of such modernisation. Indeed, during that time, there was the valid attempt to resolve the centurial social problems of Brazil: to begin fighting with poverty, to reduce deep inequality and to

V. Krasilshchikov, *Brazil - Emerging Forever?*, Societies and Political Orders in Transition, https://doi.org/10.1007/978-3-030-50208-9_9

include tens of millions of people into the process of development, thus transforming them into *citizens*. The successes were very moderate. Society did not transform but rather it changed, even though the experience of 20 years of 'social liberalism' can be viewed as very precious in all its positive and negative aspects. This experience will not disappear with the passing of time; it will have far-reaching implications for other countries and various political forces, both Left and Right (often right-wing politicians take appropriate conclusions from the Left's political experiments, carry out serious reforms and thereby prevent a revolution).

One of the main strategic mistakes of the PT, which facilitated the subsequent shift to the Right, consisted of neglecting the role of civil society movements. The attempts of the PT to look 'as all other parties' succeeded in the partial restoration of the practices of the Old Republic (*República Velha*) where many of the important decisions were taken following behind-the-scenes deals among a narrow circle of politicians.

Today, in the globalisation/information technology era, even the positive, constructive efforts of the state, aimed at *modernisation through the resolution of social problems*, may be insufficient (even when good funding is provided for respective programmes) to implement a new strategy of development. An active participation of civil society with NGOs, mass movements and volunteers is also necessary for success. Will the Left-oriented political forces of Brazil, including, of course, the PT, be capable of picking up the wave of new movements if this wave rises again, as it was in the times of the struggle for democratisation (the movement 'Diretas Já')? Meanwhile, the potential of the civil society activity is very significant for the potential resistance to the revenge of the ultra-conservative forces and solve numerous problems and further reform many aspects of the Brazilian reality. One of the acutest problems of Brazil consists in the recent taxation system.

Seemingly, this system is progressive: rich people must pay more than the poor pay, but it doesn't apply to all incomes. There are legally established tax evasions that strongly modify the apparently progressive system of taxation. For example, someone's expenditures for healthcare or medicine are deduced from his/her income subject to taxation. The similar rule spreads to the expenditures for education. Evidently, such tax exemptions are very advantageous for the rich whose expenditure for healthcare and education are much greater that the poor might expend for the same goals. In addition, the share dividends earned by physical persons are not subject to taxation. Finally, as already said in the preceding chapter, there are many indirect taxes included into the price of goods and services' tariffs (fares). As a result, the poor fund a large part of the benefits they receive via social programmes. In particular, about 50 per cent of payments to the people, who have been embraced by the *Bolsa Família* programme, return to the budget in taxes, mostly indirect, which these people pay out (Lavinas et al. 2014: 16–23; Lavinas 2015: 42–43).

The administrations of three presidents, Cardoso, Lula and Rousseff, partly attempted to approach the reform of taxation but did not attain notable success because it faced the resistance of conservative forces in Congress. At the same time, the experience of the PT rule demonstrated the limits of redistributionist social policy based mostly on income from the commodity exports. Thus, when the world economic climate began worsening, the government encountered a hard dilemma: either to use the old known model for resolving the problem, inflation, or to cut social expenditure. Any attempt to follow the previous redistributionist social policy without the additional taxation of the upper class would be impossible, yet any revision of taxes would inevitably result in serious political turbulence. In the firm realities of Brazil, taxation reform can only be enacted through the synergetic efforts of both Left/Left-centrist lawmakers and mass movements' activity.

Certainly, the change of the taxation system has a role solely within a broad framework of searching for a new model of development aimed at deliverance from the relics of conservative modernisation either in the Left or in the Right configuration. However, today it is too early to speak about the emergence of any long-term alternative in Brazil—not to the concrete policy of Bolsonaro and the recent Right forces but *to the paradigm of conservative modernisation as a whole*. The most probable vector of the Brazilian trajectory in the coming years is a continuation of the conservative policy, at best, with some pro-modernisational rhetoric. In the current conditions, all forces that worry about the future of Brazil ought to strengthen *the strategic defence* before attempting to create an effective alternative to the current situation. It will be a success of such *strategic defence* if Brazil will save the 'zones of Belgium' ('the First World') built with great difficulties and sacrifices: Embraer, nuclear energy plants, vehicles assembly production, biotechnologies, pharmaceutics, islands of electronic industry and other similar achievements, not allow them to be destroyed and to implement the new version of archaic, pre-1930 ('pre-Vargas') economic policy.

Meanwhile, there is a real danger of losing the accumulated potential, as the experience of Russia ('sub-Arctic Brazil') says. It means that Brazil risks slipping deep into the world periphery, remaining a primary goods (commodities) supplier and adjunct to the USA, EU or, more likely, China. The lack of the common border between China and Brazil is not an obstacle to Chinese exploitation of Brazilian resources. As it is known, a lack of such border between Great Britain and Latin American countries in the nineteenth century did not prevent the transformation of the former Iberian colonies into the periphery of the then *world's workshop*, although means of communication at that time were incomparably less perfect than the contemporary ones.

The marginalisation of Brazil (together with many other Latin American countries) may succeed in long-term negative effects inside of the country. In particular, it may lead to the socioeconomic disintegration of Brazil into the South/South-East and North/North-East with the subsequent political decomposition of the entire Brazilian state (a similar threat exists in Russia where the reprimarisation of the economy in the last 25–30 years has led to a seemingly paradoxical situation where the political centre and relative well-being of Moscow and St. Petersburg crucially depends on the Siberian periphery that exports gas, petroleum and raw materials for the enrichment of a narrow circles of oligarchs, top bureaucrats and their 'intellectual servants').

What then can prevent Brazil from a negative, destructive course of events? What can change the recent dangerous trajectory of Brazilian development?

At first, it is naïve to think that the recently observable frontal counter-offensive of the conservative and even frankly reactionary forces, against the social rights of most labourers in Brazil, will not face a resistance. For the full completion of this counter-offensive, it would be necessary to establish a new dictatorship: to dissolve all legislative bodies, including the National Congress; to ban activity of all, or almost all, political parties; to begin controlling mass media; and, in particular, to isolate the internet from 'subversive influence from abroad' and to subject it to state control like the Chinese authorities have done (also the Russian authorities' dream but are unable do so because of a shortage of technical resources and the poor qualification of 'executives'). However, it is difficult to imagine such a scenario today, in contemporary Brazil. For its implementation, it is also necessary to think up the image of 'external enemies' as in the 1960s–1970s when authoritarian regimes in the Southern Cone of Latin America explored—for legitimacy reasons—the theme of infiltration of Cuban guerrillas subverting the attained well-being and order. Today someone in good mental health would hardly believe in such tales of a threat of guerrillas in stone jungles of São Paulo. The regime of Maduro, with the semi-failed petrol state in Venezuela, does not reach the level of an instigator of large-scale guerrillas in Brazil.

Secondly, notwithstanding the increased significance of the internal factors of development in Latin America [i.e. a definite shift from the external-led to internal-led factors of development in Latin American countries, although the external dependency did not disappear at all (Krasilshchikov 2014)], the external conditions are important, too, and, moreover, they may play a decisive role at the turning point when a country enters the period of bifurcation. Nobody can predict with absolute clarity that Brazil and Latin America as a whole will not undergo a crisis comparable to the shock of 'the lost decade' of the 1980s or even similar to the economic earthquake of 1930–1932. Certainly, the forthcoming crisis or, at best, a moderate recession would hardly be as profound as the Great Depression or as long as 'the lost decade', but it could substantially devalue commodity exports from Latin America and aggravate social conflicts around the distribution of the shrunken pie. It might push a section of the advanced elite groups to remove the bankrupted 'masters of money' from the levers of financial-economic policy. The success of this 'removal' would depend on the activity of the alternative social forces and, also, on the correspondence of the supposed alternatives to the new global trends.

Here it is probably relevant to look on the current situation in the light of the 'big cycles' theory' originally elaborated by Kondratieff-Schumpeter-Akamatsu.

The Brazilian 'miracle' of 1967–1974 took place not only due to the 'wise policy' of the military-bureaucratic regime (its 'wisdom' is debatable up until today) but also because it coincided with the end of phase A (the ascending wave) and the beginning of phase B of the fourth big cycle in the developed, core countries. Then Brazilian industry passed through its phase A while this phase, in the core countries, came to its limit and began transforming into phase B. It facilitated an inflow of capital into Brazil, whether as foreign direct investments in manufacturing industries or as loans, and instigated the rapid growth of the new ('for Brazil!') branches of economy. Omitting here the inevitable modifications of each phase in the conditions of semi-peripheral countries like Brazil, it is worth taking into account that the fifth wave (technological set) based on microelectronics and information technology apparently comes to its objective limit because, so to speak, it had almost accomplished its 'historical mission'. The next, sixth technological set (wave), as it has been predicted in recent years, will be conditioned by the boom of biotechnologies based on all of the complement of life sciences. It will likely start in the 2020s or, a little later, in the early 2030s. It can either open up new opportunities for emerging countries (if, of course, they intensify investments in their human capital) (Grinin et al. 2016: 161–169, 171–173, 178–180) or widen the gap between the few post-industrial, technologically advanced countries and 'the rest'. Incidentally, some recently developed countries risk falling into the category 'the rest' (France and Spain, for instance). Will Brazil be able to avoid of such prospect? Rather, Brazil as well as most 'emerging countries' will experience a deep recession or, at best, a long stagnation, and it may provoke the country's profound restructure. However, will there be the social actors capable of changing the vector of development?

Can we presuppose the situation where Brazil together with some other countries of Latin America will be 'invited to development' as it occurred in the case of South Korea, Taiwan or Singapore in the 1960s? The answer 'yes' would only make sense in the conditions of the Cold War. Then the USA sought ways to build 'good capitalism' in East Asia as an efficient alternative to the Soviet and Chinese/Maoist state socialism, and said countries looked to be the best executives and experimental fields for the resolution of this strategic task. Meanwhile, such an invitation to development could only succeed in positive results if there were the local business and political elites inclined 'to accept the invitation'—to apply the proper efforts for the modernisation of their countries. For example, Uncle Sam invited his favourable ally in Southeast Asia, the Philippines, to development, too, however, with only modest results because there were the old, inherited from the Spanish colonial period, oligarchic structures but not the social actors capable of self-restriction in consumption for the sake of long-term investment and prosperity.

Today the USA is hardly interested in raising Brazil to the level of a highly developed country as it had done in regard to the just mentioned first-tier Asian 'tigers'. Brazil is too big and, if successful, might become a serious competitor to America, not only in the Western hemisphere but on a global scale. Moreover, if the USA wanted to pull Brazil into the group of the advanced countries, then it would raise the problem of a resource shortage: America has a large internal field for investment, and the US ruling class would never agree to help another big country at the cost of causing domestic problems.

Nevertheless, Brazil can potentially use the US-China controversies for real development, taking into account that USA cannot be interested in strengthening its main rival by seeing the transformation of Brazil into a raw materials supplier to the Red Dragon Empire. In particular, Brazil can feed into the global value-added chains, becoming the new *industrial* supplement to North American and/or European Union post-industrial economies. The free trade agreement between Mercosul and EU opens good opportunities for following this development path. Yes, of course, it looks as if it's the second version of *associated-dependent development*. This way is fraught with all possible deficiencies and costs, but it does not lock in the prospect of a success story in the future, as the experience of Poland and the Czech Republic demonstrated to us in the last two to three decades. Economies of these Central European countries have become the industrially developed supplements to the post-industrial part of EU, Germany in the first place, but their place in this condition requires a good system of education, engineering and scientific research (R&D) with a respective quality of human capital. In any case, such a dependency resembles more an advanced 'backwardness', than stagnation with commodity exports to China. However, even the 'improved', contemporary version of associated-dependent development presupposes the existence and activity of the actors capable of steering country on this trajectory. Unless such actors will rise, maybe as a response to huge challenges all talks about any 'emergence' of the biggest country of Ibero-America are nonsensical.

Unfortunately, today, since the powerful actors of the new development model are not seen on the horizon, *the emergence* remains as one of the myths cultivated in a framework of contemporary 'Alice-in-Wonderland social sciences'. It concerns not only Brazil. Perhaps then Brazil demonstrates today some of the features of the future for emerging countries in Asia, including India and China.

References

Grinin, L., Korotaev, A., & Tausch, A. (2016). *Economic crises, cycles, and the global periphery. With a foreword by William R. Thompson*. Preston, UK: Springer. https://doi.org/10.1007/978-3-319-41262-7.

Krasilshchikov, V. (2014). América Latina en vía para el desarrollo independiente. *Iberoamérica, 4*, 64–84 (disponible también en la vesión electrónica. Retrieved from http://iberoamericajournal.ru/iberoamerica-2014-n-4-75.html#2014-4)

Lavinas, L. (2015). A financeirização da política social: O caso brasileiro. *PolítiKa, 2*(Julho), 35–51.

Lavinas, L., Ferro, M., & Andrade, T. (2014). A *long way from tax justice: the Brazilian case. Global labour university working paper, no. 22* Geneva, Berlin: ILO, GLU. The electronic version. Viewed on 01.02.2020. Retrieved from http://www.global-labour-university.org/fileadmin/GLU_conference_2014/papers/Lavinas_Lena_GLU_WP_No.22.pdf; https://ideas.repec.org/p/ilo/ilowps/994851303402676.html

The manufacturer's authorised representative in the EU is Springer Nature Customer Service Centre GmbH, Europaplatz 3, 69115 Heidelberg, Germany. If you have any concerns regarding our products, please contact ProductSafety@springernature.com

Printed and bound by CPI Group (UK) Ltd, Croydon, CR0 4YY
22/09/2026
02221062-0004